on

Sarah Champion edited the bestselling *Disco Biscuits*.

SCEPTRE

Disco 2000

edited by
SARAH CHAMPION

SCEPTRE

Introduction and compilation © 1998 Sarah Champion

For the copyright on individual stories see pages 361–2

First published in 1998 by Hodder and Stoughton
A division of Hodder Headline PLC
A Sceptre Paperback

10 9 8 7 6 5 4 3 2 1

A CIP catalogue record for this title is available from the British Library

  ISBN 0 340 70771 2

Typeset by Palimpsest Book Production Limited,
Polmont, Stirlingshire
Printed and bound in Great Britain by
Clays Ltd, St Ives plc

Hodder and Stoughton
A division of Hodder Headline PLC
338 Euston Road
London NW1 3BH

Dedicated to Phil Champion, notorious tree-dweller and yoghurt-burglar.

Contents

'There's gonna be peace in the valley tomorrow
'Cos tonight we're going to blow it all away.
Lord we feel so twisted, we ain't ever gonna fix it,
We're just waiting for the light to shine on a brand new day ...'

Love, Love, Love, Rev D. Wayne Love and L. B. Dope

Introduction

It's weird how dates stick in your mind. To use telephone banking you have to give a string of passwords including 'memorable time and place'. Mine is 11 May 1985, Moss Side, Manchester (though I'll have to change it now). That was the night I had my first experience of pre-millennial tension . . .

At the age of fourteen, my school friend invited me to a concert at her church. I found myself the only white person in a black Pentecostal church, witnessing five hours of apocalyptic passion — end-is-nigh gospel interspersed by hell 'n' brimstone sermons with hysterical, elderly Jamaican women running down the aisle in tears, giving ten pound notes to the Pastor.

Afterwards, already spooked, I had to wait for a lift on a dodgy street corner, watching shadowy figures disappearing up a staircase above a chippy, to buy 'draw'. Then there was a siren. A burglar alarm? It couldn't be as the sound was coming from all directions. It was the siren made famous in Frankie Goes To Hollywood's 'Two Tribes' — *the four minute nuclear warning.* It sounded for twenty minutes. The streets were empty: there was no panic. Where was it being broadcast from? The street lamps? The telephone junction boxes?

Except for a tiny report in a local paper, no one commented. Sometimes, I wonder if it ever happened at all. But that night in Moss Side something changed for me. Ever since, I've lived with the eerie feeling that these really were the 'last days' — strange times that had to be lived to the full.

I wasn't alone. Not long afterwards, Acid House hit Manchester, and we partied like there was no tomorrow (presuming that there might not be and not caring if there was).

Of course, the apocalypse has been predicted for centuries: 31 December 1999, the most memorable date in our lifetimes, is at the heart of a myriad of conspiracy theories and end-of-the-world prophecies. The urgency of it seemed to escalate just before I was born, around the time of the Vietnam War. Since then, our awareness of apocalypse and chaos has been heightened by media coverage of world events, from the Gulf War 'live' on TV, to the video clip which sparked the LA riots.

All this is the background to *Disco 2000*, an anthology of fiction, in which all the stories take place in the last hours of 31 December 1999. The book is not so much about the date itself, but about the fears and fantasies of those who have lived in the date's shadow for the last thirty years.

Disco 2000 embraces all the classic end-of-the-millennium motifs — hedonism, insanity, religious mania, suicide cults, future technology, chemical excess and media conspiracies — each of them escalating as we near the mythological date. The idea was to commission exclusive new stories from cult writers whose work (whether chemical, cyberpunk, horror, or crime) embraces these themes, as well as digging up some new talent.

Of the many things predicted for the *ultimate* New Year, one is absolutely certain — it will be TV Hell. *Disco 2000* explores the ever more powerful and surreal nature of the media. In 'I'm A Policeman' by Grant Morrison (the cult DC comic writer), riots, wars and starvation have become merely advertising tools. In Steve Aylett's 'Gigantic', television is a soap-box for ever more outlandish madmen and crackpots, each with their own patented prophecy, while in Pat Cadigan's 'Witnessing The Millennium', TV cameras become all-powerful — the idea being that if you are not *seen*, you will simply disappear.

Another common theme in *Disco 2000*, not surprisingly, is time. Particularly the fact that time is an illusion — as anyone trapped in the 3.00 a.m. eternal of a bad acid trip or in the second before a car crash, will corroborate. In Paul Di Filippo's 'Mama Told Me Not To Come' the protagonist goes on a 'Bill 'n' Ted' style trip back through great parties of the past. Time plays a nasty trick in Charlie Hall's 'The Millennium Loop', while, in true apocalyptic tradition, in Jonathan Brook's 'Identity', the end of the world really is imminent.

And, if time is an illusion, then the millennium is the biggest mirage of all. To Christians, and therefore most Westerners, the 31 December 1999 is pivotal — to others it means nothing. For example, Buddhists celebrated the year 2000 over fifty years ago. And according to the ancient Mayan calendar, it is the end of 2012 which is the true date of the apocalypse, drawing a series of seemingly chaotic events towards it. Techno-shaman Terence McKenna has verified this by running the Mayan tables through a computerised version of the *I Ching* and Steve Beard's 'Retoxicity' sets it's end-of-the-millennium party in the last hours of 2012.

Disco 2000 would of course not be complete without a contribution from Robert Anton Wilson, author of the *Illuminatus* trilogy, the conspiracy theory epic in which secret societies span centuries. Bill Drummond, of KLF fame, much influenced by the *Illuminatus*, documents his and Jimmy Cauty's preparations for the end-of-the-millennium as K2 Plant Hire Ltd. They recently launched a 'Fuck The Millennium' campaign and a 'Millennium Crisis' line!

This anthology not only explores the attitudes and obsessions of the pre-millennial generation, but showcases some of its best new writers. Look out for Courttia Newland, whose 'Piece Of My Mind', the longest story in the book, is a coming-of-age novella featuring the antics of the West London kids who starred in his debut novel *The Scholar*.

Disco 2000 also features some kick-ass female writers. There are not enough in print, since the publishing industry seems to encourage women to pen novels around the cosy topics of families, relationships and romance. However, role models can be found here, such as Pat Cadigan who, alongside Paul Di Filippo, was one of the contributors to *Mirrorshades*, the definitive early 80s cyberpunk anthology. Meanwhile, Tania Glyde's characters, Bitch and Cow, go on a Tank-Girl-esque mission, proving along the way that women can be every bit as vicious as men.

As for New Orleans' Poppy Z. Brite, she may be classed as a horror writer, but *her* ghosts and vampires are skinny sexual deviants who drink whiskey, take drugs and listen to thrash. In 'Vine Of The Soul', Zac and Trevor, heroes of her novel *Drawing Blood*, turn up in Amsterdam for the end of the millennium, almost a decade after they fled the States with the FBI on their tail.

Disco 2000 is the follow up to the bestselling chemical fiction anthology *Disco Biscuits*, which captured the thoughts and excesses of a generation in print for the first time. *Disco 2000* takes things a step further: it's not just about hedonism but about the whole apocalypse vibe that characterised the eighties and nineties.

The book collects some of the most interesting writers of the late 90s. These include Douglas Coupland, whose novels document the peculiarities of American society at the end of the millennium — from the slackers of *Generation X* to the computer geeks of *Microserfs*. In *Disco 2000*, he writes about a man desperate to cleanse himself of the chemicals in his bloodstream — which to him represent the late twentieth century itself.

There's also a contribution from Neal Stephenson, whose cult classic *Snow Crash* is the most visionary cyberspace novel since William Gibson's *Count Zero*. With a typical twist, his story here is not what you might expect — but then what *should* we expect from the ending of a thousand years?

Now the end of the millennium is so close, we need to ask what it *really* means. The fact is, that most of the events in this book will *not* happen. What if the future is not a violent and apocalyptic landscape, but a bland, dull, endless suburbia? Or as J.G. Ballard explores in *Cocaine Nights*, a land of gated-communities? This sense of drab, thirty-something boredom is captured in 'reality 2' of Doug Hawes' 'A Short Archaeology of the Chemical Age'. Meanwhile, in different ways, Douglas Coupland and Neal

Stephenson also explore the alternative view of the millennium as an anti-climax.

When asked to contribute to this anthology, J.G. Ballard replied (on the back of a photograph of a motorway flyover) that he plans to 'run for the hills, or at least in the opposite direction' since it 'threatens to be hi-jacked by Tony Blair, Melvyn Bragg and co . . .' Perhaps, like a lifetime of birthdays and New Years rolled into one, the last night of 1999 can only be a let down.

And, before you ask what I'm going to be doing in the last hours of this millennium . . . *I don't know* . . . Except to say that maybe it doesn't matter, as I've already been celebrating it every night since that evening in Moss Side in 1985.

Sarah Champion
February 1998
www.discobiscuits.org

Pat Cadigan

'WITNESSING THE MILLENNIUM'

1999 is not what I expected.

Rather, 29 December 1999 is not what I expected.

To be completely accurate, the final hours of 1999 are not at all what I expected. But then when I try to think of what I might have been expecting, I come up blank. Who has any expectations of New Year's Eve but the usual party? By the time 1999 came around, I had been told repeatedly that it was not the start of the new millennium, that 31 December 2000 would mark the end of the old millennium and anyone who could count to ten would know that.

So who is it — who, or *what* — that can't count to ten? Some panel of dark gods somewhere, perhaps the millennium itself is an entity? Or did we somehow drop a stitch over the last thousand years, did somebody lose count and start over in the wrong spot, one over from where we had actually left off? Could such a mistake really go undiscovered? Or was it just covered up?

All I know is this: as of 12.01 a.m. local time, 31 December 1999, people have been disappearing. Not just in London, but in every major city around the world, in the not-so-major ones, in the rural areas, in mountain villages, resort towns, and desert camps, all beginning at 12.01 a.m. local time.

No . . . no . . . must be accurate here. This is what I have been hearing all day, on CNN, on Radio 4, even on the Internet, on BroadBand, News-On-Demand, and Daily Ticker. Media-Cast believes it's a hoax perpetrated by Microsoft as advertising for some computer game. The conspiracy newsgroups and mailing lists are exploding — long paper printouts roll out of Internet cafés like salacious white tongues. Anyone can stop and pick them up and read the theories: mass alien abductions, the Rapture, a super-secret satellite death-ray gone out of control, or activated by the CIA, MI5, the KGB, the Pope, the Republicans, the Labour Party, the Zionist-Bankers Conspiracy, the feminists, the cyberpunks, the feminist-cyberpunk-papist-aliens in the service of Elvis Presley, Marilyn Monroe, and John F. Kennedy.

It could be true, for all the difference it makes; which is to say, whether all these theories are true, only some, only one, or none at all, people are still disappearing. They say.

Meanwhile, pirate stations are fighting it out with legitimate radio for airspace, or earspace. Once in a while, one voice among the cacophony of many will cut off in mid-syllable; when everyone else realises, there is a shocked nano-pause before they go right on, braying warnings at a populace diminishing at an indefinite rate. The long white printout tongues lick out another ten feet, CNN and its imitators interrupt their previous interruption-for-a-special-bulletin with another special bulletin: one more disappearance. For every one you know of, there are an unknown number of others that occurred at just about the same time. How many for every thousand you *don't* hear of — for every disappearance you never hear about, how many more are there that you never knew existed in the first place? I wonder just to be absurd. Being absurd for the sake of being absurd — like the man said, all those years ago, *Why not?*

I have thought about going into the centre of London, except about a billion other people have the same idea and, unlike me, they are acting on it. No one wants to be alone. The belief has sprung up, apparently spontaneously, that there is safety in numbers — as long as someone can see you, you won't disappear. This is why it's best to be among as many people as possible; your chances of continuing to be visible to at least one other person increase in a crowd. Ergo, you won't disappear. Supposedly. The only reasoning behind this is that, as yet, no one has actually seen anyone else vanish — all actual vanishings, disappearances, evaporations, meltings, fadings and disintegrations have all taken place offstage, so to speak, somewhere beyond everyone's personal proscenium.

But this is not why I've thought about going into the centre of London. Well, not *really*. Well, maybe partially. Mostly, I think it is the very human desire to feel connected in a time of crisis. And, of course, I'd be hedging my bets, too. If it *were* true, then I'd be covered, I'd have as much chance as anyone of remaining in existence. And if it weren't true, I'd see the millennium in with several million of my closest friends.

Only, what if it weren't true that you wouldn't disappear if someone was looking at you? That idea rattles around in my head, wearing a groove like a hated, lingering tune caught on that oh so terribly slight obsessive proclivity we all have. What if somebody is lying about that? It's not inconceivable. We all know everyone lies. We all know incorrigible liars — we sleep with them, marry them, elect them to public office, return their lies with lies of our own. And then, when someone is caught in a lie, usually a particularly egregious lie, we act shocked, horrified, saddened, betrayed, as if no one in the history of civilisation has ever told a lie until that very moment.

And then I remember what Media-Cast said about the disappearances possibly being a Microsoft hoax. If not Microsoft, then perhaps some other company promoting software, something they earnestly want to believe is an interactive novel but is just another unoriginal variation on the old choose-your-own-adventure scheme. Except that people really do seem to have vanished while — we have been led to believe — no one was looking.

Out of sight, out of mind, and then out of existence?

If that is really the case, I am doomed, because instead of going into the centre of London, to see and be seen, to watch and be watched — wasn't that an either-or proposition once, or do I mis-remember? — I have come to Duckett's Common, to sit alone on a worn bench in the littered, pigeon-plentiful, pub-plagued, and population-prodigious borough of Haringey. Most of Haringey's residents seem to have decamped for central London; the rest have packed themselves into the pubs in numbers that are staggering even for this area, where drinking is a vocation blessed by God.

Besides myself, there are only a few of the hardier breed of crusties left outside, as well as the inveterate homeless, and the drunks too drunk to feel the December chill and too broke to get any drunker than that. The crusties can see me; I'm in their line of sight, and I must puzzle them, being neither crusty nor drunk. And I probably look too lost to be homeless.

Only I'm not *really* lost, of course. I know where I am. The question is, I guess, does anybody else know?

I can look up at the night sky and think about the spy satellites the conspiracy buffs claim can capture a recognisable image of you standing at your front door. Are there really such things?

I'm ready for my close-up, Big Brother.

The thought makes me grin at the sky as if I knew for certain there was someone up there who could appreciate the joke. But in fact, the lens is closer to home. My gaze moves to the nearest streetlamp, and then to one of the zebra-crossing poles just beyond it. No, the zebra-crossing camera will be focused on the road itself, in case of any hit-and-runs. The street-lamp is the more likely candidate for the park surveillance camera. In case of any purse-snatchings, kidnappings, dope deals, rapes, truancies, vagrancies, or unlawful expectorations, which in the era of newly resurgent tuberculosis, everyone is serious about.

The people of London demanded more surveillance cameras, as did the people of New York and Chicago, Paris, Berlin, Moscow, Tokyo, Beijing, Hong Kong. Also, Edinburgh, Reykjavik, Toronto, Rio de Janeiro, Tierra del Fuego and Honolulu. And Davenport, Iowa; Lawrence, Kansas; Fitchburg, Massachusetts; Old Dime Box, Texas; Hay-on-Wye; Stoke-on-Trent; the entire French Riviera; all the rainforest tribes in South America, and schoolyards the world over. It didn't take long.

Known as the Zapruder footage, for the name of the amateur filming the motorcade with a home-movie camera . . .

You are hereby ordered to maintain a distance of not less than five hundred yards from the plaintiff, one Jacqueline Kennedy Onassis, at all times

In VietNam today . . .

. . . and in Washington, DC, thousands of protestors . . .

. . . beating of Rodney King, captured on videotape by . . .

. . . in accordance with the recently-instituted anti-stalking laws of this jurisdiction . . .

. . . footage from this hidden camera and microphone, which clearly show how the front-man sets up victims to be taken by this scam . . .

For your protection, this transaction is being photographed . . .

Keep an eye on this, will ya?

If anyone saw the accident which occurred here at 2.45 p.m. on Monday 24th . . .

Have you seen this girl? She was last seen in the area of . . .

The store's security cameras show the robbery in progress . . .

. . . mall security camera footage clearly showing the child being led away . . .

As was the case in a previous tragedy paparazzi claimed they tried to call for help and did not resume taking photographs until after emergency vehicles were on the scene, a claim disputed by highway patrol surveillance cameras meant to catch speeders. What traffic-control cameras caught was the sight of numerous freelance photographers poking their lenses directly into the crumpled wreckage to . . .

Your Honour, these photographs taken at my client's admission to the hospital clearly show . . .

. . . murder captured on the officer's dashboard videocamera, which she left running while she got out of her patrol car to question the driver of . . .

Eyewitness News . . .

Eyewitness . . .

I, witness

CU-SeeMe.

Big Brother, are you still watching? Do I still have your attention? Do you still care, am I still entertaining enough or at least sufficiently suspicious-looking to remain interesting?

Or could I be one of the lucky ones whom the camera simply loves? Do people see my face on a monitor screen and fall instantly in love with the image?

Or, like a vampire, do I not register on a camera lens at all? Never mind that I've seen photographs of myself in the past; has *anyone else* seen them? *Lately?* Here's some pre-millennial tension for you: the fear of being watched by the wrong people and not watched by the right ones. In the last hours of 1999, with whole pockets of the world's population re-inventing the *Marie Celeste* scenario while the rest try desperately to stay in sight, you could hardly call it neurotic.

If you believe it. I'm still not sure that I do. Hysteria is our hallmark, after all, more contagious than measles — much more contagious, actually, since you can vaccinate against measles. More contagious than treatment-resistant tuberculosis, then. Able to spread through tall buildings at a single noun, mightier than documentation; facts bounce off harmlessly. And then what? They lie around on the ground, I suppose, until someone comes along, picks them up, and makes use of them in whatever way seems most advantageous. Grind your axe to a lethal sharpness on someone else's whetstone.

You, too, can be a wizard of word salad with the amazing Metaphor Mixmaster.

One of the crusties is coming to join me on the bench. His metre-length dreads are black from his scalp to just past his shoulders, where they become yellow. His clothes are, well, crusty with dirt and wear; his chapped features seem to waver between cruel and kind, while he decides about me. He's carrying a can of lager. I'd call it beer, whether it was lager, ale, stout, or porter, but that's the thing about Haringey — they know their poison, no one dies clueless. He offers me the can; dirt is caked in the lines of his hands and under what little of his fingernails he hasn't gnawed off. I'm about to refuse the offer and then it occurs to me: why not? I've done worse.

'Don't mind if I do,' I say, accepting the can from him. He looks startled but not displeased.

The lager is a surprise as well, not thin, sour and watery as I had thought it might be but lively and biting and very, very cold, colder even than this final deepening night.

'You could come over and join us,' the crusty tells me, accepting the can back and having a swig himself. 'Plenty for all over there. I think most's gone into the centre, you know. Get their pictures on the TV and the Web? What do you think, love, you think that'd be insurance against going—?' He snaps his dirty fingers.

'Dunno,' I tell him. 'I'm not really authorised to speak *ex cathedra* on anything that even remotely matters.'

'*Ex cathedra.*' He laughs. 'Thought you was one. All us Catholics know each other.'

'Maybe all of you here do,' I say. 'I can never tell.'

'You could, though,' he says. 'Just look for the ones what always look like they're bein' watched. Those're the Catholics. All Catholics grow up believin' God's got His all-seein eye on 'em all the time. Can't even wipe yer bum without God havin' a peek.' He laughed. 'We grow up under surveillance, so what's it to us if there's cameras hidden in the trees and the lamp-posts and satellites takin' spy pictures, alla that. We know His eye is on the sparrow, like.'

'If you're going to lecture me, you can at least offer me another sip of beer.'

He obligingly hands the can to me. 'And you're American. Thought so.'

'It's not like the accent is hard to place.'

'Well, you coulda been either Canadian or American, but when you asked me for another drink, I knew you was American for sure. You called it "beer", not "lager", and you didn't say "please".' He laughs again as he takes the can back from me.

'How do they do without you in the diplomatic corps?'

'Dunno. I'm not there, am I?' He finds this hilarious. Then his gaze drifts past me and his smile fades. I turn to look.

The three-person crew entering the park is like any of those I've seen in Covent Garden — a woman to ask questions, someone to film it, and a third person on sound duties, which usually involves a fur-covered microphone the size of an uncut Bologna sausage. I never knew exactly what they were up to in Covent Garden, whether they were interviewing tourists, taking a survey, or doing a project for a class in broadcasting.

They come right for us without hesitating. My crusty friend sits up straighter, pulling his can of lager close to his body in a protective way. Is he afraid they're going to ask for a swig? I'm bewildered. There are plenty more people in central London to interview, that's where the story's gone. What did they think they were going to find here? I look at the crusty, thinking he might share another insight with me, but he is eyeing the crew as they arrange themselves in front of us, all the potential cruelty in his face coming out unchecked.

'Hello,' says the woman pleasantly. She is dressed like a newscaster, or like she thinks she's a newscaster — tasteful wool coat, orderly blue blouse with a graceful scarf tie at the throat, long slender navy-blue skirt with a kick pleat in the back. 'Do you have a minute or two?'

The sound tech, also a woman, looks up at her with a pained grimace. 'No, Molly, they're sittin' there because they're in a big fookin' 'urry to be on London Bridge at straight-up midnight.'

Molly is unperturbed. 'Kit never talks about the weather, either. Light conversation completely escapes her, she can't throw a dinner party to save her own life. Would you mind if I asked you some questions for a New Year's Day news programme on BBC I?'

'You think anyone'll be around to see it?' asks the crusty.

Molly makes a couple of practised gestures and the furry Bologna is floating on its boom just over our knees, while the cameraman, who seems only old enough to have just started shaving, aims the lens at us as if it were a bazooka he's learning to fire. 'Could you two move closer together?'

The crusty and I look at each other and stay where we were. 'We ain't demonstrative,' he explains.

'I'm not asking for a demonstration, I just want to get both of you in the picture.'

'Oh.' The crusty slides over so that his shoulder touches mine. 'Why'ntcha say so?'

'I just did.' Molly smooths her sleek henna-ed cap of glossy hair with such a careful touch that she doesn't actually disturb a strand, and whirls on the camera. 'In these final hours of 1999, when most of London is packing itself into Trafalgar Square and The Strand, as well as along the banks of the Thames, there are a few hardy souls who seem determined to test fate, to sneer in the face of possible doom, to—'

'Shouldn't that be *tempt* fate?' says the sound tech suddenly.

'Dub it in later, who cares?' Molly says and clears her throat. 'To sneer in the face of possible doom, to defy, uh, what everybody else is afraid of — namely, not to have been seen by enough people to prevent them from disappearing. Tell me, sir, are you *not* afraid of disappearing, or are you perhaps hoping that you will? And if so, why?'

'Uh . . .' The crusty glances at me. 'What?'

'Take it in steps, Barbara Walters,' says the sound tech boredly.

'Barbara?' says the crusty. 'Thought you said her name was Molly.'

The cameraman laughs. 'Shut up,' Molly says without turning around. 'Okay. One thing at a time, then. Aren't you afraid of disappearing?'

The crusty shrugs. 'Never have done so can't imagine I will.'

The woman turns to me. 'What about you, madam?'

Madam? If there is any justice, she'll disappear, I think, and deliberately look down at my lap. 'I'm a fatalist. I figure if I'm going to disappear, I will no matter what I do. And if I'm not, I won't.'

Molly pushes her face down close to mine so that I have to look at her. She has brown eyes that turn down at the outer corners; her eyelids have fallen as well, giving her a tired and sincere look. In the part of America I come from, women go into television journalism when they decide their modelling careers have foundered, with the hope of achieving the only pinnacle left to them: anchorwoman. Molly, on the other hand, has probably gone into television journalism out of a desire to go into television journalism. She is not six feet tall, one hundred pounds; she would not get so much as a second look at the bottom-rated station in the city where I used to live. I should like her for that, at least, but I only feel annoyed.

'When people do disappear,' she says to me firmly, in a school-teacher's pay-attention-this-is-going-to-be-on-the-final tone, 'where do *you* think they go?'

I shrug. 'Nirvana?'

The crusty elbows me hard. 'She said "disappear", not "kill themselves with a shotgun".' He throws back his head and roars laughter at God. A few moments later, he notices he's the only one laughing.

'God, that is so cold,' Molly tells him. 'Where do you think they go?'

He stares at her in disbelief. 'Where they go? Same place a soap bubble goes when *it* disappears, where'd you think?'

'Where do you think that is?' Molly persists.

The crusty folds his arms carefully, without spilling any lager. 'It's a trick question, innit?'

Molly looks at me, and then at the cameraman and sound tech. All of us burst out laughing and this time the crusty is the only one who isn't laughing. The sound tech has to wipe her eyes with a sweatshirt cuff. 'Jesus,' she says, all but hiccuping. 'The things you'll do just to stay in existence.'

'Hey! *Hey!*' A new voice, distant, somewhere behind me. 'Hey, come on — it's a telly crew! They've got a camera, they're *broadcasting!*' The pub behind the common is emptying, its patrons spilling out every available exit, possibly some windows as well. They stagger, sway, tumble, but inexorably advance on us. Actually, on the telly crew.

Molly rolls her eyes. 'Well, actually we're not broadcasting . . .'

'Shut up, Moll,' the sound tech says, watching the drunken horde approach. 'If they say we're broadcasting, we're broad-casting. That is, if you want to get out of this one *unspliced* as it were.'

Molly had been about to get annoyed; now she decides to go

pale instead. 'Why don't we just give them the camera and get out of here?'

'Oh, great,' the cameraman says. 'I'll lose my bond.'

'Your bond or your balls,' says the sound tech, still watching the on-coming mob. 'It's your choice, lad.'

Only there's no more time to choose; funny how fast an unruly crowd of drunks can move on the eve of what they believe is the millennium, especially when they're heading for something they're drunk enough to think will save their lives. Or possibly their souls. My father used to move that fast, usually from one drink to another, attacking each glass as if the secret of the universe were waiting at the bottom of each measure of liquid. I have no idea if he was still in existence.

'You,' burps a man in shirt sleeves, pointing at Molly unsteadily. Alcohol has every muscle in his face sagging into every other muscle; he looks like a bloodhound, or one of that even more wrinkly breed. 'Whaddaya, uh, what, you wanna interview some people?'

'Oh, mad for it, us,' says the sound tech, pointing the furry Bologna at him. 'Tell us your take on all this, all of England is waiting to hear.'

'That's funny, you don't look like CNN,' someone else says.

'Nah, they're Sky News,' says the man in shirt sleeves. I wonder when it's going to occur to him that he's cold, but I think he's drunk enough that he'd freeze to death before he could start shivering. He starts shaking his index finger at the sound tech, getting ready to lecture her on something and then remembers, somehow, that he should talk to the camera. It takes a minute, but he finds the lens pointing at him. It's not much steadier than he is, at the moment; the cameraman doesn't like the way the pub crowd is surrounding us, and I don't blame him. You can see how hungry their faces are; they look more like they want to rape the camera than be filmed by it. They also look like they're not sure what raping the camera would involve, but they're willing to experiment. All night, if necessary.

Memo for the new millennium, I think to myself, provided I survive that long: never give a bunch of drunks a sense of purpose.

The aroma of alcohol in all its various fermented forms and flavours, hops, malts, juniper, grapes, sugars, is overwhelming. They must have a nice assortment in that pub — *had* a nice assortment. Something tells me that the only reason someone noticed the telly crew out here was that everything on the shelves and in the kegs behind the bar ran out.

'I been givin' this disappearing stuff a lotta thought, a *lotta* thought,' the guy says, shaking his finger at the camera lens. 'People just disappear, no one knows why? *I* know why. *I know.* It's because the bloody media's got too much power, that's why—'

Immediately, the crowd starts shouting him down. Well, shouting *at* him, anyway — it's hard to tell exactly what the general sentiment is, as there seem to be as many people hollering in agreement as there are insisting he's full of shit, and they're all at least as inebriated as he is, many probably more so. I'm starting to feel disoriented; perhaps drunken hysteria is even more contagious than the sober variety.

Molly surprises me by suddenly jumping up on the park bench beside me and motioning for quiet; even more surprising, the racket dies down for her and that startles her as much as it does anyone, including me.

She clears her throat. 'Let him finish,' she enunciates.

There's a long moment while this sinks in. Our media theorist in shirt sleeves clambers up on the bench next to the crusty and looks around. 'Yeah,' he says, sounding pleased. 'Lemme finish, this's important. It's the *media* it's got *too much* bloody *power*. It's got *so much* goddamn power now that you ain't *nothin'* unless you got a bloody fuckin' *camera* pointed at you. And *now*, they fixed it so that if you *ain't* got a camera focused on you, you're just *poof!*'

'Who are *you* callin' a poof, ya bloody bastard!' someone shouts.

'I *dint* say that . . .' the guy yells but everyone is hollering and yelling again and someone pulls him down off the bench. A wire-thin woman with badly dyed copper hair takes his place and raises both her stick-like arms for quiet.

'It's not just the media,' she brays, her voice gravelly but full-bodied, a pipe-organ with a three-pack-a-day habit. 'It's the *paparazzi*, it's their revenge! They been in league with the dark forces for a long time now, and when we tried to get rid a them couple years ago, they swore they'd fix us once and for all. *And they did!*'

The crusty looks at me, alarmed. 'Jeez, who left the bleedin' cage door open?'

I can't help smiling back at him. 'Who says there ever was a door?'

'The bleedin' *paparazzi!*' our new spokeswoman brays. 'They got them new digital cameras, what scans stuff right into the bleedin' computers! That's where everybody's gone, they're on bleedin' *computers!* You don't want to have no camera on you, you don't want none a them lenses on you! You gotta *smash* 'em before they hoover you up like bleedin' *dustbunnies* and stick you on some wanker's *hard-drive* so he can molest your *children* like they all want to on the bleedin' *Internet* . . .'

I'm not sure whether to laugh or applaud the humour and creativity in this one, except I suddenly realise I'd be the only one laughing or clapping. Everyone else has swarmed over the camera-man and the sound tech in a spontaneous, heart-felt human-wave attack you used to see only in gladiator epics.

'*Stop! Stop!*' Molly screams, at first meaning the attack on her colleagues, and then meaning the many horrible drunken hands pulling her down from the bench. She goes over backwards and accidentally kicks me in the head, knocking me into the crusty. We hit the ground together and I'm not sure whether he's trying to attack me or help me or defend himself because he thinks I'm attacking him. Or maybe those aren't his hands at all.

I roll under the bench and curl up tight, clenching my eyes, my teeth, my sphincter, trying to block out the sounds of the television crew being torn to pieces, waiting for the sound of broken glass as they do something unspeakable to the camera . . .

Time goes away; in the distance, I hear gunshots. No, this is

England, and it's New Year's Eve, I'm hearing fireworks, I'm hearing—

I'm hearing nothing but the blood roaring in my ears. At first I don't believe it, and then I listen carefully. Fireworks in the distance; no screams, no breaking glass, no sirens. It takes forever, but I finally force myself to uncurl and unclench everything except my eyes. Because I don't want to see what the drunken horde with a sense of purpose has done to eradicate paedophilia on the Internet.

But when I finally do bring myself to open my eyes, after another span of forever, there's nothing to see except the camera on the grass. There's no sign of anyone else, no sign that anyone else was ever there, except for the tipped-over can of lager that belonged to the crusty. Whatever was left has poured out.

I crawl out from under the bench and look around. The homeless are gone; the crusty's other friends are nowhere in sight.

I go over to the camera and pick it up. It's even heavier than I thought it would be, and no wonder. When I look through the lens, I see, superimposed over the sharp-focused sight of the grass of Duckett's Common, large red letters, blinking on and off:

FULL.

I look over at the street lamp and the zebra-crossing pole. The same red letters flashing the same word on and off have appeared on them as well.

FULL. FULL. FULL.

I put the camera down on the grass very carefully and sit down on the bench again. I don't have a watch, but I'm pretty sure it must be after midnight now. It's the new year, century, millennium and I can't help it — I've come this far, I might as well wait and see who's going to come round and unload those cameras.

I'm curious as to what exposure they've been using.

Nicholas Blincoe

'ENGLISH ASTRONAUT'

Harry was counting heads by the dance floor when this bouncing, healthy guy came over, saying 'Fuck man. I don't believe this.'

Harry looked up. He saw a wide-mouth smile splitting a face framed by dense curly hair, the closest a white guy could get to an afro. Then, on his chin, a fluff-ball of a goatee. Harry's best guess, the guy stretched to about ten feet tall. The hair-do gave him the extra height. Anyone who looked like that, it would take a major blackout before you forgot him. All Harry could do was shrug.

'You got to remember me: Mobi, man. Last year in Goa, you were down with Yoni's crew. I was with Arno ... Yigal, yeah? All those guys?'

Harry nodded, Maybe. He said, 'We're all fellow travellers, all trying to follow the signs.'

That was it for now. Who could talk over the music? Anyway, so far as Harry was concerned, it was Goa, Goa, Gone. White beaches, white heat, white-out. He smiled, *Peace*, and turned back to the club floor. On his count, he reckoned 5 per cent of the people dancing were carrying automatic weapons, mostly rifles but with a few machine-pistols stirred into the mix. Harry was numerological. He took the firearm percentage as a correlation and a proof of the prophecy. What he called the 5 per cent apostles. It was an article of mathematics and faith: there were the 5 per cent who lit the candles, the 10 per cent who blew them out and the 85 per cent who were for ever lost to the struggle and the light.

The Mobi guy was still craning over Harry's shoulder, bending low to catch his ear. 'Freaks you out, man.'

'Huh?'

'You know, coming here, seeing all these guys with guns.' The way he spoke, it was one of those *accents-plus* . . . meaning an accent plus an American inflexion. He even spoke American: when he said '*guys*' he also meant girls.

One girl walked past. She was wearing a pair of army shorts and a bikini top, a machine-gun hanging from her shoulder and a spare clip fastened to the barrel with elastic bands. Mobi smiled at her and held up his hand: like '*Five Minutes*'. He turned back to Harry saying: 'My girl friend. Since she's drafted, I don't get to see her. It's real bad.'

Harry said, 'You got to be prepared.'

'For sure.' The guy said it with a shrug: *it's a fact.*

Harry was thinking, 'Be Prepared'? Wasn't that the cub-scout motto? There had to be a misalignment somewhere; all kinds of extraneous shit hexing his head.

Now the guy was asking, 'So how long you been in Israel?'

'I got here . . . the day before day before yesterday,' Harry decided the guy could do the numbers for himself.

'What? The twenty-seventh, yeah? Where did you come from?'

Harry tried to think back but it was just a ball of confusion: times, dates and places with no index.

The guy started twitching into giggles. 'Shit, man. You don't remember? Whatever you're on, I got to try it. You Brits, you're all fucking crazy.'

Harry flashed a short grin and slid away. Not crazy . . . attuned. It was just that, sometimes, the tunes were out of synch. The numbers were playing out of sequence. Maybe dancing would help.

Back at the bar, Mobi was telling his girl friend, 'This guy is unbelievable, you know. He has no idea where he's come from. He says he just fucking dropped down.'

Mobi turned and pointed. Harry was out there, trancing across the floor, his hands criss-crossing the air like *yogi-a-go-go*. The club was set in the basement of a two-storey building off Jaffa Road in the centre of West Jerusalem. It was kind of cramped but there weren't many places that played trance. Anyway, Mobi liked it. If anyone asked, he'd say you could meet some real cool types, like the guys he met during his last vacation in Goa. Mobi visited the club once a week, using his folks' car to drive the thirteen kilometres from their villa in Abu Gosh.

Mobi said, 'The guy's been all over: Koh Phang Nga, Goa, the Mountains of the Moon. He's touched down here for the millennium.'

Illy nodded, checked her watch. The music was boring and she was due back at the barracks in the morning. She swung her Uzi round so it hung at her back, stood up and said, 'I need a lift, Mobi.'

Mobi said, 'You hear about this mental New Year's Eve party they got planned, out in the Negev?'

She had. But she was on duty that night. Anyway, she wasn't sure she was into partying for the millennium ... she couldn't decide. She'd read an article in the paper against it, saying that it was of no significance to an Israeli. Then a few politicians had got up in the Knesset and said they were going to get a boycott deal going. They said the same thing again, outside of parliament, on the TV news. The way Illy saw it, as long as she was on duty, she didn't have to make a decision whether the millennium was a blasphemy or un-Israeli or whatever.

She dragged Mobi to his feet, telling him, 'Come on.'

Mobi stood and followed her out, hoping the Brit guy Harry saw him wave. As he caught Illy at the door, he remembered he still had some of that mental Dutch weed. He asked her, 'You want to drive over to Shoresh, sit out and smoke it?'

Illy thought. 'Yeah, okay.'

Harry left the club about an hour later but didn't go far. He checked his record player out of the cloakroom and sat on top of it, out in Zion Square. After the airless fug of the club, it was a chance to enjoy the night air. He'd been told Jerusalem was unseasonably warm for December. The weather was good, like a perfect English spring. There were plenty of other people slumped around the square, either in clumps or in couples. One slim, wiry guy stood and walked over. When he reached Harry, he asked if he was the Brit. Harry nodded.

'So how do you like it here, man?'

'It's pure history, ten thousand years in the making.'

The guy nodded, 'Yeah ... close on, close on. It all happens here. The hub, the nub, the centre of the fucking world.'

Harry corrected him. 'The fucking cosmos.'

'That's right. So what do you want: acid, X or K? I also got some hash and a quantity of the local herbs.'

He stuffed his hands in the pockets of his coat, jangling one side and then the other. Whatever Harry wanted, it was all wrapped and ready to go. Harry decided on a couple of Ketamine tablets and also asked what the acid was like. The guy told him it was cool, not so visual you couldn't function. It was popular with the army guys 'cos it segued just as well with rock 'n' roll as it did with trance: 'You can either make out you're in 'Nam or back in Goa. Whichever you prefer. Call it versatile, its works every which way.' He nodded at Harry's hand, clutched round the K tabs. 'You thinking of taking those now?'

Harry shook his head. 'No, I'll wait for the Millennium.'

'Yeah? You going out to the desert party? Mobi mention it to you?'

Harry took a moment to call up Mobi's picture. Then he nodded: the tall one, yeah, they spoke for a while. He remembered now, the kid definitely mentioned a desert event. At the time Harry wasn't sure whether that meant a rave, a festival or some kind of spiritual lift-off.

The dealer said, 'You want to get Mobi to drive you. His

parents got a Cherokee so there's plenty of room and no chance of you getting stranded.' A pause, then: 'Where you staying?'

Harry had the address written on a piece of paper. He read it out, 'Salah ed-Din Street.'

'Out with the Arabs, yeah? Well, you'll be safe, Blondie.' The dealer grinned. 'You should ask Mobi to put you up. His folks' place is amazing. Like it's part medieval fucking castle, part jet-port. His old man's the Israeli Bill Gates or something.'

They were just about done now. But as the dealer nodded and turned to go, Harry said, 'Hey.'

'Yeah?'

'Where can I get an adaptor plug?'

'At three in the morning, no-fucking-where. Why?'

'My record player, it's got an English plug.'

Harry tapped the box he was sitting on. The guy bent over and saw what looked like a square trunk, or maybe an outsize vanity case. It was covered in red leatherette, stretched over plywood. Then the guy noticed the dials and the circular cut-outs which the speaker sat behind. It was an old mono-player, like a Dansette.

'You brought a record player with you?'

'An Elisabethan Astronaut.' Harry pointed out the name, written above the dials in a sixties idea of sci-fi script.

'So what do they say at your hotel, you start cranking this thing up?'

'Nothing,' Harry said. 'I haven't got it working yet.'

It was seven in the morning when the wailing started. Harry's room was level with the top of the nearest minaret. He could look over and see the guy who did the chanting, yelling his head off. Harry wasn't complaining, he didn't want to waste time sleeping when he was travelling. The Elisabethan Astronaut sat open on the table by the window. Harry repacked his books inside the box. They fitted neatly around the spindle, on top of the turntable. Then he hefted the whole thing down the stairs to the main lobby.

The man at the desk nodded hello, giving the record player a sideways look as he said, '*Keef alak?*'

Harry smiled, said, 'Right on.'

He had been careful so far. He had even paid for his room up-front on the day he arrived. That way no one would worry that he took all his belongings with him every time he left the room. The joke was, he booked the room straight through to 2 January 2000, even though the world was scheduled for termination the night before.

Harry said, 'Electrical shop?'

The desk man shook his head. 'Electrics?'

Harry thought for a moment and decided to mime shaving with an electric shaver, followed through with a question-shrug. The man said, Ah, and walked round from his desk. He was wearing a short white Arab smock, otherwise a normal pair of chinos and a pair of Italian loafers. At the door of his hotel he pointed Harry to the right and said, 'The Colon's Gate.' Then chopped with his hand, 'Straight. Electric shop.'

It was a bright, sunny-cool morning, close enough to dawn for the walls of the Old City to still have a pink dawn-blush. The closest landmark was the mosque they called the Dome of the Rock. High up above the city walls, its gold-leafed dome was studded with pin-spots of lights, rotating like a slo-mo glitter ball. Harry looked up, got his bearings.

The hotel guy had pointed down the road, towards the second gate along; the one facing the run-down arcade of fast-food stalls and music shops, just past the bus station. Harry didn't know anything about the buses, most people seemed to use the service-taxis parked beside the arcade. The taxis were all long wheel-base Mercedes, for some reason coloured safari-suit tan. This early in the morning, they were leaving the rank half full. If any driver looked across and saw Harry carrying the Elisabethan Astronaut, they assumed he was packed for a journey. They called across, shouting, 'Jericho? Ramallah? Beth'lem?'

Harry shook his head, he was travelling in time not space.

All he needed were a few pieces of electrical kit. He crossed the road, through the gate and passed into the stone crush of the Old City. Here, the busiest streets were maybe twelve feet wide, like trenches thrown between the old buildings, the paving slabs worn to a footless glaze, some worn through completely. The worst of the cracks and holes had been repaired with hand-mixed concrete. Harry didn't see an electrical shop but, so far, only one shop in four was open. The rest had security shutters as blank as garage doors: no signs out front giving you opening times, just Arabic graffiti with a distinct political sheen to it.

Harry peeled off the main drag, El-Wad Road, and through a series of turns until he was in a covered section of the city. A few of the slowly opening shops pushed postcards and gifts, the rest sold food; general consumer lines, household necessities. A spice shop had powders in all the colours of dirt set out in bin-sized tubs. Next door was decorated with dangling strings of plastic pan-scrubs, like squeezy sea anemones. Then there was one shop piled high with shoes; the next with carpets; then music cassettes and videos. Everywhere, market-style dross sold right alongside premium brands.

This covered street was set on a hill, climbing in a series of long flat steps. As the steps went up, the roof seemed to get lower and lower. Harry put on a turn of speed. When he broke into the open he found himself on the Via Dolorosa. He read the street sign and decided this was a good place for a sit-down. He set the Elisabethan Astronaut on its edge and took up a position by the Second Station of the Cross: the Chapels of the Condemnation and Flagellation. As he sat, he watched the visitors work out which way to genuflect, right for flagellation, left for condemnation.

A man leaned up beside him. He was wearing an English hat, like a cricket umpire, but spoke in an American accent. He asked if Harry was a pilgrim. Harry said he guessed he was ... 'in the deepest sense.'

The man said, 'You know the world ends tonight.'

Harry nodded, 'I know.'

'What are you gonna do?'

Harry had his own agenda. All he said, 'It's not fully decided, not yet.'

'Me, I'll go to Golgotha to await His judgement.'

Harry nodded: 'Sounds good.'

A group of monks were coming up the street, faces hooded-up like extras out of *Star Wars*, all singing in off-key, alien voices. As they passed, the American man turned to Harry and said, 'I reckon I'll follow these gentlemen.'

Harry pointed, 'I'll try this-a-way.'

Harry found the electrical shop about five minutes later. It took the electrical shop guy a while to clue-in to Harry's needs. When he did, he suggested Harry try a tourist shop. There was one just around the corner, owned and run by his cousin. It was no problem, he would come along, even help with the translation. The plug cable was folded up inside the Elisabethan Astronaut's case. Harry opened it up for the new shop-keeper to see.

'It's got to fit this.'

He held up the three-prong plug. The man prodded the earth pin, turned the plug around and then went to a shoebox at the back of his shop. He returned with an adaptor plug and handed it to Harry who tried it for size. It fitted.

The first guy, the electrical shop man, said: 'Do you want to test it?' There was a mains socket halfway up the wall. The man smiled, open and helpful: 'Test it now. So we know there is no mistake.'

Harry shook his head. 'Not here.'

'No problem. My cousin makes no charge for electricity.' The man tugged the plug out of Harry's hands and was almost at the wall before Harry stopped him.

'NOT HERE.'

The two men were knocked back by Harry's ferocity. They were both big. Between them they'd seen all kinds of action. They didn't know what to make of this skinny English kid. He had to be one of those *crazies*, come to Jerusalem to lose his head. After he paid and left, they watched him walk down El Wad Road towards Temple Mount before they decided to send a boy ahead of him. Better warn the security team if there was a crazy around.

Temple Mount, what the Jews called the Holy of the Holies because Solomon built his temple there, was now the site of two mosques; El-Aqsa and the more splendid Dome of the Rock. It was always Harry's plan to head for the Rock. The way he saw it, the place was a nexus for all the prophecies: if anything it was over-coded with meaning. Now Harry was almost there, he was bouncing. But as he rounded the next corner, he was almost knocked down by a little kid, about ten years old. The kid was going full pelt. One elbow grazed Harry's legs as his arms pumped up and down, his skinny legs splaying out as he ran. Ahead were the heavy iron gates of the Temple Mount compound. These gates were kept locked, visitors entered through a smaller door cut into the right-hand side gate. The kid hardly slowed, just jumped through the little door with his arms outstretched like he was diving into a hole. On the far side of the gates, there was a desk and a group of volunteers who took care of security. When Harry stepped through the doorway, the little kid was standing behind the security desk, among the older youths and men. Everyone was looking straight at Harry.

'We need to see inside your case, sir.' The man who spoke was thick-set, moustached. One side of his head was creased, either by a bullet or a baton. He slapped a hand on the table, just to encourage Harry. 'Security, sir.'

Harry looked at the kid then around the rest of the faces. He lifted the Elisabethan Astronaut on to the table, flipped open the two catches and left it for one of the men to open. Apparently, that wasn't good enough. Harry had to open the lid himself.

The security guys pored over the books stacked inside the box. Harry looked away, across the marble-paved compound to the Dome of the Rock. The gold of the dome was shining even brighter as the sun climbed higher.

'This, sir? What is this?'

Harry looked back. The security chief was holding up the book on numerology. Harry nodded hard, he didn't go anywhere without it. He said, 'It's my Bible.'

'And this?' Holding a plastic jacketed book, imprinted with a burnished cross.

'Yeah well, that is the Bible. But it's nothing without the code book.' Like Harry always said, the Bible had the raw data but it was like something seen through sunglasses after dark. It required decipherisation. That was why Harry always carried the book of numerology, to access the Bible's thirty-six levels of meaning. Over time, he developed a good way of explaining the concept. He turned his serene look on the security guy and said: 'Like, everyone knows the Bible is the Word, but not that it is also the Number. That's the hidden knowledge, that's why I need the second book.'

The security chief tossed the book on the table and shrugged at his men. There were another couple of books inside the record player case, besides toothpaste and Harry's alternate pair of socks, but none of the men seemed interested in further reading. They couldn't feel the mathematics: neither the word nor its digit-double. Harry decided to leave them to their darkness. There was so little time, not everyone could join the 5 per cent. They didn't have any more questions, anyway. Just shifted through his gear.

Harry looked back across the compound. There were groups milling around the doors of El-Aqsa Mosque, opposite the Dome of the Rock. It looked as though prayers were about to start.

The security chief broke in again, 'Leave this here.'

'What?'

'If you want to complete your sightseeing, you may leave your record player here. I will give it back to you as you leave.'

'That's no good. That can't be done.'

'Your decision. You will not come in here with this thing.'

Harry looked him over. The security man and his crew. Harry

wondered what his chances were if he picked up the case, made to leave but fakied, took a run for the Dome of the Rock with the Astronaut under his arm. He might make twenty-five yards. Not much more, the box was too heavy.

He tried another tack, 'You think this is a bomb?'

The man shrugged.

Harry said, 'You think I'd walk round with it if it was a bomb? Risk blowing myself up so close to the Two Triple-O? Like I'm really going to kill myself the day before the end?'

No one said anything.

'I mean, you see the fucking irony, don't you?' Harry said. 'Missing the whole fucking finale.'

The security chief said, 'Get out.'

'What?'

His men were moving into position now, gripping hold of his arms and leading him back to the door in the gate.

Harry was screaming, 'Why are you throwing me out? I've not done nothing to you, you fucking twats. Get off me.'

He was lifted bodily over the lip of the door, stumbling as he was dropped to the street. He kept the Elisabethan Astronaut clutched to his chest for safety, it's why he couldn't keep his balance. He stumbled to the side wall, clattering shoulder-first to the old stones. He was still shouting, 'Twats. Fucking twats.'

The security guards followed him through the doorway, partly encircling him. He had a choice, he could clear off down El Wad Road. If he was as crazy as he sounded, he could stick around and continue shouting his theory about the end of the world. The crowd milling round the entrance to El-Aqsa Mosque had already seen the beginnings of the trouble. Sergeant Alawi, head of the volunteer security force, could hold back his own men but there was no way he could stop the crowd if they decided this was another one of those fundamentalist lunatics, convinced that Judgement Day would never happen until Temple Mount was cleared of Muslims.

Harry was shouting, 'Know the numbers: the three sixes, the

three to the six. Two thousand divided by three is all the sixes, divided by six is all the threes. That's a judgement on you, you bastards. You know it by it's number. Two thousand divided by thirty-six reveals all the fives. That's the 5 per cent who know His judgement is at hand. So get ready, you twats.'

Sergeant Alawi turned to one of his men and said, 'Get him out of here. I don't want anyone kicked to death on my watch.'

'Right, chief.' The man nodded, made to go but turned back. 'Shall we tell the Jews?'

Sergeant Alawi thought. 'Yes, okay. Run over to the police over at the Wall and give them a description. Give them one more headbanger to look out for.'

Harry was shouting, 'Got it, you bastards: a message from the 5 per cent. Get your fucking hands off me.'

A man of about twenty-five with a mad moustache and mad hair was pulling at Harry's arm, dragging him back into the Old City. Harry tried to wrench himself free but caught something in the man's eyes, a pause for thought. The man tapped the side of his head, threw a look back towards the entrance to Temple Mount, an implied question, like: *Do you really need to stay?* Harry looked, the doorway was a mass of bodies, almost climbing on top of each other to get a look at him. Harry decided to go, regroup at least.

East Jerusalem was dark, the street lights were shut down and the whole area had a spooky, tourist-unfriendly look. It was a different story in West Jerusalem and most of the Old City. The electricity was working fine and the crowds had followed the light. The ugliest crowd was pushing around the Church of the Holy Sepulchre, waiting to get into one of the masses. The problem, though, an American tourist was barricaded into one of the smaller chapels and until the Israeli police prised him out, the millennium celebrations were on hold. The chapel was built on a platform inside the main church and had been identified as the site of Golgotha and Calvary. The American had the idea that the place where Christ died was the place most likely to see His Second Coming and the guy wanted to be sure he was the first in line for a blessing. The only way into the chapel was up a couple of steep staircases and the man easily covered both with his shotgun.

Illy Ered was in the IDF barracks at the tourist resort on Har Homa, high above Bethlehem. She was working the radio when the news came through from Jerusalem. Illy wasn't surprised. She already knew about a similar incident in the Church of the Nativity, Bethlehem, which was closer to her platoon's beat. Their guy was believed to be Brazilian and seemed to be working on the theory that Jesus was more likely to return to the place he was born. So far as Illy knew, the guy was alive and safe in the custody of the Palestinian Authority. Bethlehem was a PA town, so if her captain wanted a full briefing he was going to have to ask the Palestinians. Illy was certain the platoon would never go down there. There were an estimated two million people in Bethlehem tonight, most of them crowded into Manger Square outside the Nativity Church. According to the schedule, they were watching a firework display but soon the Roman and Orthodox Patriarchs were going to climb on the church roof and give their sermons. On top of which, Illy had just relayed the news that Yasser Arafat was likely to show. It was probably true: Arafat loved getting his photo taken with the local Patriarchs. The way things stood, there was no chance of the Israeli Defence Force swooping into action.

At 10.45, she got the alarm and her platoon scrambled. Half of them were convinced they were going to attack Bethlehem. One guy was so pumped, he was sitting in the back of the truck hammering his rifle against his head. The sentries were pulling open the barracks' gates when the captain swung into the back of the truck. He saw the guy beating himself up and grabbed him by the neck.

'Asshole.'

'We're going in, yeah? We're gonna fuck Yasser sideways, man, sir?'

'Shut up.' The captain turned to Illy, 'What's the news?'

Illy wore the headphones lopsided, on one ear only. She said, 'We're being sent to the Negev. Await orders en route.'

The headbanger said, 'No way, no way. Not fucking desert manoeuvres while we got Yasser's paramilitaries pissing in our fucking face.'

Illy shook her head. 'This is not a manoeuvre.'

The second she said it, everyone turned on her, mouths open.

The captain saying, 'Cool it. We don't know what's happening yet.' But you could tell everyone was thinking: the fucking Egyptians are invading again.

Illy was shaking. She managed to say, 'Not Egyptians. A group of Israeli settlers. They've attacked a rave party.'

All she could think about was Mobi, stranded in the Negev. Clueless and defenceless, probably drugged out of compos mentis. What could he do to save himself?

Further details came through as their truck dropped down on to the new bypass and headed for Hebron and the desert beyond. By now, they weren't just listening to the army radio but also to the eleven o'clock radio news. A whole platoon straining towards one cheap transistor radio as their truck cannoned down the highway.

A woman's voice saying: '*It is still not entirely clear why the hardline group from the settlers community opened fire on the party-goers. Speculation centres on their opposition to any form of celebration of the beginning of the third millennium of the Common Era.*'

Illy listened, trying to catch a mention of the party organisers or the desert location, hoping that when she heard either, it would not sound familiar. She tried to remember what Mobi had said before he left for the Negev.

The voice continuing its statistics: '*Reports of fifteen dead remain unsubstantiated . . .*'

Illy's headphones crackled, cutting across the news report. 'Go to Jerusalem. Repeat, turn around and head for Jerusalem.'

Her captain caught the look on her face and tried to read it. He was shouting, *'What's up?'* Illy shook her head. She had one hand clamped on her left earphone, trying to block out all the clamour while she confirmed the message. Tonight's secure codeword was Mordechai. She heard it, repeated it, and banged on the back of the driver's cab.

Their driver pulled a U-turn by bumping across the central reservation of the road. They were only just outside Bethlehem now and the mouth of the first of the bypass tunnels opened ahead of them. Jerusalem was ten minutes away, straight through the mountain.

The newscaster's voice continued: *'IDF personnel stationed in the Negev ...'* the tunnel swallowed the rest of the radio report. The platoon listened to static until they heard *'... all settlers believed to be dead.'*

One soldier, the platoon headcase, was shouting, 'We're killing Israelis? I'm not fucking killing Israelis.'

The captain told him to shut up. No one was asking him to, they were heading for East Jerusalem.

The radio again, *'... claims that the rave was organised by sun or devil-worshippers contrast with reports that it was staged by drug dealers associated with the so-called Israeli Beach Mafia of Goa ...'* The truck drove into the second and longest tunnel and the radio shorted into static once more.

The captain said, 'What's happening in Jerusalem, Ered? What have you heard?'

Illy wasn't even on the right wavelength, she was searching for the channel used by the South Negev unit.

'Ered!'

She snapped to, 'Captain.'

'Stick to Jerusalem, soldier.'

'Sorry, sir.' She refocused, told herself to keep it compart-mentalised: file Mobi under *'civilian'* and turn the page.

She finally came up with a message from Jerusalem: 'Someone's broken into the Temple Mount area, sir. The city police may need back-up in case it develops into a situation with the Arab irregulars.'

Back in Jerusalem, Sergeant Alawi's opposite number on the official Jerusalem police force had received his orders. He began by saying, 'I've been instructed to recognise you.'

Alawi thanked him. 'You look familiar, too, Sergeant.'

They crossed the Temple Mount compound together, the Israeli sergeant pointing to the tops of the walls: 'I can get snipers up there.'

'Then we'll certainly have a riot.' The last time the Israeli put shooters up on the walls, they were shooting Palestinians.

'What then?'

'I don't know. I didn't even think you were allowed in here.' The Chief Rabbi had ruled the Temple Mount off-limits to Jews ... claiming the place was too holy.

The Israeli sergeant said, 'There's been a rethink, only the Dome of the Rock is off-limits now.'

'That's too bad. The intruder is in the Dome of the Rock. He's sat on top of the Rock.'

'What's he doing?'

'Waiting to ascend to Heaven on his record player.'

The sergeant was impressed. That was way loonier than anything he had heard before.

'How did he get in?'

Sergeant Alawi shrugged. 'The important thing is, getting him out.'

As they crossed the threshold of the mosque, the Israeli sergeant got a quick chill along his spine. He counted himself an atheist but still, no Jew was supposed to enter the site of the temple, the place that received the first spot of light when God illuminated the world. The place that would be lit once more, so he'd been told, when the Messiah appeared. Already, he believed he could hear a kind of sweet heavenly music. As he reached the centre of the mosque he recognised the voice of Karen Carpenter: 'Calling Occupants of Inter Planetary Craft.' In the centre of the great round hall, he stopped at the edge of a balustrade and looked down, into a hole and the old caves below. He was surprised, the caves looked nothing like caves ... they were so ornate, so elaborately decorated. The only clue that they were natural was the great flat rock directly below: the Rock, where Abraham almost sacrificed his son and, later, where Mohammed's soul had lingered in a dream before flying on to Heaven. And sitting on top of it, a stupid-looking kid holding a red leatherette box.

Harry looked up, saw them looking down, so waved. Then he turned the volume knob, just a touch. The music lifted him up. He could almost feel himself tearing free of his Earth chains and rising up to become infinite. In the ideal sphere, among all the numbers, he would be a number without end ...

He felt a piercing shock followed by a spreading pain. He never thought that his transportation would be so painful. But then, as Karen Carpenter's voice dipped to a whisper, he saw a pin-spot of light open ahead of him. He could actually feel his thoughts slipping away, losing the jagged peaks and troughs that swung up and down. He was becoming just one frequency, one flat line, extending on and on and on ...

At 12.03, just three minutes into the Third Millennium Anno Domini or Common Era, Illy Ered stood shoulder-to-shoulder with men she knew were trained Palestinian Authority soldiers, even though there weren't supposed to be any in Jerusalem. Their chief, a man named Alawi, was giving the orders: they were to block off access from either direction of El Wad Road. Once her captain confirmed Alawi's order, Illy's platoon got to work.

Mobi met her later and asked, 'What was happening?'

Illy said, 'I wish I knew. They were smuggling something out of the Temple Mount but I couldn't tell what it was. Some of the guys reckoned it was the body of someone killed inside the mosque — but you know what they're like, every one a conspiracy theorist.' What she thought was she had seen the Palestinian sergeant carrying a battered old suitcase, an old-style wood one covered in imitation leather.

She shrugged: 'Whatever, it had to be important if the Arabs were co-operating.' Then she looked at Mobi. 'I was sure you were killed.'

Mobi stood there, giving an enormous shoulder-heave of disbelief: 'As it got towards midnight, we had our heads turned towards the sky, watching this laser move across the face of the moon, ticking away the seconds. Then, suddenly, these lunatics are rising up on the rocks above us, opening fire with fucking assault rifles. Fucking psychopathic, fucking Orthodox twats. They come over like they're so spiritual, they know it all. And then they try and kill us. I tell you, I've had it with all that hard-line shit. What we had in the desert, it was purer, more spiritual, *closer* ... you know what I'm saying?'

Illy tried to follow. She didn't feel it was down to her to draw a line, decide exactly when Mobi began talking nonsense. She thought it was a miracle he wasn't even scratched when the shooting started.

Mobi tried again, 'It's like that guy said, the one I was speaking to at the club last night. Yeah?'

Illy nodded. She thought she remembered.

'What he was saying is, we're on the verge of a new realisation. If you got eyes to see, you just gotta open them because the numbers are all racked up in alignment.'

'Oh?'

'He told me, we're the first to understand, not the last. Soon everyone will know that man can move between Heaven and Earth like an astronaut.' Mobi pulled a piece of paper out of his pocket. 'I even wrote it down. He said, when the first man disappears, maybe no one will even realise he's made the journey. But once we put it together, we will know anything is possible.

Man can move between Heaven and Earth at will, like that first astronaut.'

'Do you believe that?'

'Yeah. What I reckon, *Why not?* That's my philosophy.'

Grant Morrison

'I'M A POLICEMAN'

'How about a newly-born baby with *'Fuck me! It's Diet Cloke!'* felt-tipped on its tit?' Id yells. 'Sort of like a message from God, you know? The way people keep finding the name of Allah when they cut marrows in half . . .'

'Benetton did that one ages ago,' I mutter. I know she can't hear me; the party's beginning to peak now as the nation's hippest young band take to the stage and launch into their Christmas number one 'A Binary Precursor for SN 1987A'. Already the anthem of a generation, the song is the first to openly hint at an explanation for the curiously axisymmetric rings of Supernova 1987A. The group, Microbiology In Clinical Practice, are two girls, two boys, a gender transient and a dog; it's an almost perfect blend and their brand of 'Hexstasy-fuelled Concrete Jungle has defined the "commence de siècle" (sic) spirit of a post-techno generation desperate to throw off the oppressive shackles of hand-me-down baggy psychedelia in the wake of the murder of the Moon Goddess by the Sun King, which signalled, as did the American moon landing in 1969, an attempt by rigidly patriarchal power structures to regain control over an increasingly fluid and feminine tendency in Western art and culture . . .' (as I wrote in the liner notes for their debut CD-ROM 'Hello Boys', the cover of which features a starving Rwandan waif holding two crudely carved begging bowls at chest height).

I decide to go out on to the balcony. I feel like playing with my gun.

As I emerge into the cryogenic chill from the colossal storm of light particles and sound waves that is the party, a Nuremberg-style cheer goes up. A millions-strong human traffic jam, stretching all the way back down the Mall, bubbles and ripples like the surface of the archaic tar pits which once consumed the dinosaurs.

THEY COULDN'T GO BACK TO SCHOOL

We've been trying to think of ways to market Cloaca-Cola, the *arriviste* soft-drink sensation from the newly-emerging economic superstate that is the Indian sub-continent. Cloke derives its piquant and surprising aftertaste from an infusion of ashes; the by-product of burning tonnes of human excrement in huge cremation pyres. Citing the great Tantric masters, Cloke bosses are selling their product on the proven health and longevity benefits of consuming powdered human faeces.

'I'm thinking we should keep it simple,' I say.

Id weaves through the Jarmanesque turmoil of dancing clergy-men, defrocked coppers and exotic Go-Go Girl Guides, trailing clouds of 'Conformity' by Calvin Klein (a fragrance so potent it's almost visible). Four hundred miles away, dogs in Scotland smell her coming and whimper in their sleep.

PLENTY OF EXCITEMENT

'I'm the country's greatest living writer, for fuck's sake! My ad campaigns are mainstays of the sixth year studies English curriculum! Why am I having deadline trouble with this Cloke gig?'

No one answers.

All I need is a slogan. The clock runs out at midnight. If I don't modem the goods to New Delhi by then, the shit flies like *Challenger* flew: I blow the biggest publicity coup of all time.

I've decided to make them sweat a little.

I swing my leg over the balcony and get comfy before taking aim. The motion of the crowd simulates peristalsis.

'Starorzewski! Starorzewski!' they cry with one voice, spotting me.

Relenting for a moment, I cradle the rifle in my lap and lift a bright red megaphone to my lips. Words shall be my weapons.

'YOU'RE ALL BEING DUPED BY THE CAPITALIST MEDIA MACHINE!' I scream. 'FORCE-FED A DIET OF OTHER PEOPLE'S LIVES, YOU SIT CHAINED TO YOUR TELEVISION SETS, AVIDLY CONSUMING THE LATEST MEANINGLESS FICTIONS WHILE YOUR OWN DEVALUED EXISTENCES ARE CONDENSED INTO MINUTE-LONG "VIDEO NATION" CLIPS ON BBC 2! LET TEN MEN AND WOMEN MEET WHO ARE RESOLVED ON THE LIGHTNING OF VIOLENCE RATHER THAN THE AGONY OF SURVIVAL; FROM THIS MOMENT DESPAIR ENDS AND TACTICS BEGIN!'

The crowd cheers and the sound is like an avalanche of bass drums. I swiftly snatch up the gun, discouraged, and glue my eye to the scope. Caught in the precision cross-hairs of my telescopic sight, a hysterically-haemmorhaging novice nun moulds a life-size photograph of my face to the contours of her own and forces her tongue through my unsmiling lips.

Now I've seen everything.

A NICE EVENING'S WORK

'They can't hear a word you're saying,' Id tells me, lounging into view stage left. 'Christ! It's freezing out here!'

She's right but I don't care. I'm generating *Tum-mo*, the psychic heat of the Tibetan Lamas. Far from being cold, I'm producing enough heat energy to light a cigarette.

'Every word you say is being monitored and electronically *détourned* by MI6 Anti-Situationists, using Negative Sound tech-nology,' Id goes on, baiting me. (The French bioterrorist cell that hothouse-cloned her from a stain on the blacktop created a monster.) 'Nothing you just came out with has anything to do with what they hear.'

'I love Big Brother.'

'Me too.' I can see Id's wearing contact lenses with three-element multi-coated air-spaced optics, which allow her to see far beyond the range of the naked eye. 'You're missing all the fun, you know,' she says. Her lenses whir as they zoom in on the crowd. 'They're waiting for the End of the World. In fifteen minutes, the nineties will be over. It'll all be over. For them anyway.'

'I love technology,' I say with genuine feeling, and look back into the huge state room where the last and greatest party of the Age of Pisces is in full swing.

ALL GOOD THINGS END!

On screen are some of Id's latest *Hello!* photospreads blown up to epic, Hitlerian proportions:

Here, in a Rei Kawabuko tank dress, daintily regurgitating a tiny roasted quail into the chirping open mouth of her eldest son. Here, artlessly toasting her ex with champagne at 7gs in a NASA centrifuge. Here again, glittering, nailed to a spinning atom in the simulated crucifixion which ended her run as Unified Field Theory in Andrew Lloyd Webber's musical adaptation of Stephen Hawking's bestselling *A Brief History of Time*. And here — the money shot — Id stripped to the waist, passionately French-kissing a terminal AIDS patient in Bangkok.

'You don't think they're too much?' she asks nervously.

'You look gorgeous darling!' I say.

'Even the one of me shitting on Mother Teresa's grave?'

'It's a fucking masterpiece,' I assure her, 'Lichfield outdid himself.'

'You think so?' she says, brightening. I can always win her over.

'Of course,' I say. 'I mean, let's face it, at least it's not ...' I don't have to say another word. We both smile, recalling Tamara Beckwith's ill-advised photo-diary of her participation in a pro-celebrity baby seal cull organised by the Norwegian Minster for Culture and his son.

'I know what you mean,' Id says, spoiling the moment.

DOWN THE SECRET PASSAGE IN THE MIDDLE OF THE NIGHT

Resuming my telescopic scan of the record-breaking crowd, I try to imagine it as seen from one of the orbital spy satellites which constantly supply the tabloids with pictures of Id, myself and our dazzling army of human refuse. Seen from a geo-synchronous orbit, 39,000 miles out into space, the surging biomass might appear as a grotesque cephalopod, jammed uncomfortably into the streets of London. How quickly surveillance surrenders to surrealism! I hover on the brink of epiphany then re-sight, targeting a dwarf in a red coat, exactly like the one from *Don't Look Now*.

A WONDERFUL DAY

As though somehow reading my mind, Id has activated the random channel surfer. The Philips Liquid Crystal Wallpaper display flutters madly, presenting horrific images from Paris's autumn collections. Top marks for a refusal to compromise with even the basic tenets of civilised society have to be awarded to the Neo-Anti-Nazi Radical Animal Rights designer Klaus Shreck, who set the seal on his status as the *enfant terrible* of the international rag trade when he sent *überwaif* Little Nikita the catwalk wearing the expertly-flayed skin of Naomi Campbell as a pair of culottes. Shreck in that one shocking photo-opportunity was immediately exposed as the international terrorist and sadistic serial killer, Leatherneck. Seized by the police of five countries, amid the popping of champagne corks and flashbulbs, he jeered at reporters, vowing he'd be back to highlight further animal rights abuses.

Little Nikita, after claiming 'I was so high on Hex I could have been fucking a giant ant for all I know,' was released on bail, wearing a mirror latex spray-on catsuit. Everyone felt sorry for her; Steven Meisel's groundbreaking PET scan shots of her brain in the preceding May's *Vogue* had resulted in a fashion-conscious doctor's timely identification of the early stages of Creutzfeldt-Jakob Disease.

'Can't we have the adverts on?' I whine.

HITCH-HIKING ALL THE WAY

'This is my favourite!' Id says, pointing at the screen.

I snake through the crowd with my scope. The negative Union Jack is everywhere. It feels like Altamont.

I feel like the Omega Man.

'Is this what it's come to?' I muse bitterly through the mega-phone.

A NIGHT OF SURPRISES

When I look back from my reverie, Id's laughing loudly.

'What's it an advert for?'

'Instant coffee,' she says, searching in her purse for the two pink DMT capsules she knows she put there last night. 'It's that new coffee, made from South American holly. It's got five times the caffeine so you have to vomit it up as soon as you've drunk it.'

I'm watching a Dobermann 'devil dog' savaging ET. The terrified alien's blood splatters the screen with explosive ferocity. It's no contest; the innocent visitor from a gentler world is rapidly pawed and chewed to a bloody psychedelic mess in hi-fidelity slo-mo detail.

With mingled nausea and fascination I stare, entranced. I'm captivated by the director's pornographic fascination with the little alien's viscera, which seem, in shamanic fashion, to actually spell out the name of the coffee product. I can't bear to look away as CGI technology contrives to put the viewer directly into the action through the fear-maddened eyes of the slavering canine. The whole thing arouses deep, sullen electricity in my reptile backbrain; I long to fuck, to defecate, to protect my territory.

'I'm sure these adverts are designed to provoke aggressive territorial responses,' I say.

No one dares contradict me.

THE WARNING OF THE BELLS

The merciless stars shine down. Quasar transmissions from the distant Lyman-Alpha clouds on the rim of the observable universe seem to mock me.

I mow my skull with the Remington. Black plastic jacket. 'Smart Thug' T-shirt. Bunker boots. I look like a *Sweeney* villain.

I look the part.

I've got minutes to go. My PocketMac, with its 64 billion K data storage capacity (not forgetting the adjustable holographic display, voice-activated virtual mouse and liquid disk drive), is in my hand. I flip open the case and activate the encrypted display with the fool-proof password, 'I'm just a lousy no-good faggot.'

'*I'm okay! You're not okay!*' I chant, remembering the joys of the loudhailer for a moment.

GRANDAD'S OLD BOX

On the wall some typically gorgeous post-op TS in a Vivienne Westwood is wanking across the windscreen of a car while a man drives it into a truck filled with United Nations' peace-keeping troops. Something about the scenario is oddly moving; I feel that I've really come to know these people and as the ad ends, I suddenly miss them; the outwardly tough but deeply sensitive and vulnerable she-male; the young soldiers, nervously exchanging jokes and fags in the face of their own mortality; and, perhaps most poignant of all, the ambiguous figure of the driver, hurled into a world he could never hope to comprehend. It all seems so cruel, so far from the bucolic idylls of Papa and Nicole in the timeless Renault Clio series.

'It's for the new Honda Cursor,' Id yells.

'It's a fucking award-winner,' I whisper, dabbing at my eyes. 'I was there. It was like the end of *Death in Venice*.'

A GREAT DEAL OF NEWS

I tap a few words on the Mac screen. It looks promising. I can hear helicopter rotors now as ten HH-GOA Desert Hawks arrive to airlift the 24-hour party guests out to the next location.

MTV's got Nip-Hop band Octylcyanoacrylate, articulating the rage and frustration of middle management white-collar salary men in the computer software sales division of a multinational. Somehow we've heard it all before. I fire a shot into the crowd and nobody seems to mind. Gamely, somebody shoots back and takes a chunk out of my shoulder with a semi-jacketed hollow point shell.

'I'm thinking of brain surgery,' I say laconically, to mask the dreadful pain of cauterised flesh, chipped bone (although I'm only bringing up the subject to get Id horny, I have been considering a discreet visit to one of the new cosmetic neuro-surgery clinics). 'I thought maybe get some prefrontal cortex work done; you know what my memory's like. Then maybe I could get them to take a look at my IQ. It's big but it's not as big as I'd like.'

THE TIME GOES BY

EastEnders is on the wall now and Grant Mitchell's having a shockingly convincing nervous breakdown. He's just turned on his telly at 8 p.m. on a Thursday and seen himself watching himself, infinitely regressing. Tiffany arrives at the door, anxious to make up, eager to tell him she's thought of a name for their latest — Conjunctivitis Associated With Methicillin-Resistant *Staphylococcus Aureus* In a Long-Term Care Facility, after her grandad — but Grant's gone, his mind folded up and put away like a game of draughts.

Tiff walks into the living room to find him sobbing, in existential crisis. Synth drums sound the crack of doom.

The band are coming to the end of their set with the storming, anthemic 'I'm A Policeman'. Id uses the International Sign Language for the Deaf to tell me that it's time to go.

ALL VERY PECULIAR

Helicopters are beginning to land in the courtyard. The changing of the guard is performed swiftly and with extreme prejudice.

On the wall now, unseen by anyone as the state room empties counter-clockwise down the stairs, a veteran comedian is performing a routine in front of a silent audience of men and women wearing cut-out masks of the Big Brother face from the BBC television version of *1984*, starring Peter Cushing. The entertainer's nerve is beginning to crack after three televised hours of this terrifying psychological ordeal. He's exhausted his supply of jokes and impressions and is now tearfully confessing to a series of shocking assaults on old age pensioners which he apparently carried out a few years ago to help make ends meet between series.

'It's pulling eighteen million viewers a week,' Id tells me on the way to the helicopters.

IN THE MORNING WHAT MORE COULD ANYONE WANT?

We float up over the cheering crowd, swooping in low over the Palace gates. Everything goes into drifting slow motion. They're playing Id's song, the finale of Elgar's Variations on an Original Theme ('Enigma'). The crowd breaks like a wave against the railings, mouths opening and closing with no sound. Hundreds are trampled as we glide overhead and strobe spotlights transform the Mall into a Grand Guignol disco. I reach for my megaphone in an attempt to comfort the bereaved and dying but it's too late. These choppers move fast.

Id has her contacts trained on the Palace as it recedes into classical perspective. Our successors, a group of identically dressed children with white hair and luminous eyes, stand waving on the balcony. I can feel the telekinetic gravity of their unearthly minds, even from here.

'I'm sure they'll do a brilliant job,' I say.

ALONG COMES AN ADVENTURE

The helicopters swing like bells as élite Delta force commandos dance with demented party-goers.

Overhead I can hear the thrumming engines of the fluorescent saffron B-29 bomber the Cloaca-Cola Corporation has chartered for the century's grand finale.

'I can't wait to get to New York!' Id shouts, happily, placing a pink capsule on her tongue. 'By the time we've finished there, it'll look like the end of *Planet of the Apes*.

HEADLONG INTO TROUBLE

On the portable telly I've brought, just in case, the end credits of *Rape, She Wrote* are fading on a tinkled harpsichord riff. A little Channel O logo yaps six tones and then all is still.

Bees buzz, idly labouring. Deep summer in the Home Counties. An elderly man is sitting in an idyllic English country garden. He could almost be Sir John Betjeman or perhaps Benny Hill, if Benny had lived. He glances skyward, his geriatric features briefly eclipsed by an uncanny, scalloped shadow. In a quavering voice he begins:

> *I'm terribly sure it's not England;*
> *Those churches look awfully strange.*
> *And ... Dear God Almighty! Some chap in a nightie's*
> *been strung from the spire of the Grange.*

> *I'm terribly sure it's not England;*
> *The Archbishop's fucking the Dean.*
> *And Hitler's delighted, for Churchill's been sighted,*
> *defiling a child on the Green ...*

Off camera, we hear barked commands and the sounds of a firing squad taking aim.

'I've got it!' I say. 'Put me through to India!'

Big Ben is gonging the closing seconds of the last thousand years.

ALL GOOD THINGS END!

We're on every channel in the world and thanks to negative sound broadcasts, everyone will hear exactly what they want to hear.

Id hands me a mike, connected to massive Bose speakers mounted on the chopper's fuselage. She's fucked on Hexstasy but she'll be fine in five minutes.

High above the fragile cirro-stratus layer, the bomb-bay doors of the B-29 flap open. A thousand gallons of Cloaca-Cola rain down from the upper atmosphere in glorious, biblical torrents.

'NEW DIET CLOKE!' I scream, shattering windows. 'FOR PEOPLE WHO WON'T JUST SWALLOW ANY OLD SHIT!'

They're cheering and dancing in the streets. Airborne cameras swoop and dive. Everyone's an extra in the greatest ad of all time.

MAROONED BESIDE THE WHIRLPOOL

The choppers swing around over the oil fires and the burning wicker men, bisecting the meridian line at Greenwich, heading west with the new millennium.

All over London, Cloaca-Cola is crystallising in the cold air and falling exactly like the snow at the end of that film *The Dead*.

Jonathan Brook

'IDENTITY'

I

James was driving, in from the North, in the boxster. He had the top down and after the shower the city was fresh, the metal and glass of other cars was all colour, splintered light from the wet asphalt, even the sky was a clean blue. His hands were shaking slightly and the boxster pulsed past the trees and wooden gates of the houses in their avenues as he moved westward, towards the bar he wanted. It would be full of light and people now. He would sit at the bar in his suit and proffer a silent toast to the changing times. Eddie and Stasia would come over, slap him on the back and buy some champagne.

He stopped at a light. There was a car next to him, a new two-seat Merc with two black guys riding in the front. He stared at them. They stared back, their mouths were open, suddenly shouting to him but he didn't register the words. They seemed angry with him and he couldn't understand the reason for this.

They challenged him to race with them but when the lights changed he let them pull away and watched as they turned round to taunt him. His hands were shaking and his back was wet against the leather of the seat. Let it go. But they pulled in to the side of the road and waited for him to pass, then followed him. He drove slowly, studying them in the rear-view, as though they were some odd specimen of life he found intriguing but repulsive. They were outside his world and this thought made him feel sad as he knew he had made the world for himself. Perhaps he had excluded them from its design.

They pulled close to the bumper of the boxster and he thought they would nudge him forward and he drove very slowly now, waiting for them to do it but very anxious now as he knew Eddie would shout at him if the car was scratched. He could hear them screaming at him. He tried to imagine that he was them but he could feel none of their hate or enthusiasm for what was about to happen. He began to laugh at them because he didn't want this to happen and neither should they.

They didn't like his laughter so they accelerated to his side and blocked his way at another set of lights. He couldn't reverse and get lost in the giant web of streets around him that was the city. There was another car close behind in the traffic queue, a frightened woman, scrabbling for her phone, leaning over to lock her doors. He felt as though the options open to him, from which he could select a sensible course of action, were being gradually removed from the reality frame and this made him feel uncomfortable. One of the black guys was getting out of the Merc, purposeful, determined, pathetic. Across the pavement a shoeless and shirtless derelict watched the scene, sitting on the step of a grocery store. He stared at the derelict. The black man leaned over the door frame and spat at him.

He pushed the boxster up on to the pavement and pulled around the Merc, sank the accelerator to the floor and the car roared through the red light, pushing him deep into the seat. There was a box of tissues on the front seat, Stasia wiping Eddie's come out of her mouth, fixing her lipstick, wiping the rim of a quick-chill Coke can because Eddie thinks they get dirty in storage, taking a quick gulp after the gas canister has cooled the liquid down to six degrees, to kill the taste, smoothing the brown drops of the drink from her powdered cheeks, laughing softly. He yanked one out and wiped the man's brown-flecked spittle from his jacket. He must try to suppress these thoughts of Stasia. In the rear-view now, cinematic, the black man rapidly climbing back into the Merc like a furious insect and the Merc lurching after him.

He knew the boxster was quicker than their car. But he had already done enough to prevent it. And he thought the spitting was taking things too far. He took a corner, braked and blocked the street diagonally with the car, then stepped out and reached in for the baseball bat that lay across the rear of the grey-carpet cabin. The car was so new it still had the heavy, showroom smell of leather and carpet. He filled his lungs with the scent.

When the Merc arrived the driver hit the brakes and the wheels locked and they slid into a parked car. They tried to get out to attack him but he beat the car with the bat and they changed their minds. They stared up at him with big eyes. He smashed the lights, the screens, beat the doors until the paint fell off in long strips. He smashed the wheel spokes and knocked the door handles off. He broke the driver's arm as he tried to steer the Merc backwards, leaning across the door-frame and arcing the bat across the carmine leather interior. The engine stalled. It was a quiet street with lots of glass and trees, dark little porches and cool shaded rooms. Bookcases and white fireplaces with dried flowers. There was no one but the two men to witness his violence.

The passenger crawled across the bonnet of the parked car and into the street and he beat him on the head, not too hard, and broke his knee with a side blow that nearly ripped the limb from its socket. When they had stopped crying and were quiet he got back into the boxster, threw the bat into the back cabin and drove away. His hands were still shaking.

On the way to the bar he tried to consider what had happened. He wanted to know if the event could have been changed, if it was as transient as the city, its efforts with brick and stone so fragile. It should have been his choice. But some had told him all would happen as it had been planned, even the most seemingly minor events and all their opposites and all the wide scope of chance. Nothing is insignificant. Everything is known and set, just as vast and ineluctable as the form of the hidden mantle of this world beneath him. But he could not believe this, it meant that there must be a God figure. He could not accept this, even though the idea was attractive to him, and he felt limited. He grew confused and he stopped the car for a few moments to try to think of it all but he could not. There was simply too much to consider, like trying to taste all the flavour of an ocean, a sip at a time. After a few minutes he became very thirsty and drove on.

2

The bar was full. They had seats by a window, walled-in by a crowd of drinkers. Eddie was talking but his words were of little interest to James. James watched his mentor's chubby fingers stroking Stasia's knee and had thoughts of his own. There were only two hours to kill before the end of the last two thousand years. The idea made James shiver in his seat. Line time.

Before visiting the bar he'd hidden the bat in the garden of Eddie's flat, wrapped it snugly in a roll of felt and then a plastic bag, positioned it behind an evergreen. Knowing it was there made him feel secure.

In the last few weeks he had realised many things about himself and the planet. Eddie was studying him, nervous for some reason, and James felt the surges and moods inside his head which he knew were the very thing his guardian feared. And they were strong these feelings. James had stopped sleeping months ago. With the night he would close his eyes and lie still as Stasia came in to his room to stroke his brow and check he was sleeping. He would wait, sometimes for an hour, his restlessness caged, stored like electricity, until springing from the bed and leaving the building, stealthy as a cat. He would locate the bat and wander through the sodium orange streets of the city, sensing the blood in his body as lava, his thoughts accelerated, contradictory, furious. Eddie's lessons were becoming harder to digest and accept. James would strike for the river and the projects. There he found his tournaments and challengers, the arena of blood that exhilarated his psyche. Broken bones and defeated screams were his truths. He was changing his language. Eddie's words were like dust beneath his feet.

It was in the projects that he felt he was a child of fire. The long block buildings that housed the detritus of the city, the last people with spirit, with the will to conquer and fight. The city elders committed them to the projects where they were urged to climb the long ladder to social integration, the 'step programme' that promised improved housing, temporary vehicle rights, city zone permits and increased subsidies, carefully supervised, monitored, rewarded by monthly progress reports. But James had scaled the project walls and shadowed the guards. They were not expecting intruders. Their focus was set on those attempting to escape. And inside the projects there was no harmony, none of the images flashed across the screens on the outside city were present. The people were refusing to comply with the 'step programme'. There were fires and open pits of garbage, crowds of young men and women under the lights, drunk and profane, rolling in the scarred earth between the buildings, resistant. Here was his domain. And his harem. The painted and smeared women he pushed against graffitied walls as his spoils but no liquid sprang from his groin. Eddie had seen to that. And Eddie had told him that these things were of no concern to him.

He had discovered them. His senses were growing acute. He had heard them in the car, hidden in the drive and watched them, watched her head bobbing at his guardian's waist. And he had felt nothing but a mild revulsion, as might one who watches field animals fornicate. Until that evening and his pretence of sleep had brought Stasia to his room. It was only with his full concentration that he could prevent himself reacting to her touch. He could smell her hair and body in his stuffy room for hours afterwards. And each evening she came to him, his desire for her was doubled. The women of the projects were a diversion. But what he could not have, he wanted more than anything. Sex. Identity. An equal.

3

'Well it would seem that your prognosis was correct, Dr Spence.'

'Indeed?'

'The men I used were assaulted with a near-deadly force.'

'Of course they were. It's getting close. With a weapon?'

'A wooden baseball bat.'

'How fitting. James has taken to the club already.'

Spence wished he could still smoke. He wanted to watch the plume of blue-grey air thread through the coned tunnels of the spotlights in the suite. He'd always enjoyed watching smoke swirl in the path of bright light. It reminded him of fuel dynamics, flow patterns, the qualities of air. It reminded him of a clean science. 'What time is it?' he asked.

'It's half an hour past ten, Dr Spence.'

'They won't give me a watch, you know?'

'I know.'

'And do you know where James is now?'

'He's with Foster and his girlfriend. In a bar,' said the man at the desk.

'Eddie would want to drink the new year in. Eddie with his sports cars and women, a practising hedonist. It'll be quite a surprise for him, the midnight bell.'

'We're going to detain him before the line time. It's in progress now.' Spence was fiddling with the hairs of his eyebrows. He was trying to think of a way to stop them taking this action but he was too tired to be tactical.

'That would be foolish.'

'None the less, that is what will happen. We followed your

advice to observe and provoke up to this point but after the attack this afternoon it's been decided that the line time poses too many risks. He has to be contained before then. You will assist us in his subsequent interrogation I hope.'

'You put my daughter in the projects. I'm in no position to be unco-operative.'

'She's in the projects, Dr Spence, because she had a father who was devoid of any social morality. She can return if she demonstrates the necessary "step" improvements.'

'We both know it's a ghetto down there. The "step programme" is a farce.'

'You were describing the problems you had with the accelerator agent. Would you continue please, doctor.'

Dr Spence had been living in suites like this one for the last two months, since his arrest. He slept badly and he was losing weight. In the mornings he had headaches and cramps in his groin and his upper chest, where the incisions had been made. The young man opposite him — he knew none of their names — was unaware that he was dying. He would die and if his daughter were not dead already then without his influence she would die too. Only James was to live, taking Spence's vitality away with him, carried in his veins, in his very cells. Spence found their confidence in containing him ludicrous.

'I need something to eat. I can't relax and talk with you if I'm hungry.'

'I'll call it up.'

Spence leaned back in his chair and wished he could still smoke.

In Mexico they had sat in their white concrete square, over-looking the Sea of Cortez, smoking and laughing. They were walled in with glass, on a scrub hillside. The laboratory was built into the rock below them, cool and brilliantly lit. There were no technicians. Their preliminary research had shown that the two of them alone were capable of the task ahead and so the halls and rooms echoed only with their talk and the dynamo hum of the refrigeration equipment. It was a private world. He and Eddie had been close friends then. Their discussions roamed the parameters of James and what he would represent.

He was thinking of what James had asked him, the night before Eddie took him away from the laboratory compound. The walk out into the black sky and the ocean below. James beside him on the concrete parapet, a mind evolved beyond anything Spence could comprehend.

'Dr Spence.'

'Yes, James.'

'How old am I? Am I older than the sun?'

4

James could sense movement outside the building. A girl's eye flickered with a reflection, a shape beyond the glass in motion. He felt tense. And in the crowded bar, the clamour and the stretched skin of laughter, the alcohol kick fleshing the faces and making the chrome plating dance in the lights. The noise. Eddie was talking again but James ignored him.

'I have to take a piss.' And he stood and started walking towards the back of the room.

The line time is the big bang in reverse.

He was thinking of what the doctor had told him. That he would be all men. That he was a composite man, a collage of the dead. He was probing the pattern and there was a flash of images, suspicions, insecurities, the breakthrough of thought that had created him. He remembered these words. The doctor was one of the infinite strands of which he was composed and the doctor mistrusted him. James knew there were men outside who wanted to hurt him. The doctor would have known.

He pushed through the group at the bar, moving for the door

but already there were shapes forcing their way among the crowd. They wore black and they carried batons like the guards at the projects. They were shouting. Eddie rose behind him and called out his name but James did not turn to recognise him, that was finished now. He clung to the bar and the guards began to hack at the crowd with their batons, trying to reach him. He watched as they knocked people to the ground and sank the batons into bare flesh to emit their charges. And the crowd broke into panic. They struggled and pushed for space. Some clung on to the guards and asked them what it was they wanted here and were struck down. Some even fought with them, lashing out in confusion, punching and kicking. James saw one man tapping a bottle on the bar top, a look of amazement on his face that it would not smash and provide him with a weapon. Two girls next to him removed their shoes and clambered up on to the bar. They stood there, spectators not sure what to do next. James bent low and slid between the back of the crowd and the wooden boards and found himself under a table facing the outside door.

He rushed past the guards and the bodies on the floor and stepped through the door. There was a shot. Beside his head the wood exploded and he felt a splinter of the door-frame enter his neck. He could taste it in his throat.

If outside the bar the clone is judged uncontainable and deadly force is sanctioned.

As James stepped on to the pavement, the other side of the street lit up with flashes from small arms fire directed against him. But he was behind a car now, trying to work the splinter free from his soft flesh. It was stuck. He could taste the blood trickling towards his lungs. He followed the line of the car until he reached the entrance to a house next to the bar. Stooping, he rushed the door and forced his way through. He was in a hallway, yellow carpets and pictures of period aircraft on the cream walls. He paced through the house, opened another door and wandered into the rear garden. He scaled a low wall and fell into the next garden, kicked against the tall windows with his boot. A man opened it for him and he stepped into a living room. The man and a woman, still in their after-office gloom, a bottle of wine on a coffee table, a loosened tie and laddered tights. The television murmured in the corner of the room. They watched as he walked past them and into the dark of their hallway, tugging the front door and stepping out into the next street. Engines were revving in the bar street. Cries from the wounded. Frightened sobs.

He moved to the middle of the road and fell into a jog. With each step the splinter tickled some flap of skin deep in his neck. He began to cough, under the black canopy of space, heading for his bat and the projects. Security. Older than the sun.

5

'The line time is the big bang in reverse.'

'He has no genetic counterpoint. He can't even ejaculate.'

'That may not be necessary. I think we've allowed it to go beyond that.'

Eddie was still trembling. The charge had knocked him cold and his brain was tingling from the energy surge it had received. He was wondering if this was how James must feel all the time. He was worried that Spence could be correct. The young man at the desk looked more worried than either of them.

'After our failure to contain your clone, I must ask you to be more direct with your comments, doctor. There is only one hour until the Greenwich millennium start.'

Spence was still focused on speaking with his former colleague. They had not met since Spence had been arrested. 'I don't think your crank sermonising has helped much, has it Eddie?'

'It was an attempt. It was creative. More than you were capable of doing.'

'You were just playing games. I'm the one who's suffered. Don't forget it was me who provided the primary strand. My death knell, not yours.'

Eddie rocked forward in his chair. 'He knows. In the last few weeks he's been unresponsive. He can taste it coming.'

'What Eddie is saying, is that the big bang is about to go into reverse.'

'No. You're wrong, Spence. James is of the future. He's progressive.'

'Ignore him, he's in shock. But don't ignore the warning.'

The man behind the desk smiled at Spence.

'He's a very violent teenager that's for sure, but little else. And the safe gene that Professor Foster installed into the pattern precludes regeneration. Even if we don't catch him, he'll die. You aged him nineteen years in only one and the process will continue at that rate. Will it not?'

'But not with his progeny.'

'There will be no progeny.'

'As you say.'

6

Before. There he lived in a land of pictures, frames from hidden films, dusty rooms in his consciousness that had been left, forgotten, draped in sheets, locked away. There had been moods, shifting feelings of loss and reunion, grief, isolated thoughts, a man climbing a long hill to where a woman waited for him, a black crag under a blood-red sky, witches and warlocks in solemn observance, the scent and the memory of their encounter fresh in his mind, the king of this land, reverberating in all the space, the capacity of his psyche, tall towers and huge slabs of stone, furled flags on the ramparts. There was nervousness and courage and bleak fields of mud with the clouds the colour of piss, poems in his head, casualties and machinery, the silent panic of industry, rusting presses and steel platforms and winches reaching off to skylights, links in the chain sparkling in the sun. There were seasons and storms and mighty seas crashing against white rock. There were deserts and plains of smooth glassy crystal beneath his feet, black mountains at the world's rim, a lambent moon. There were open expanses of grass so high it reached his chin and he heard laughter, children playing beyond the horizons, hidden from view in the deep waving green, the sun the colour of butter. All was colour and shape. And there were thoughts. He could conceptualise infinity. It was akin to an emotion. But how can you describe infinity to one who cannot comprehend it? He was imprisoned in a school for dunces and found a diagram of a radio set and he built it from bits of tin and scraps of watches, his brain working into all the gaps of the drawing. It was a poor drawing. He would redesign the drawing. And the teachers surrounded him and lifted him up to the light, smiling, congratulating one another on their find, as though he were some nugget or sparkling gem found in the bank of a river. He who had been locked away, written off, rejected. And he was a teenager fumbling with his shirt, shoving toast into his mouth, late to meet his brother, a test, another test, in the sandy wastes where they could not be disturbed. Derided for cranks but they would soar into the air, he and Wilbur, up above the world, like the gods sitting in Olympus. And he was the man with the world in his head, reaction, inter-reaction, psychology, phrenology, relativity, relativism. He was a dendrochronologist. A man counting the circles in a violated oak, noting the discolouration, a swarm of insects perhaps, a cyclone, a drought, reading the patterns of life into the trunk, making his move on history, moulding it to his shape. All it had seen, that tree. All its firm hours as a sentinel in the woods. And now its viscera ripped open for the man to study, the hungry man, the searching man. And he was in ports and cities, in mountains and lakes, binoculars, microscopes, notebooks full of neat coded writing, the paranoid academic. And he wandered back inside his mind to visit other rooms. The doors were beginning to open to him. There were no limits to the secret information latent there, the circles and colours. These were not memories. These were living feelings, actual, real. How can words fill his ocean, fit his needs. He was all languages and language is thought, it governs thought. The linguists may argue but when you see an object there is a word in your head for this object. Someone has placed it there when you were a child, before you could argue and say 'no. I will not have that word. I deny you this word.' We agree and take the word. Try now not to think in words. But James is beyond this distinction of word and object. He is beyond any petty altered state or noble religious system, the monks who spend their lives trying to appreciate each object as a fresh sensation, virgin on their consciousness. All is known and all is fresh to James. He needs no tuition.

James stopped running and spat blood in the street.

At the core of his thinking the spark of what he himself is, the plaything, the model for the two geneticists, seeking his own soul amid all the rubble with which they have filled his mind. He would find it in their ashes. Another flood of images, another room opening. More rapidly now. The doors were rocking off their hinges, clattering to the ground. Random now, images, colours flooding out, bombarding him, speeding, narcotic. Tear open the streets, let the rock run out and cover the buildings. Let the trees spring back. We need more trees. Let the air clear, soak the stench from the skies. Let the ice come back.

He ran quickly through the streets.

7

'I think this guy could be a freak.'

'Maybe you're right. Is that jewellery he's wearing?'

The two guards watched the figure loping towards them. Their batons were a blue flicker at the end of their wrists. Behind them was the project perimeter, a fourteen-foot steel door set into a six mile wall. There were lights and wire, steel poles protecting the guard house. Up in a watchtower another guard leaned over the parapet and spat. He gazed at the shape of the man take on colour as he ran into the compound. He stopped a few feet from the two men.

'Open up.'

James was panting. Blood was streaking his suit, the collar was black and greasy. Blood lined his throat and there was a pink foam around his mouth as it mixed with the air pumping up from his lungs. The splinter stuck out at a mad angle from the side of his neck, wobbling as he spoke. The guards looked at each other and had nothing to say. One of them paced round to the side of the barrier and punched a code into an illuminated keyboard. The steel door swung open.

James could see the fires and the dancing shadows of figures projected on to the concrete slabs of the project buildings. The noise swept across the compound, screams and maniac laughter, howling, shuffling feet. On the assembly green there were groups of men shouting, gangs screaming taunts and picking off the vulnerable from the rival mass like pack predators. He saw the flash of a bottle among them, in the spotlight glare from the wall, the project alcohol, distilled in bath tubs, industrial ethanol and liquorice, a huge tub prepared for this evening's celebrations, a dark and malevolent liquid hidden in every stairwell. Favours and promises were bought with this drink. There is no money in the projects. The crowd moved as one force, drunk and rabid, motiveless but aroused. They had seen the door to the outside crack apart and they drifted across the grass towards it. Above the buildings and the huge, seething assembly point there was a layer of black smoke, ink in the sky, blocking out the stars.

'You still want to go in?'

James watched the anarchy within, salivating. The guard lifted an arm, alerting the man in the tower. His confidence was returning. A water cannon was mounted on the tower. James could hear the top man clicking the restraints away, checking the pressure, swinging the barrel around, the flood bearing down on him. He jogged past the bemused guard, picked up speed as he heard the door start to close and sprinted towards the desperate faces of his followers before him.

8

'Doctor Spence. Are you feeling all right, doctor?'

Spence felt as though there was a fire smouldering in his chest. His skin was wet with sweat and his body flashed with pains, cramps and swellings, aches and burning tissue. The other scientist stepped across to the sick man and placed his hand on his temple. The skin was ice-cold.

'Spence is dying'.

'Why is he sick?'

Eddie returned to his chair. 'Spence gave his own DNA to form the core matrix for James, from which we linked all our other material, the thousands of patterns that we'd isolated. Spence was the donor. He was the trunk of the tree from which the branches grow, so to speak.'

Spence was curled in a ball now. His muscles were locking him into a foetus position in his chair. The man at the desk was tapping his fingers together, hard enough for them to click.

'There's a chance that James marks the end of evolution. I have rejected this theory, I believe James is suffering from a form of mental distress with his genetic maturity approaching and after this point he will come back to us. I still have faith in him. However, if the doctor dies, we could have problems.'

'Really?'

'It could mean that James has evolved to the point that DNA itself goes into reverse. Spence was the primary agent so he'd be the first to, well, decay.'

'Decay?'

'Yes, all of us. The planet's occupants. But it's unlikely.'

They both watched the doctor.

'Do you believe in coincidence?'

'I'm sorry?'

'We are interconnected in ways that are only coming to light now. Coincidence may just be one aspect of this interconnection, a genetic 'flow'. Some of this was revealed to us by our initial research, it was central to our ability to make James a composite clone. People may be one. We all come from one chemical structure, it develops but retains its original essence. This was the belief of the doctor — that external reality is all perceived, is all within the brain and the populace itself is a family of brains, all perceiving that reality. The doctor was terrified of James. But I knew that if there was decay it would be limited to the primary agent.'

'Why?'

'Because James cannot link with another strand apart from the doctor's. The doctor is close to him, within him and so James can touch him, hurt him. But I took away his ability to reproduce, to enter the genetic playing field. The only way he could link to other strands would be to exchange cellular structure with a female pattern identical to his primary agent's. He could then join the wider genetic pool and would dominate it. You did isolate the daughter? As I requested.'

'But he can't produce sperm.'

'He wouldn't need to. The accelerator we developed is a fertility agent. Any cellular contact would be sufficient to impregnate the woman. If his cells were able to reach her womb that is. Where's the daughter?'

'She's contained. But what risk?'

'I'm not sure. Spence thought the whole galaxy could be a genetic structure. It's only something we see or feel. We believe it's there in our heads. But it's a life perception. If life is reversed, then I can't say. Have you found James yet?' There was a screen on the desk. It carried a report about the sighting at the perimeter, the successful containment of the clone.

'We have.'

'I suggest you bring him to me. To be safe. If you hadn't burst in when you did I'd be with him now. And I wouldn't have been assaulted by your moronic guards.'

'Noted.'

'Then don't let me stop you.'

The man at the desk stood up and walked out of the room. Eddie watched his old colleague shivering on the other side of the room.

9

The first offensive by the authorities was crushed a few minutes before his line time. He had led his ragged warriors by imitation methods at first, his fearlessness impressing them, they joined him. As with the images clicking together, forming shapes in his mind, the final clarity to his being, so did his inchoate army take on form and division. He appointed officers and gave orders. Dissent was met with brutal punishment. On the battle field he was supreme. He taught them their tactics, how to draw the uniformed men into the arena and then separate them from their vehicles. He showed them how the batons could be seized and turned on their keepers. The intruders were massacred. His army was bloodstained now, adorned in scraps of clothing and equipment from the butchered troops sent to suppress them. A man with wild streaming hair ran past him, naked bar a helmet and radio set taken from a dead enemy. Another man comes to request orders for an assault on the wall position, waits patiently for his commander to notice him outside the group of officers surrounding him in conference. James approaches him. His breath stinks of the liquorice drink and his eyes are balls of white. He carries the severed head of a policeman hanging from his waistband, a trophy.

The army is structured in its hate for the guards and its reverence for James but the soldiers are demented, lunatics wielding the scythe. James stands in the quiet group of his officers and watches the mayhem, the figures criss-crossing the midnight assembly ground, the burning vehicles and the tracking lights, the water hose, the bastion of the entrance gate standing high in opposition. The forces are massing there for another attack.

At the last line time, crowds of peasants gathered around the cathedrals and ripped out their hair, scared that the sun would not rise in the morning. They beat their heads on the cobbles and wailed. Priests threw themselves into deep rivers and drowned. But there was to be another stage before his line time arrived. Now it had. All over the city, the people were expectant now, channelling their thoughts into the one conduit. The new age only a few minutes away, what would it bring? This mental energy surging throughout the metropolis gave him the strength he needed. Millions of his subjects were focused on this one concern, giving it enormous power and significance. James was able to tap into this power, use it for his purposes. All minds were thinking as one. At line time his year of birth would be celebrated, the future would be initiated.

The girl was reaching up to his neck. He had not sensed her presence and this confused him. She touched the splinter.

'Let me take this from you.' She led him from his officers. At the gates the authorities were sweeping through, he could see the lights and weaponry, the massed force.

'I have no time for this.'

'You must have the strength. Allow me.' Only seconds from the line time. Her touch on his neck is soft and penetrating, as though she strokes his soul. He cannot read her. She kneels on the grass and he sits beside her. She begins to work the spike free from the fleshy hole in his neck. James feels no pain. He is experiencing a wash of connections, of thoughts, inter-related, realisations. The girl is touching him, rolling him over into the grass.

'Be with me.'

And he moves her skirts, sweeps his hand to the warm bank of her thigh. She kisses him. The lovers amid the delirium of the battlefield, the black estate blocks forming their horizon, the muddy earth their bed. And James is within her, within himself. He feels the ecstasy of union for the first time in his brief life. And high above the entwined lovers, sister brother, mother father, above the scenes of violence and hate that surround their tiny pocket of bliss, up in the majestic heavens, very slowly, the stars begin to fizzle and fade, one by one, going out across the night skies. The stars begin to die.

Poppy Z. Brite

'VINE OF THE SOUL'

The canals were completely frozen over that winter. All sorts of shit was embedded in the ice — either dropped in while the water was still in the chocolate-pudding stage, or else squeezed from the bowels of the canals by upheavals deep within the mud. Old bicycles, ladder-back chairs, toilets, even a human leg had been seen (though the last was soon chipped out and disposed of).

It was a cold season, but we were as warm as always. Even if we hadn't both had the South in our blood, I think we created enough cumulative friction to outdo a hundred Georgia summer afternoons. Amsterdam in December was nothing to us.

We'd been together for seven years then, Trevor and I. After we left the States and shook off the Secret Service, we spent eight months fucking around rural Jamaica until we found out most Jamaicans weren't as queer-tolerant as our friends who ran the pot plantation, and we had to leave in kind of a hurry. This being the second time we'd had to more or less get airlifted out of a place, we decided to try and make it the last. We scored black-market US passports in Buenos Aires, caught an actual scheduled flight on a real airline, and ended up here in the land of subsidised art, legalised drugs, obscene amounts of money available for the asking to anybody who knows a lot about computers, like me.

It was easy to catch up on the stuff I'd missed during eight months in the Third World. Even if it hadn't been, I was ahead of these jocks, because I knew my way over, under, around and through the American systems. The hard part was learning Dutch. It took me almost three weeks. Trevor's brain isn't wired for Dutch, apparently, but his Aryan colouring, his broad shoulders and his vaguely hippieish look get him mistaken for an Amsterdammer even though all he can say after nearly seven years is 'Sprecht U Engels?'

Maybe because we'd never actually 'dated', we had this habit of making 'dates'. Trevor would be home all day drawing, and I'd be off tweaking machines, and we'd arrange to meet somewhere. On the last day of 1999, we hooked up at the Heavy Scene Coffee Shop in the red-light district for the express purpose of getting blasted on hash and watching the throngs rage as the century changed. I made my way down the winding stairs into the basement space that was the Heavy Scene: flashing Christmas bulbs, European MTV on the box with the sound turned off so the stereo could blare, fragrant with sweet smoke and already crowded.

There was always this little thrill upon seeing each other, as if this were a real date, two people meeting to size up their possibilities, two people who didn't have seven years of history and love and irritation and sharing a bathroom. All in all, I wouldn't trade the seven years. But that little illicit thrill gave me an under-the-table boner every time.

Trev was already at a table with an espresso and a joint in front of him. The joint was untouched, the coffee about half gone. He had his hair in a loose pony-tail and a pencil smudge on the bridge of his nose. He'd spent the day pencilling Goth Squad, the DC comic he drew purely for cash. It wasn't a bad comic, but it was scripted by a hefty deathrock princess from Minneapolis who hadn't stopped writing little mash notes to Trevor in her margins ever since she'd seen his picture in Comics Journal. I thought it was pretty funny, but it wasn't the kind of thing he could ever see the humour in.

His weary-watchful expression cleared when he saw me. 'Hey,' we said at the same time, and he half-rose as I started to sit, and we kissed lightly. A few tourists made wide eyes at us, but they knew they were in Amsterdam and had to Practise Tolerance while they smoked their legal pot.

I went to the bar, liking the sensation of Trev's eyes on me from behind. '*Een Heineken, stublieft*,' I told the blue-haired black girl serving drinks.

'*Nee bier*,' she said, slightly annoyed.

'*Oh ja* — pardon.' There had been a law passed a few years ago that establishments couldn't sell cannabis and alcohol together — to keep the fuckups on the move, I guess. The tourists didn't know about it, and the foreign potheads never remembered. I ordered a can of fizzy mineral water and another espresso for Trevor, and turned around to see a tall, bleached-blond man in black leather leaning down to kiss Trevor on both cheeks.

'Franzz fucking Quaffka,' I said, coming up behind him.

He turned with a grin that would've made a shark step back. I took a step back myself to avoid his kisses — not because I disliked them, but because I could never receive them without wanting to grab the guy's ass. It was just some kind of pheromone he put out.

'*I vass born to keel und make love!*' he cried, as if to prove my point. Everyone in the coffee shop turned to investigate this claim, but Franzz's glittering black eyes were fixed on me. 'Zach! It is so good to see you *zwei* out to zelebrate zee new millennium!'

'I'm sure you can help with our celebration,' I said. 'Why don't you sit down, Franzz?'

'Ah, I am too restless! I cannot sit down! I stay here, fine!' And so he hovered, gesticulating, carving his own space in the crowd, at some point casually taking up and lighting the joint Trevor had rolled, which turned out to be at least half crumbly black hash. And he filled us in on his amazing life since the last time he'd been in town.

Franzz was a fashion designer of international repute and the attendant fame you'd expect; he and his more business-minded sister, Vittoria, had launched lines of ladies' wear, jewellery and cosmetics that were huge status symbols all over the world.

But Franzz couldn't be counted on for anything except artistic inspiration. He would disappear from Quaffka headquarters in Milan with no notice and no entourage and only twenty credit cards, surfacing days or weeks later in, say, Amsterdam for New Year's Eve 1999.

And he sought out the company of other designers. But not the ones who made dresses, jewellery, or perfume. He generally found them a boring lot. Franzz liked chemists.

He liked all science-minded types, really, which was why he had collected me. He said that our talent was electric, whereas his and Trevor's was like a swathe of watercolour across a piece of raw silk. He talked like that, too. But best of all he liked attic alchemists and basement wizards, those who combined esoteric and often deadly ingredients to create, not gold, but buzzes. Franzz collected drug designers — funded them too, probably, though I'd never ask and he'd never tell — and I knew he'd have something special planned for tonight.

Just as we were finishing the hash joint, I felt my micropager vibrating in my pocket, right against my left nut. I didn't even want the thing with me, but I'd come from a job in the Noord and hadn't wanted to go all the way to our flat on Reguliersgracht to drop off my stuff.

It was Piet at Systems Centrum Europa, a company I'd done a lot of freelance upsetting for. I considered ignoring the page, then felt sorry for him sitting out there in the silicon 'burbs on New Year's Eve and went to the pay phone to see if something interesting was up.

It wasn't. When I went back to the table, Franzz was illustrating some point by sweeping his arms in a great circle and shouting, 'SUNDAY, BLOODY SUNDAY!' I ducked past him into my chair.

'What's up?' Trevor asked.

'Nothing. Boring.'

'No, no, tell uz,' said Franzz, and I could see he really wanted to know.

'Well, see, a lot of people are convinced that all the computer networks are going to go down at midnight. The machines won't understand the changing of the dates, see, because computer years only happen in two digits. So supposedly they'll think it's 1900, which will cause them to go haywire in all sorts of interesting ways.'

'Yes, I have heard of this.' Franzz pursed his lips. 'But I have been hearing it for years.'

'They've *known* about it for years, but no one has any idea what to *do* about it. Piet's out there with a bunch of techs, just to watch his own little network, and they want to be ready for . . .' I shrugged. 'Whatever. The techs have spent the past half of the decade trying to figure out exactly what's going to happen, and they don't even really know that.'

'But you have an idea, as always.' Franzz pointed a perfectly manicured, silver-varnished nail at me. 'So, vhat happens to zee computers at midnight, Zach?'

'Probably a lot of them *will* go down. I don't think planes will start falling out of the sky, like the apocalyptics say, because people have manual control of that. But I believe all the records are going to be fucked up for a very long time.'

'Records of vhat?'

'Everything.'

'Und you don't vanna help?' Franzz enquired — with barely suppressed amusement, I thought.

'No way. I want to see exactly what happens, and then I want to go in and see what I can do with it.'

Franzz's grin was approving. Trevor just shook his head and mouthed a word that looked like *Extradition*, which I thought was pretty fucking unlikely after seven years. I hadn't even been old enough to prosecute as an adult when I did my worst stuff stateside. Anyway, Trevor knew he couldn't stop me. Something that big, I couldn't even stop myself.

'So,' I asked Franzz, 'what chemicals do you plan to be on tonight?'

He glanced around nervously, even though no one at the surrounding tables could have heard me over the guitarwall of the latest big hit off 'Foo Fighters 10'. 'Come back to my room. I show you.'

'Yeah, I bet you'll show us.'

'I show you that too, if you like. But first I show you new drug.'

Franzz's 'room' was an enormous luxury flat overlooking the gaudiest stretch of Oudezijds Voorburgwal, lent to him by an unnamed friend who had chosen to bring in the millennium elsewhere. Through a vast picture-window the pink smear of neon, the stone arches lit with globes of electric red, the shimmering black canal, the peristalsis of the crowds could be seen or blotted out with the touch of a button that turned the glass into a mirror. We left the view on.

Never one to waste time, Franzz produced a tiny plastic bag from somewhere and tapped its contents on to a glass coffee table. A scatter of white powder, which he began to caress with a razor blade. Trevor looked interested, but I backed off.

'Nuh, nuh, you guys. Not if it's any kind of coke or speed, or even X, you never know what that shit's cut with. You know me and stimulants.'

Franzz didn't look up from his task, but spoke without moving his lips to avoid blowing the powder, which made his indefinable accent even weirder. 'Yezzz, yezzz, ZZach. I know you and stimulants. No coffee, no crystal, no Coca-Cola. This is something safe for you high-strung types.'

I let that one pass, since my personality isn't particularly high-strung but my body undoubtedly is. 'So what exactly—'

Franzz interrupted me with something so full of Z's that I could make no sense of it.

'Say again?'

He looked up, pronounced the two words carefully. '*Sssynthetic ayahuasca.*'

Trevor really perked up then. 'That's in Burroughs.'

'Impossible,' said Franzz, 'since it was only synthesised to perfection one week ago.'

'Not the designer version. The real article in the rain forest. He called it *yage*, and he went to Colombia to look for it at the end of *Junky*.'

'*Und?*'

'Well, he found it, of course. He's written some stuff about it since then. A strange hallucinogen.' Trev frowned. 'Doesn't it cause projectile vomiting?'

'Fortunately,' said Franzz, 'they have synthesised that out.'

He scraped up three large, sloppy lines. I noticed that the powder didn't have the icy glint of coke or the eggshell tint of heroin; rather, it gave off a pearly, subtle iridescence that I could have been imagining but didn't think I was.

'Gentlemen?'

Franzz was holding out, I swear to God, a gold-plated cocaine straw. Probably a vintage model from the seventies. What the hell. I turned my head and exhaled, put a finger over my left nostril, bent over the coffee table and snorted my line of jungle powder.

I was ready for pain. The handful of times I'd snorted anything, my sinuses always seemed to think I'd jammed a flamethrower up my nose. But this went down *cool*.

'A touch of eucalyptus,' said Franzz.

'That sounds healthy.'

'Yezzz. Drugs are zo good for you.'

I watched Trevor do his line, stray pieces of ginger-coloured hair escaping his pony-tail and dabbling in the powder. He threw his head back, closed his eyes, inhaled sharply, and smiled. I reached over and squeezed his hand as Franzz did up his own dose. His long pencil-callused fingers enfolded mine in a familiar grip. Whatever happened, he was there. I knew he was thinking the same thing.

'Zee very first thing this drug does,' Franzz announced, 'is to make you unbearably horny.'

I glanced at Trev. His eyes were open, but narrowed. Was Franzz going to hit us up for a *ménage à trois*? He'd never tried anything like that before — seemed to know better. And, hell, he was in Amsterdam; he could have younger, kinkier stuff than us. 'So,' Franzz continued with a smile, perhaps sensing our apprehension, 'I leave you *zwei* alone for a little while. Maybe I bring someone back later. I will enjoy using the bed more if I know two beautiful boys have warmed it!'

Snapping up the collar of his leather jacket for emphasis, he strode over to the door, tipped us a salute, and left the flat before either of us could say anything.

'Uh,' I finally managed, and then the ayahuasca hit. *White*, but iridescent, like the powder: a streaming, swarming rush of it. White white white, and maybe a fleck of colour here and there but you couldn't be sure, it was all going so fast, it was so white, it dazzled the mind. I felt something warm and wet against my lips, realised it was Trevor's mouth, realised Franzz had been right.

We didn't warm up the bed for him, because we never made it that far: we fucked in front of the big picture-window with the neon going insane down below. I could taste every pore of his cock in my mouth; I could feel the heat of his come pulsing through the various tubes and up and out over my tongue in a flood of sweet and salt.

Then Trevor was fucking me, inside me, and our eyes were locked, and suddenly time slid sideways and we were both looking at this television set. It was a rounded, small-screened model from the fifties, a Jetsons TV, and William S. Burroughs was on it.

'Yage,' he intoned. 'Ayahuasca. Harmine. Vine of the soul.' He looked thinner and gloomier than he ever was when he was alive. 'Said to increase telepathic sensitivity. A Colombian scientist isolated from yage, a chemical he called "telepathine". Legend claims that the Sun-father impregnated a woman through the eyesocket and the foetus became yage, the narcotic plant, while still in the womb. Yage is the god of semen, both sexual and foetal. Yage may be the final fix.'

'That last line was from *Junky*,' Trevor said, and then Bill and the cartoon TV were gone and there we were on the soft carpet in front of the window, bodies intertwined, nerves thrumming in synchronicity. I grabbed his ass and pulled him deeper into me, and we came at the same time and could *feel* each other coming, feel every jot and fiber of all the voltage flowing between us, and it was so intense I think we lost consciousness.

Thunder woke us. We could feel the vibrations in our bones. The sky over the whorehouses blossomed with multicoloured points of light. Fireworks. Midnight.

We pulled a comforter off the sofa and wrapped ourselves up in front of the window to watch the show. The fireworks were purple, green, gold, Mardi Gras colours, making me briefly homesick. Trevor looked at me, looked *into* me the way he always has, only this time there was something more to it. For an instant I sensed a kind of tattered aura surrounding us, connecting us, smoky blue and rent with electricity.

'Mardi Gras colours,' he said.

I just smiled and hugged him closer.

It wasn't more than another half hour before Franzz came back. He was alone, but in good spirits. We were treated to '*I vass born to keel und make love!*' again, in case we had forgotten, but we felt comfortable enough unwrapping the comforter from our sticky bodies and getting dressed in front of him. He'd been kinder than we could have expected.

'So did you see any planes falling out of the sky?' I asked.

Franzz thought about it. 'No . . . only a cashier who couldn't ring up my Dr Pepper because his machine, his register was broken.'

Only one thing about this really surprised me. 'You drink Dr Pepper, Franzz?'

He shrugged, and this time his grin wasn't so much wicked as faintly embarrassed. 'I had a boyfriend once who came from Texas. My boyfriends all leave, but their bad habits live on in me.'

A pang of sadness flashed between me and Trevor. Was Franzz lonely? We had never imagined him so. The idea depressed us, and we responded — not deliberately — by flashing on a scrap of an old Beatles song that stayed stuck in our heads for hours. *'Can't buy me looo-love, nonono, NO ...'*

'Oh yes,' said Franzz, 'and many of the prostitutes have signs in their windows: No Credit Cards. Tonight Only.'

'I don't blame them,' I said.

Charlie Hall

'THE MILLENNIUM LOOP'

I see him before my eyes discover his form. Like a flash of light that burns the retina, his shifty image slides over my vision as I bring the van past the trees.

They are the only Scots pines in the Northern Australian desert, left perhaps by an original settler choking his last scratches of breath out and flinging a handful of desiccated hope over the red sand, a sad unforgotten promise made unsuspecting to the kinfolk at home ('*Well if ye must leave us here in Auchterarder take a wee bit of Bonnie Scotland with ye!*'). Or maybe a migrant bird dropped seeds; they arrived, took root and survived. All I know is that they are here now, our only witnesses, ageless and mysterious. Unknown trees that shoulder swathes of green-black shadow against the sun and watch the fizzing wheel of time.

I tense without knowing why and, as a burst of White Cockatoos splits the foliage, there's a strange lurch like disappointment in my heart, the call of a distant voice. I turn my face away and see my feet gnarled and travel-stained at the pedals of the van and notice the faded blue button badge by the accelerator and without looking I know it reads 'WELCOME TO THE TWENTY-FIRST CENTURY'. I look up at the red road and I know you're waiting, sardonic smile and bent thumb crooked at Tetsuo and me, and I feel a quiver that is the echo of that feeling and we're already in the groove that only leads to your thumb and your smiling face, not looking at the road but staring up at the liquid sun, slaking your thirst on the crazy beams. I feel that I must drive past you but we're all locked in. I glance at Tets as a freak blast of wind barks through a gap in the windows and screams an indecipherable word and we shift in our seats, and Tets smiles and, as the morning light cuts his face, for a tiny second, too swift to grasp, I see The Loop come round.

I started seeing the spiders in Nepal, I bought a gun in Pakistan and I ran out of ammunition in Malaysia. That we've made it all the way here is a miracle, an epic of stumbles.

The plan was for Tetsuo and me to take the camper from London to Warning Mountain near Byron Bay in Eastern Australia, the first part of the land mass, to catch the dawn of the year 2000. We were both due to be playing at a massive rave there and we had decided to make the trip by land. We had contacted all our promoter friends in Europe, Scandinavia, Russia and the Beach Party belt of South Eastern Asia and worked out a schedule that had us DJing in all the major clubs and parties en route. It became a twisted and convoluted trail, crossing and recrossing the continents but we had vowed to cover the ground, get all the clubs and events under our belts and make it a retirement tour, ending up with the Warning Mountain dawn rave. My plan concluded with easy retirement in the rainforest behind Byron Bay selling leatherwood honey and dope.

Tets was thinking about going back to Japan where we had initially met, back to his family and friends. But I was ready to begin a new life, I had no more business in the UK, I wanted to make a fresh start and this Millennium story, this viral fever that had the world gripped, seemed a good enough reason to make a dramatic and permanent exit that wouldn't be interpreted as running away and would be in keeping with the unrooted, unplanned nomadic life of the DJ.

I had met Tetsuo, as I mentioned, in Japan on a tour. The air-conditioning had broken down at a party in The Liquid Rooms. A thousand devoted Japanese techno kids stripped to the waists like English ravers, sleeping on bass bins, collapsing as they danced, the sodden air squeaking and crackling with cyber static. It was in this scary dream scene, in a nightclub on the seventh floor of a block in Discotown, Tokyo that we had come across each other, banging knees and heads together as we simultaneously ducked down for our record boxes. Tetsuo was on the bill with me that night, his English was good and afterwards we had become friends. Two months later he had phoned me from Heathrow, came round to my flat with his record boxes and studio equipment and stayed. We had planned this trip after I had got back from Melbourne once, buzzing with Tsunami fever, desperate to break the cyclical life of airports and exchange rates, like an old gunslinger unable to put his sixshooters away but running out of time, desperate to go out in a blaze.

We purred through Europe; the van was as good as new and we did our gigs and accepted the embraces of friends like currency, gazing into their faces, grasping hands, kneading flesh, drowning in the sad glory of our disappearance. Not once did we think to stay; we weighed our love (and that of our vanishing friends) carefully like flat stones at the seaside, before skimming them all out and tasting the catch in our throats as our images quivered and faded, and then it wasn't us at the shoreline it was our friends who looked out and smiled and pointed at the last splash. Out of sight in the cooling murky water, we continued to spin gently as we headed for the bottom, time and time again.

The main roads across the continents were busy, occasionally the ghastly hump of panic emerging like the ancient scabrous back of a surfacing whale. Refugees filled cars and buses as well-established educated civilisations had begun to listen to the seductive whispers of mystics who claimed to have messages, people previously shrugged away as eccentrics with obsessive interests in ancient texts and interpretations of passages in old holy manuscripts. Gossip and speculation spread, heated by the virus. Bright lights in the sky, mysterious portents and signs, a casual word let slip in a bar. Any of these occurrences could appear the next day as fact on the front page of a national newspaper. Governments and the once omnipotent media were too slow and tightly structured to intercept these random and illogical idea bugs. Sub-cults emerged, advising and guiding their believers. They turned their backs on the hegemony of the consensus and struck out on their own. Countries fell into states of lethargic anarchy and the people made their own decisions, took their own routes and gradually fractured into thousands of micro-communities. This wasn't particularly radical, no one took to the streets with flags and barricades, but after work the population would slip furtively to their PCs to check their latest e-mail instructions, log into chat rooms, minds narrow and frightened, defiant and belligerent. There were nods and winks, secret signals and signs that made outcasts of everyone. There was no common purpose, no reason to obey, to fear, to aspire. Society began to rot.

Better, then, to take to the road, to be a stranger among genuine strangers. Better to have a goal in a world surrounded by aimless people. Better the knife than the butter.

The first gigs were virtually as per normal, the same as ever. But we brought with us a *frisson* of the virus and would remind people of what was coming, rolling across space towards us, as inevitable as gravity, and as we headed east the energy picked up.

In the rich panic of Naples, a red city dripping with reliquaries, the Virgin had her finger raised as she kept her eyes lowered but none could fail to see the admonishment in her tone as she warned of *what might come*. And Naples fell to its knees and prayed, slammed back past the days of the Conception to mysterious times when gods walked in the olive groves and temples were built around bleached bones encrusted with gold. We all ate from bare wooden tables swilled and washed with the best wines; hunks of uncut Parmesan and fresh mozzarellas. We ate the last suppers and gripped one another in the booming poised hyperenergy of the clubs. We left the young gangster kids and trainspotters, scary with teenage pimpled faces, expensive designer jackets weighed down with metal weaponry and naïve eager smiles, and sped on, skimming over the waves, spinning in the cool water.

We heard cries under the midnight sun when we played in the ruined palaces along the Baltic coast by St Petersburg and found a group of old people standing round a fire. As they threw their possessions into the grinning maw of flames they shrieked gently, an invocation, a song of release. Some had lived through the Second World War, they had watched Hitler and Stalin's forces destroy their lives and had closed their hearts and saved themselves for a day when they could be free of the memory and the responsibility of remembering and nurturing the past, which matured like a cruel hungry child gnawing at the breast, keeping it good for the moment of abandonment, of flinging out. So they shrieked as their chattels burned and the shrieks were little creatures that popped from between their old trembling lips and fluttered like Disney bluebirds over the fire and singed their wings and the heat took them up into the pink sky of the white night to freedom and weightlessness.

We played in the insufferable heat of the bunker basement of a Moscow bank where the Intellectual Set slam-danced to Jeff Mills and the gangsters who hired us laughed and passed round the vodka and cocaine, and we saw the sadness in their smiles as they knew the Dog Days were over before they had even matured. And outside, as we stood freezing and sweaty in the brown-snowed street, we smelled the hot fetid breath of the Dog and we stayed and grasped the hands of these people and the same flashing skimming spinning gentle intensity flickered in our eyes and as we turned away we/they immediately withered and turned brown and became dust and blew sand and were gone, never to touch again.

In Tashkent we played in the old airport where as a backpacker I'd waited three days for my connecting flight to Bangkok. Our music was alien and familiar to them, a call. Unease and sporadic revolution sat over the area like the unsettling stench from a downwind factory and I thought I saw a spider, but it was the dried-up severed hand of an unknown victim, lying lonely by a petrol pump.

In Nepal the van broke down properly for the first time. Dead. We were scared and cold, darkness was pulling the mountains around us and for a flickering second we stared into the chasm of our foolhardy mission; we had just got to the *difficult* bit and we were already in trouble. Tetsuo climbed under the vehicle and began pulling and prodding. I paced and watched the purple and orange sunset soak the snowed peaks. I didn't like this, it wasn't working and I felt a familiar sick feeling of being alone and afraid and fucked-up.

But Tets dragged his long skinny body out from under the van and ran oily fingers through his ludicrous mop of blue hair. He held up something that looked like a dead snake and said he knew what was wrong, maybe, but then the lid of darkness slammed over us and we were little children. Desperation nagged us and as we ran out of options, I found a pale blue worn-out badge in my pocket. I'd written a number on the paper reverse and it was still legible.

Tetsuo said that he recognised the number, some e-mail address, but he couldn't identify it.

'It is Australian number. Look. Ah, maybe we call, maybe a friend will pick up.'

I pulled the laptop out and activated the modem. Out in the cold big bluish mountains there was virtually no signal but with a ten-second power boost from the van batteries our beam got to the remains of MIR, bounced off and found the satellite. Back to Earth and the screen's static began to form patterns, froze, scrambled the codes and the ringing window appeared.

'Ah! Ringing I think. Good!' Tetsuo smiled and hope lit up his clear, unmarked face.

The phone picked up, connected, and the image began to stream across space.

I'm not saying I was never afraid of spiders; the darkness, dirt and random evil they represent struck me at the age of eleven.

I'm not avoiding responsibility for Tetsuo or for anything that happened after that, but I do remember those last lost moments of happy ignorance, those precious few seconds as the digital signal rushed through the air to resound off the spastic hull of that revolving contorted space tomb, that monument to idiocy, that modern-day Tower of Babel. Those dripping seconds like a gently overflowing jar. The whole world unfurled around us and we were plugged into eternity, at one with all creation, part of the same animal message, all tingling with space dust. Even then I felt something momentous stir me but misinterpreted it as the simple wonder of technology and nature, but now I see those moments as the sweetest and saddest of my long life as Tets and I grinned at each other and without our knowledge the simple innocence of blind life trickled away out of the jar.

The image was blurred, bit-mapped over that distance, probably using low band-width, jerky but unmistakable.

The figure suddenly loomed into view, staring with sightless eyes in the direction of the C-U-C-Me camera and mike, hands fluttering birdlike, brushing webs of blindness away.

The image faded and flirted, hard to decipher through space dust and static. The voice came through, parched, coughing and muffled.

'Mmmphf. Hek! Hek! Nehh, it's real! The Loop!' it creaked, 'The Loop! Nahh! Don hang up, lissen, you've seen it, stop The Loop, it'll come, find a way not to meet it ... he's watching the sun ... the trees. Find a way to stop!! ...' Exhausted, the speaker fell back.

I hit Send, 'Hey! Hey! We need help, we're stuck! Stop your fucking nonsense! Shut up, we need HELP!! We ... I ...'

'It's just message. Person not there I think. Only message ...'

Tets pulled me away from the computer. He put his arm round my shoulder in a clumsy impression of Western solidarity, the poignancy of it biting me.

'Yeah Tets. But did you see?'

'Your voice ... and perhaps the face ... it was you.'

We glanced at each other. I felt my liquid stomach bubble. Seconds became hours and our voices were frozen in our throats. Against the moon the mountains tilted and toppled, and like a theatrical joke the backdrop of the sky snagged and was ripped down.

Tets was bowing nervously, trying not to catch my eye but needing to monitor me at the same time. He saw my anger, confusion and fear like a Godzilla in me; raging, blowing fire and trampling suburbs. We both felt the moments stretch and tear and in the purpling moonlight I saw a tree festooned with trembling spiders.

How did I get to leave a message in an Australian mail-box? How had I even got that number I'd dialled? It had to be a weird coincidence, a mistake. We were spooked.

'I must've e-mailed a message . . . can't remember leaving one. I've got a double somewhere . . . haha . . . I—' I was sweating. A skin of oily perspiration ran over me. I forced myself to grip on, got my breathing near normal as I slowly squeezed the panic out of me and away. A mysterious coincidence but no more. There was no chance that I had left that message. We hadn't got to Australia yet.

A few hours later we lay listening to the wind come booming through the pass. The van rocked on its suspension, as if we were in a heavy boat. The frazzled sensation we both felt after the message incident had faded and we had been able to crack a few feeble jokes about it. But a shadow of that same look of humbled fear remained in Tetsuo's face so I was relieved to be lying in the dark listening to my friend's ragged altitude breathing.

'Here,' he passed me the chillum and I drew on it. 'We start the van when we wake. Now we begin our *holiday* and spend our money on Charas and, uh *bhaji!*'

'Yeah, but what'll happen if we can't start the van, what then? What if we can't even get out of this country? We could be here for ever!' I noticed my voice rising and I fought the panic back.

'Not such a bad place to be. Perhaps we become monks,'

Tetsuo laughed and a flash, a blur of yellow feathers shot through my vision.

'No! We're on a mission T., we've got to get to Warning Mountain, I don't want this to be like my whole life; false starts and sidetracks, I want to correct it, do something *right* and see it through.'

'But your way. Have you not considered your life in a Taoist perspective? Maybe you are right and those you see as right are wrong. We have a saying, "The reed that bends with the wind is stronger than the wind, and more powerful than the mighty oak that the wind can topple." If you move with your life you live it right and if you force yourself to bend you become unnatural. Maybe we celebrate Millennium here, maybe we bring the first light to us instead of forever chasing the light . . .'

The message, we kept coming back to that message. It made me deeply uncomfortable and apprehensive. I picked up the badge and rolled it in my hand, pricking the pin into my thumb, lucid dreaming. I knew there was more, a voice . . .

'What is all this crap about anyway, time and calendars, they're all a concept, what's real is this. Hey! Maybe we're *supposed* to be here, maybe this is where it all happens anyway, maybe that message . . .' I didn't want to start discussing that again. 'It's all bollocks, it's only the invention of Greenwich Mean Time that says it's eleven-fifteen in the night here and that the dawn starts at the Date Line. I mean it's all a human concept. And a Western European one at that. Time. And the calendar.'

'Ah, but we must have common understanding of a few basic matters. That is civilisation. And remember, it is that "concept" that says we get paid double to work New Year's Eve, that says the day even exists.' Tets chuckled into the darkness. 'We both know it's bollocks. But we make benefit from it too.'

'Okay, okay.' I was grinning too. 'But if we don't get the fucking van going tomorrow we'd better start dismantling our common understanding and form a new civilisation of two. Like all those sorry fools behind us. We'd better quickly arrange to have the dawn of the Millennium this morning from over there,' and I waved my hand towards the mountains in the east.

'I think, no problem for mending van. In daylight I can see. Maybe we build new petrol line. No problem.'

And we slipped into sleep.

I awoke needing a piss. It was still dark and utterly silent now that the wind had died away. I struggled out of the van and found a rock to urinate on. I was stoned and when I closed my eyes I got flashes on my vision like blipverts. I saw a group of trees in red sand; I saw my laptop, the screen in C-U-C-Me mode and that scruffy intense face peering out like a Stone Age man staring at the machine and seeing it for the first time. As the screen flickered and flashed with each burst of vision in my head I heard the words again, '. . . The Loop . . . he's watching the sun . . . find a way to stop . . . I . . .' and then another flash . . . the face stared out and was in my head '. . . unless you get out of The Loop you'll be in it for ever. Stay put! The dawn will come to you, don't chase it! If you pursue your dream too far it will fold back on you. Listen to the words of your friend! He knows without knowing . . . How can you be told; who can make you listen . . . ?'

Panic gripped me in a horrible intimate embrace and I rushed to finish my piss. It wouldn't come and I squeezed the panic away and did it. As I turned back to the van I saw that the rock I'd relieved myself on was an oozing mass of quivering brown spiders. If I'd had a gun I'd've started blasting away at them there and then.

In the morning, as promised, Tetsuo made another petrol line, from a roll of tubing which he'd wisely packed. We got the van started and headed off into the rising sun. But something had changed; the mysterious message incident had burned us both, we moved warily and there was a new apprehension, just a small shadow that we both mistook for 'vision hangover' at the time, but it would grow and grow as we approached our goal.

Oh yeah, and I bought a gun and started shooting at the spiders at night.

✻   ✻   ✻

The Beach Party Belt was festering with delusion and we pushed through, weighed down with a sense of something else. All the tripping fools shuffling to the beats in the moonlit sand filled us with an exhausting hopelessness and we played, took our wages and hurried on. The parties slipped by in blur. We were treading water while our future crunched through time towards us.

I tense without knowing why and as a burst of white cockatoos splits the foliage there's a strange lurch like disappointment in my heart, an unanswered call from a distant voice.

'—*The Trees!* — *Turn Back!*—'

The dark trees, an explosion of feathers, and as I looked at my feet, the badge . . .

(Fuck! Look at the— 'Fuck! Look at the old geezer!' yelled Tetsuo. He pointed at a grey shape at the roadside. 'He will burn his eyes. Look! See him stare at sun!' (—at sun!) 'Should we stop? Or maybe drive on, he looks dangerous. Maybe he's a nutter?'

But I had already started pulling over.

We were one day away from Byron, we were going to make it and these pangs of dread and distant foreboding could be dismissed. Maybe it was white line fever, or just the hangover of the crazy times that had settled over us since that night in the Himalayas. We hadn't really talked about it. We'd let it lie, an unattended casualty in the battle zone that we'd strolled into, an eight-legged hell of spiders; fat, squashy, quivering and dark, in which we'd had no spare moments to discuss the ramifications of our message from outer space as I'd attempted to clear the world of my private arachnids with a crate of homemade bullets, while Tets hung on to me, pulling me back down to the ground, ducking the metal and flying debris.

The geezer pulled open the door of the van and slid right in next to Tets on the bench seat. He scanned the interior as if he was seeking something out and as I engaged the gears he bent down. He found and brandished the blue button badge, pale eyes searching my face, waiting for an answer.

'Eh? Eh?' he waved the badge at me.

'Where you headed, geezer?' I ignored this display; he was either a genuine and quite possibly dangerous psycho or he was on to me. Either way, I wasn't going to get involved with his game. But I felt his ghost swoop and strafe my spirit which huddled vulnerable and exposed.

He smirked, smirked!, 'Where you goin'? Well I'm goin' there too.'

'We're off to the Edge of the World!' Tetsuo blurted. 'We are going to see millennium at, ah Warning Mountain, only one day left in Twentieth Century!'

'If you count time by our contemporary calendar and clock,' I added, getting the last word in and at once feeling pathetic and childish.

The old geezer was looking at the badge. He turned it over in his hands and let out a great sigh.

'Why you goin' to search for the Edge of the World?' he asked Tetsuo, 'Didn't no one tell ye, Earth's round, keeps goin' round, mate.'

'We play at party for welcoming 2000,' he was into his stride and never noticed the sarcasm or clue. He was buzzing with the excitement as the stress of six months' travelling with me had begun to unravel. 'Where we go,' he added conspiratorially, 'is the edge of the world, the first continental landmass to see the new dawn of the Twenty-First Century yes, it is so!' He nodded at me, I was frozen, wired on the tightrope-tense energy as the grinding roar of our future boomed in my head. 'We come all this way in this van from UK in Volkswagen Camper. My first time in Camper. Most Impressive.' He patted the dashboard and smiled.

'How come you're right out here sunbathing in the desert, you old geezer? Where you come from? I never saw any towns, what's your story? Get chucked out of another van for being nosy?' I said.

'So many questions. You ask the wrong questions. Why not look into the sun, let the light in.' His face, his eyes, suggested cool sanity but his words were definitely tripped out. He made me feel uncomfortable, I wanted to boot him out but as with a tramp in a doorway, you don't want to be always turning your face, so I let the bugger stay. He didn't look physically dangerous and I couldn't really turf him out into the desert just because he made me feel bad. We were stuck with him and he was going all the way with us.

We drove silently and the wariness that had fluttered into our hearts in cold Nepal came back to roost, feathers clicking with fear lice. The road ahead began to resemble a deep rut that we seemed doomed to roll along.

'D'ye mind . . . ?' he held the badge.

'What? You want *that*? Yeah, sure, don't even know how it got in here, probably some hitch-hiker we picked up.'

'Have a swap,' he said and took a badge off his hat. 'Look, it's a new one. That one's worn out,' and he pinned it to my shirt, leaning right over Tetsuo, who grimaced at his sharp Outback odour.

'Ah! See, we are in the next century already!' Tets laughed and read the badge (WELCOME TO THE TWENTY-FIRST CENTURY). The geezer glanced quickly at Tetsuo's face but only saw open childish humour and wonder.

'Ah, Time,' began Tets. He stared ahead at the red road and fell silent as the geezer and I waited . . . 'Does it flow straight?' and the geezer snatched another unrewarded glimpse at the enigmatic face. 'Look at this road. We would say "This road is straight, it goes in a straight line to Byron. We have seen this on a map," but there are bends. And gradients, and it does not go quite straight. And if it not straight then what is it? Is "not straight" a good definition? Maybe in my language but not in yours, perhaps. You have one word for "straight" but many words for "not straight". And the people who developed your language also developed the notion of time and place. Most worrying I think.'

Tetsuo was incapable of irony and the old geezer and I stared at him.

'It's all a fact,' I said. 'Time exists but we just have to agree on one definition of it. It happened to be ours. I'm not satisfied either. But it exists without definition, a day passes in the desert even if there is no one there to prove it.'

'Ah! But there is only present tense. This is all we know. For sure. We *believe* that the past exists, we must honour our ancestors and we hope that the future is there, but all we *know* is the present, all we can *prove* is that which we can feel, see, smell, hear or taste. We have no way to know that time really proceeds in an ordered way.'

'Reality is subjective,' I quoted sarcastically. 'It relies on our common understanding of it, is that it?'

I wanted something more, I had got so fed up with meeting all the cyber-hippies, self-help manual searchers and cynical nihilists on our trail who drivelled the usual mantras and were content to weave their own webs of reality, shoring up their excuses for laziness and lack of purpose and love with this collective, protective nonsense. We have to work so hard just to find purpose, a reason to carry on when the alternative of merely biding one's time, filling in the gap between birth and death with anything that helps seems so seductive. And the answer's never given but people keep searching. That's Life; bloody questions.

We continued driving. The desert had started to give way to scrubland, farmland, woods and the blue of the forest in the distance. The heat slackened, but the sun was still peaking and I wanted to escape from our passenger. Tetsuo took over driving and I slumped in the back, pretending to be asleep, watching the bristling wizened neck of the old geezer until I drifted off.

When I woke I burst like a newborn baby into a land of confusion. I couldn't see. There was only whiteness and pain. My face was on fire, wet with sweat, maybe tears as well. My laptop vision had returned and I surfaced from the dream crying.

'—*the sun . . . find a way to stop!*—'

I was blind (but at last I could see). All this *déjà vu*, recognising things, the badge, the phone message. Everything had happened before it had happened. The Loop was something to do with time. How else could I remember events before they happened?

I felt hands on me, they pressed my body back so that I remained supine. Everything shuddered as Tets brought the van sliding to a halt. I struggled and heard familiar voices.

'Relax! It's Tets. You fell asleep with your eyes open and you burn in sun. Sorry man, never saw, looking at road. You'll be all right, we nearly there. It's okay, don't worry.'

I felt the old geezer, he had come into the back of the van with me and his civet smell was everywhere like dashing spiders, I was entangled and helpless. Revolted by that spider image as his busy warm hands ran over my face, damp and fast.

'You see! You see! You can, can't you?!' There was an edge of pleading; no danger, but I was suffocating with his proximity. He wanted me to say yes.

'Mnnurh, nnh. Yeahhhn. I can shee—' There was something in my mouth and it stuck to my teeth, choking me. The images kept flashing. I saw the ocean and the tiny green speck of the first light. A cheer mutated to a wail, then static. White and yellow birds, thousands, millions flung like crows in the air, a metallic wall like ice rose out of the water. I had the impression of something folding back.

'You saw! You let the light come in! Now you know, but it's too late this time!' I could feel the man crouching by me, pouring his words into my ear. 'But you can try!' He was dragging my laptop out of its bag, I heard bits of equipment falling and breaking, then he booted it up, I heard the drive whirring. Then I heard him tapping a number in. It connected fast. I saw thousands of expectant faces turned towards the rising sun, the dust purple in the new dawn and a midnight sun looping towards us all and the sigh rising like a cheer, then the fold coming round, racing round the planet.

The laptop beeped, connected, and my hands were guided to the camera-mike. 'Leave a message! Speak into it!' I could scarcely hear his voice, the crushing grinding sound of The Loop was drowning everything out.

I hunched forward. My mind was spinning and I was frozen with panic: I couldn't decide if I was still dreaming; no time to think, brain throbbing with the enormity of what I'd discovered. I obeyed, leaning forward with old man's hands, hacking and wheezing. I had to go along with events.

'The Loop ... no, don't hang up ... Listen, you've seen it already, it'll come, find a way not to meet it!' I had to make myself think in that broken-down van ... I remembered Tetsuo's Taoist thoughts ... '—*listen to the words of your friend, he knows without knowing*—', I knew the futility, I would continue this loop until I worked it out myself ... 'How can you be told? Who can make you listen?' and I collapsed, drained of energy.

Tetsuo pulled me out of the sweaty mess of the van and into the cooling evening air. Scraps of vision returned, little darts of movement and colour. He pressed a bottle of water into my quivering hands and I drank.

Soon I could see again. The sun had shone in through the rooflight of the camper and I had fried, exposed for three hours or more. As we cooled down, the impossibility of the situation began to emerge and the old geezer bid us *au revoir* until tomorrow.

'We never see the dawn of the Twenty-first Century. These badges are a hoax. When midnight comes up everything meets a timewall and slips back to the dawn of this morning. The matter of Time is so exact that it cannot get through to the Twenty-first Century, something has to interfere but no one can remember that. They are in The Loop, everyone is doomed to continue. There's no way out, but there's a chance if you can start remembering. You travel this road every day, you two. I wait by it every day. The party is held every night, and is allowed to continue as if it has never happened or will ever happen before or again: It never finishes. See you by the trees,' and he slid into the gathering darkness.

I looked up. The light had faded away and a glorious sunset was throwing colours at the sky; pinks and yellows, a dash of purple and some burning red. A grand finale for a life that ends in eternity. A meaningless plot that is trapped like a jammed needle on a record, repeating the last few bars endlessly as we live those moments as if each one is fresh. How long have we been on this last day? A year of days? A thousand years? And what of the past — is the whole story just this last repetitive groove embellished with false memories? Is our folly a dash towards a future that never comes, missing hints and clues because we won't accept the truth or can't cope with it? Where have we come from and for what purpose, and is life as pointless and empty as the hippies and wasters like to say? Are we best off just smashing our minds and ignoring The Loop, or accepting it and not fighting it? The sun sets. Tetsuo and I stand alone. Ahead of us we see the split peak of Warning Mountain, faint flashes of strobe lights playing like summer lightning over the dark face. Ravers and celebrants gathered from all over the world, chai mats and beer tents, everything arranged in a massive crescent to acknowledge and welcome the dawn that never comes, the ultimate proof of mankind's arrogance and folly. Ahead of that, the blank grey metallic fold we all think is the sky. We climb back into the van and Tets starts the engine. Perhaps we can trick The Loop. Maybe it's not even there anyway, maybe it just won't *happen*. Tets rubs his cheek.

The memory is strong now, no more spookiness of *déjà vu* now that we know we're in The Loop. I write the phone number on the back of the badge and Tets pulls over to let me pin it on to a roadsign. A traveller already heading this way will pass us and notice it and take it to Russia and we will find it again in a petrol station, because just as time collapses it's not just the last day that loops, and there's no more day as the concept dissolves and it all becomes one.

Wearily we head towards the fold in time. We are confident.

Doug Hawes

'A SHORT ARCHAEOLOGY OF THE CHEMICAL AGE'

4.10 p.m.

Whenever someone says you can definitely borrow a sound system, remember: they have also promised the same pleasure to at least two other people.

So, to get the decks means a dash into Manchester, speedo at forty, petrol gauge at zero and Randall holding the Herald's passenger door shut all the way. Braving the cold, we sit outside Manto's two storeys of chrome and plate glass in the last glow of fragile winter sunshine.

As we watch the worked-out bodies slipping past along the canal, we sip Spanish lager from German bottles with pieces of Ecuadorian lime stuffed in the neck. The village is sucking in its stomach, flexing its muscles and (says Randall) choosing its sarongs for the big night, the party to end all parties.

Lara turns up late. She is wearing a shaggy Day-Glo orange fur coat and matching hat.

'Wow. How's wombling these days?'

'It's amazing what you can pick up — Hiya boys.'

'Who are you calling boys?'

'Boys,' she says, definitely, 'your decks are in Castlefield.'

'Not the straight village!'

'Now, now, liberate your confused bisexual side.'

'What other side is there?'

She points her sunglasses in my direction: 'Good point. Remember.'

We sit a while longer, as the street begins to fill up early with the more impatient or less well sorted and desperate. Soon, there will be standing room only. One by one, the bars and clubs will crank up the volume of competing beats. Voices will become louder and glances longer as collective expectation approaches critical mass.

In a hundred clubs and parties, molecules will wrench apart and recombine in now-familiar ways, as chemically-upgraded minds vibrate with the rich harmonies of desire. As hearts quicken under hard muscles eager to dance, recalibrated eyes will register the richly velvet texture of skin and capture the bright certainties in fresh-beaded sweat. Ears tuned to new frequencies, harsher truths will cease their whispering and all that we will feel is everything.

Bare-chested ravers will congregate cheesily in toilets that have become living rooms, smiling and rushing, leaning over to feel the icy-coldness of the mirror flatten tingling backs.

Old lovers will mutually lock-on as great mountains and icy lakes form in their pupils. New lovers will recognise one another from long ago. Mouth to mouth, flesh on flesh, they will travel from the bright dance floor to sensuously shadowed corners and back again.

We drive down to Castlefield, while the canal water takes the slow route along the tow-path, leaking down through the nine locks of the Rochdale Canal, past dark, desired places of anonymity and generosity. We drink more lager in the vast courtyard of Dukes, Lara cuddled between us in her soft coat. Craning our necks for a worm's-eye view of the great grey-black iron girders of the railway viaducts, bolted together (says Lara) like hideously outsized Meccano.

'Cathedrals of the industrial age.'

'Where are the choirboys?'

'And girls, please.'

'Look at it! Imagine, it's 1850 and you've just moved here from some rural hole where the biggest thing you ever saw had four legs, and the first thing you see is that! Wouldn't you get down on your knees?'

'That depends.'

'Cathedrals should be six hundred years old and look like York Minster, not Meccano.'

'I prefer my cathedrals with a late licence if you don't mind.'

We sit back and watch the girders arch over the still waters of the Castlefield basin. Soon the millennium that built our myriad cathedrals will be gone. And where will we worship then?

Tonight we may witness more than just another millennium.

But, of course, we don't know this as we head back up the A6, our precious cargo nestled snugly among duvets in the boot as the very last light fades. Behind us, the canal slips quietly through the last lock and out on to the long straight waterways of the Cheshire ring.

11.10 p.m.

Place one sprig of *petro selenum crispum* (aka parsley) in the centre of a small but attractive plate, quite likely given to you by your mother. Arrange one to two generous handfuls of *methylenedioxymethylamphetamine* (aka you-know-what) in a heaped bank around the outside. Serve with style.

Presentation is nine-tenths of the law.

Naturally, these aren't the first, and there's more in the fridge along with the acid and M & S Cava nestling there patiently for the first morning of the next millennium, but things should always be special — and today is very special indeed.

But, as I said, we don't know that, not yet, not now.

I wander out into the hallway, where light from the candles is repeated a thousand times in the tiny lenses of the decorations hanging from the ceiling. Alex and Randall are sitting on the stairs, dangling strands of gold and silver through the banisters.

'We're playing with Kitten.'

'She's in the living room. Cats like cat food.' I offer them the plate.

'We're all cats. Miaow.'

I feed Alex an E, watching his eyes. But his engorged pupils are still wavering with that hint of anxiety that says: ME ME ME — it's not time yet.

I walk through into my ordinarily spacious, stripped and stranded living room, into which have been inserted twenty-seven candles, a sound system, two cast-iron trees and a variety of bizarre ornaments. Multicoloured stars and silver flying saucers cover one wall, opposite the holographic silver portholes of an enormous mushroom-inspired yellow submarine. The head and torso of a tailor's dummy rises from a speaker, snaking metallic shower hose replacing one arm. The enormous silver star on the chimneybreast watches, and waits.

Also watching the dancers, Kevin sprawls over a chair, waving a joint airily in front of Tom and Cal. His flowing hair contrasts with the short, serious-raver crops of his brothers. Saz slips from her perch on the chair back and bubbles over. She examines the plate for a moment, as if these were home-made scones — looking for the perfect one.

'Nice presentation,' she says, popping her selection into her mouth.

Karen is bent over the borrowed decks that fill one corner, brow furrowed in concentration as she matches high beats in the earphones with the muffled thumping she can hear through them.

I twist my body among the hanging signs which say 'perfect' and 'imperfect'. Bright papier mâché fish and holo-suns pass me as I pass the plate around guests. Each of them may take a small white tablet of guaranteed pure MDMA. In twenty minutes, we will each resolve our personal confusions the ways only we know how. In thirty our pupils will be dilated and our mooring ropes tearing loose, and in fifty — if my mathematics are correct, we will celebrate the new year like some lost tribe in the desert, drugged-up.

11.27 p.m.

Lara comes gambolling into the kitchen and scurries up the stepladders to sit with her head in the billowing clouds we made with a roll of some weird white foamy stuff.

'Dan Dare, pilot of the future,' she says, smugly. I offer her the plate. 'Golly! What wonders lie in store for us, Dan?'

'By the middle of the next century, everybody will be working for nothing on a two day rolling contract and an endless comedown. However, we will each own a recycled Ka and a satellite-linked traffic computer. We will be happy avoiding each other the whole time.'

'Charming.'

'Cynic. Globalisation and drugs, my friend. A heady combination, you mark me.'

I reach up and gently scratch the warm roots behind her ear. I stop when she nearly falls off the ladder with ecstasy, and rest my hand on her neck. Her arms snake round and link behind my back. A surge of energy runs up my spine and sets off a hundred tiny pinpricks of pleasure somewhere in my brain. Time pauses to watch us.

It's starting.

I unwind myself from arms that seem to have already grown stronger, pick up the plate.

'I have an important mission.'

'Go talk to the space cadets, Digby.'

*　　*　　*

11.34 p.m.

I'm sitting on the stairs now, warbling away with more friends in an idle way. What would the peasants, only just getting used to new villages and self-styled Lords of the manor, have been thinking a thousand years ago? If they had had an *Eagle* annual, says Ted, would it have included 'Cathedrals of the Future', 'Build your own General Dynamics Crusader', 'How to make a real working model water-mill' or 'Amazing facts about God'?

An old classic is kicking in in the background:

> *He said that Change must come . . .*
> *Yep, you got it . . . Change must come . . . c'mon now.*

I look through banisters into the living room. Laughter and the forms of friends bold and bright, some lounging on the imported old sofas torn to pieces by generations of semi-homeless cats. How strange that only one room in my house is called the living room: what do I do in the rest of it then?

Reality number two, the place I fear most, answers me:

High walls topped with razor-wire surround the small housing estate. A bored security guard concentrates on his flickering gameboy. A car approaches. He tenses slightly, then relaxes as the registration number pops up on the VDU, underneath the flashing word 'Cleared'. Still, his eyes cannot help following it suspiciously as it crawls past the barrier and into the brightly lit warren of identically individual semi-detached houses.

It stops in front of the third house on the left. Two young men get out. The one with long black hair glances nervously up at the clouded sky. They hurry past the undersized patch of Astroturf that serves as a lawn and into the security of the double-glazed porch.

A woman wearing orange dungarees sits hypnotised in front of the television set. The patterns she trawls through so desperately tell her nothing she can hear. The sounds from the speaker hiss over the top of a harsh demanding baby voice echoing down the hallway, and between them they whisper:

When you made me you promised me life.

He is wearing Levis and a check shirt, coldness in his heart and a can of lager is in his hand as he opens the front door. 'Alex, Randall, come in,' he says in an over-jovial voice, and immediately takes a big swig of beer. They wait till he's finished gulping and slip quietly inside with their familiar bottles-of-wine-in-carrier-bags.

As the front door closes, she drags herself back from the strange place she has been and frowns twice, screwing up her eyes as tight as she can, as though she was looking into a very bright light. The evidence of pain temporarily erased, she draws her lips into a smile that is neither too harsh nor too innocent.

From the hallway she hears Randall's voice asking about Lada repairs. She tenses and prepares herself for the party to start . . .

Okay, okay, coming up fast:

> *Change must come through the barrel of a gun, (that's right)*
> *CHANGE MUST COME THROUGH THE BARREL OF A*
> *GUN . . .*

From underneath, a four/four beat picks up the chaotic mass of overlain 303s and syncopated arpeggios and God-knows-what and slams it into our brains. Opening minds buzz with formless thoughts, their impulses expertly channelled through recharged ganglia. They whip through synaptic clefts like invincible joyriders crashing the last red lights before the open highways. Long, straight, empty nerves carry them effortlessly to destinations where smooth muscles scoop them up and outwards without hesitation.

Repetition matched only by deviation, sensual codes flash back up nerve pathways telling us that our CPUs have just been MMXd and all systems are on-line. Saz's silver dress sucks in the light from the candles, holds it for a moment and sends it flying outwards again, framing her white eyes and Paradise Factory grin. It glances off jewels of sweat mined from hard muscles that coat Alex's chest. Eyes tight, lips half-open, his arms restructure reality as he moves. Above him, a sign says 'THE CHANCE OF A LIFETIME'. Randall bounces wildly round making a pioneering attempt at powered flight. Lara stands in the dead centre, strips of bright material falling round her head, quizzical – listening to a voice only she can hear.

Karen's wide eyes follow the swirls in the loose material of her dress – intricate patterns that may explain why Josh laughs wildly, and why Rich, upside down, shouts 'ohmyGodohmyGodohmyGod' in time to the music; Tom and Cal are making hot-knife eyes at each other; Kevin pauses somewhere off the trail – his hand gathers ringlets of hair back from his face, his brow furrowed as he waits for the answer.

Gavin shimmers bald-headed through the chaos like our druid. He encourages the madness with delighted eyes, then plucks sanity out of the air in mid-flight, taming it with the memories of pink orchids and Canal Street pints on hot summer days.

11.44 p.m.

Alex's long hair flows around me. The stubble on his jawbone is soothed by my hand, bristling again as it slides by. His lips are heavy and engulfing, then light and playful. Saz nuzzles Randall's neck as he winds his legs tightly round her stomach. A flashbulb goes off inside my head and time freezes in its glare.

*　　*　　*

11.46 p.m.

Time to sort out drinks for zero hour. Back to the kitchen for a tray of miniature crystal glasses and the bottle of Jamesons. As I pour, the Jamesons shimmers, liquid drags over the edge of the bottle awkwardly . . .

Reality number two:

Inside my head, Bulgarian cabernet sauvignon splashes into a glass.

Nine people sit uncomfortably in a living room designed for four point four people. Fortunately, as well as the three-piece suite, there are two battered deckchairs and a pouffe. They are all drinking too fast, not to get them high but to keep them low, as they talk in high monotones.

The conversation has moved on from Lada repairs. It meanders awkwardly around the likelihood of a second Blair term, precipitating several short speeches which conclude it is either inevitable or impossible. It touches uneasily on the stays of execution granted today as part of 'Project Clemency' and comes to rest, as always these days, with the weather. As they speak, a thin, grey rain scratches at the newly-leaded windows and they shiver, remembering the post-Sizewell dictum: 100,000 drops till you drop. Always wear your overalls.

But now someone has drunk too much or too little or whatever. Someone is choking back a sob for the ridiculous, romantic loss they have suffered. Someone, in short, has remembered.

They stare at the floor like someone has shat on the carpet. They were doing so well, now none of them has anything left to say to drown out the voice that each of them can hear whining inside their heads:

You promised me LIFE . . .

Remember?

Randall pulls his fingernails from my hair and pulls me close.

'Been walking in the rain?'

'Yeah.'

'Oh, shit. Remember. It's nearly time.'

Held tight by strong muscles: muscles made to dance; muscles made for a passion no emptiness can waste.

I remember these things. I remember the way things were and the way things will be. It's nearly time.

11.48 p.m.

A voice comes through from the dining room:

'God, I love this drug — it should be called mellow!'

I laugh, that's Ant's catchphrase. Ant is peculiar in that he has never had the madness, or if he has, he has never admitted to it. The closest he's come to drug-induced psychosis was when we were tripping once and he stated, very matter of fact, that all drinks were composed mainly of vitamin C.

Through the open door, I can see him and Lara with half a dozen others. They have got hold of an enormous ragged white sheet. We stuffed the room full of them and hung powder-blue drapes around the walls so it looks like Iceworld. As they dance, it rises and falls slowly, billowing white clouds reach up to touch a brittle blue sky. Lara lets go of her corner and dances into the centre, eyes closed as she sways, a parachutist in magical freefall.

He's right though, everything's a piece of the jigsaw and it is a drug to love. Maybe not for everyone. Maybe not even for me as

Reality number two cuts in:

A small group of people sit drunkenly in an undersized living room. A pile of pinkish salt lies on the carpet — despite accumulated evidence to the contrary, they believe it will erase the evidence of red wine. That it can take away stains. One of them surreptitiously drys her eyes on a sleeve. They are placing things that look like miniature plastic Dairylea cheese boxes on a complicated board that resembles a star map.

'Are you okay?' says one, 'You do look a little pale.'

Stalled at red traffic lights, system finally crashed. She nods helplessly, 'Yeah, fine, just . . . you know.'

They lean forward understanding now, concerned and slightly censorious.

'Perhaps a little stout?'

A stilted lout.

I giggle.

Rocketing back again, and just in time, fending off the élite crack forces of paranoia, holding the urban defences firm, the civilian population shrinking back . . . Jesus, I was about to drink a little stout and play Trivial Pursuit! Talk about 2000 compliant . . .

Someone, Ted, puts a spliff in my hand and a hand on my shoulder.

'Playing the genius version now?'

I acknowledge him with a grateful smile and something between a wave, sigh and shrug.

Reality number two. Heads are shaking and hurt faces cajole:

'Such things are illusory. You remember, don't you, the way that the highs got lower and stranger and the lows just stranger. Watching ourselves slowly become caricatures of our supposedly liberated selves, we said — no more. Better stout and Trivial Pursuits. Better anything than forever reaching desperately over that great grey gulf of water which separates us all for ever, whose treacherous currents flow only down and down and down.'

*   *   *

11.57 p.m.

Twenty-seven bright pinpoints of candlelight multiply in the oily surfaces of whiskey in the glasses. Kevin's hands cease their perpetual description of the indescribable, one resting on angular hip as the other holds the gift aloft for inspection. Rich says 'Why thank you!' and drinks his straight down. Light disperses over his tongue and vanishes down his throat. Lara and Josh stop giggling and just stare at the silver tray like it's a flying saucer.

'Whiskey. Drink.'

'Oh, I see.' Josh turns to Lara: 'It's whiskey and you drink it.'

Her face clears: 'Aha! Let's drink it then.'

As the Jamesons goes round, so does the message that it is nearly time. It reaches Cal at the decks: hard backbeats mutate slowly — incredibly — into one of those weightless, string-chord-and-diva tracks. The bright lights inside our heads fill the room. For one long final moment, we are at peace.

11.59 p.m.

Alex reaches with his eyes through a curtain of jet-black hair. He knows. Karen licks Ted's lips a final time. She is ready. Randall wipes sweat from his mad eyes and looks pleadingly. Reach forwards and gather his neck, open palmed, head down on to bare chest. Lips caress nipple ring a brief second, then he too is back.

Lines of energy snake out through the room as we open ourselves ready to receive. Numbers multiply as we sense it is time, materialising into the empty spaces in the room until there are no empty spaces left, just expectant, generous flesh.

*   *   *

The door of a house swings open, revealing a curiously familiar tableaux to the nine people, who hesitate outside for a moment. One of them, a woman in orange dungarees, is carrying a baby. The rain drips down the fringe of her hair, and her eyes say:

It's time

All over the city, we pause, still grasping our lager with a piece of lime in it and look up for a moment, convinced we heard something like a call to arms.

11.59:59 p.m.

I take my finger off the pause button.

Paul Di Filippo

'MAMA TOLD ME NOT TO COME'

'Aren't you having fun yet, Loren?'

I lifted my head slowly. It felt like it belonged to someone else. Some sadomasochist who had stuffed it with sand, used the tongue for a doormat and the eyesockets for a photobath, then left the whole mess out in a cold autumn rain.

Ann Marie, my hostess, towered over me, glass in hand. The numerous drinks she had consumed that night had done little to mute her incorrigible perkiness.

'Do I look like I'm having "fun" yet, Ann Marie?'

I was sitting on the floor in a corner of Ann Marie's living room, clasping my upraised knees. I was wearing the same stained suit I had worn for the past week, twenty-four hours a day. My hair resembled a haystack pitched by one of the less competent Snopeses. The stubble on my face was patched with dried mustard from a steady diet of cart-vendor hot dogs.

All around me swirled and bubbled, perked and pooled, churned and chortled, shrieked and shouted, guffawed and gasped, tinkled and crashed that strange human activity known as — a party.

A party I was in no way a party to.

Ann Marie tried to focus her chipmunk-bright gaze on me, and, after womanful concentration, succeeded.

'Hmmm, well, now that you mention it, Loren, I have seen you look happier, not to mention more smartly dressed . . .'

From a far-off room came the noise of breaking glass, followed by yelps, cheers and what sounded like curtains being ripped off their rods.

'Ann Marie,' I said wearily, 'don't you think you'd better see what's going on with your other guests? It sounds like they're demolishing your lovely apartment.'

I believe it was one of the more feeble-minded kings of England of whom it was said: 'Be careful what idea you put into the King's head, for once inserted it is nigh impossible to dislodge.' Ann Marie, especially after a certain amount of booze, was similarly singleminded. And now I was the sole object of her concern.

'Oh, I'm not worried about anything,' she said blithely. 'I bought a special party insurance just for tonight. After all, it's not every day you get the chance to welcome in a new century.'

'An astute and unarguable observation, Ann Marie.'

'You see, I don't care what anyone does tonight, as long as they're having fun! And that's why I'm worried about you. You're obviously not having fun!'

'Fun' was a concept I could no longer wrap my mind around. It seemed to me now in my despair that I had never understood the word. I doubted anyone really did. All I wanted was to be left alone until midnight. Locking eyes with Ann Marie, I tried to communicate this. 'Ann Marie, do you know why I came to your party tonight?'

'Why, to have fun with your friends, of course.'

'No, Ann Marie. Although that might have been true at one time, it is unfortunately not so now. I came, Ann Marie, simply because you live on the forty-ninth floor.' A look of absolute bewilderment instantly transformed Ann Marie's face, as if she were one of those dolls with a button in their backs that swapped their expressions.

'It is a nice view of the city, Loren, but you've seen it a hundred times before—'

'Tonight, Ann Marie, I intend to see it "up close and personal", you might say. At midnight, when everyone else is celebrating the beginning of a glorious new century, I am going to open your sliding glass door — assuming none of these "party animals" has broken it before then, in which case I shall simply step through the shard-filled frame — and emerge on to that small square of unadorned concrete you insist on calling a "patio", from the railing of which I shall instantly hurl myself into space, thus ending my complete and utter misery.'

Someone twisted the button in Ann Marie's back, dialing up an expression of shocked disgust. 'Do you have any idea, Loren, of what a bummer that would be for everyone who's trying to enjoy themselves?'

'I am not too keen on the notion myself, Ann Marie. But it seems like the only thing left for me to do.'

Ann Marie dropped into a squat beside me, sloshing some of her drink on my trouser leg in the process. Not that it mattered.

'Tell ol' Annie all about it, Loren. What's wrong?'

'It's quite simple. Precisely one week ago, my whole life fell apart like a dollar wristwatch. In the space of a single hour, Jenny left me and I lost my job.'

'I wondered why she wasn't with you. What happened?'

'I still don't know. I got home and found a note. It said that she was flying to El Ay with someone named Reynaldo.'

'Uh-oh.'

'You knew about Reynaldo?'

'She swore it was just a fling—'

I dropped my head into my hands and listened to someone moan for about thirty seconds before realising it was me.

'There, there, Loren,' said Ann Marie, patting my shoulder. 'She was never good enough for you.'

'But I still love her, damn it!'

'You'll find someone else, I'm sure. Once you get your-self looking respectable again. Why, the new love of your life could even be here tonight! And I'm sure you'll land another job.'

My laugh must have been awfully loud and eerie-sounding, to cause everyone in the immediate vicinity to look at me as they did. Even Ann Marie appeared shocked, and she knew what I was feeling.

'Don't tell me—' she began.

I feared I was shouting, but I couldn't help it. 'Yes! I've been replaced by an expert system! A thousand-dollar software package has taken my place! Six years of higher education down the fucking tubes! There's nothing left for me but a government retraining camp—'

'I hear the meals are great,' said Ann Marie half-heartedly.

I scrambled awkwardly to my feet. Seven nights of sleeping on park benches and steam gratings had taken their toll. 'I don't care if they serve stuffed fucking pheasant! I'm going to kill myself! Do you all hear me? I'm going to take the big dive! Tickets on sale now!'

'Loren, please! People are trying to start the new millennium off with a cheerful attitude!'

All the spirit went out of me. To say I felt like a sack full of shit would have been to err on the side of cheerfulness. I felt like an empty sack that had once held shit. 'Okay, Ann Marie, you win. I'll be a good boy. Until the clock strikes twelve. And then I'm going to make like a crippled pigeon.'

Ann Marie's native idiot exuberance reasserted itself. 'That's wonderful, Loren. I'm sure something will make you change your mind before you do anything rash. Now, let me see. First you need a little drink. Then, we'll introduce you to someone exciting. Who would you like to talk to?'

'No one.'

'Oh, don't be a poop! I know! There's this real character that Sam brought with him. The guy claims to be a Greek god of some sort. Imagine! Now, he'll make you forget about your teensy-weensy troubles.'

'Is he Charon? That's the only one I feel like meeting.'

'Sharon? I told you, he's a guy! Now, c'mon.'

I let Ann Marie lead me away. I didn't have anything planned for an hour yet.

All around us the party was accelerating like a piano dropped from a penthouse suite, promising as spectacularly clangorous a finale.

Five people were monopolising the middle of the living room with a game of Co-ed Naked Twister. A bottle of baby oil seemed to be involved. Their audience were the people sitting three-deep on the couch, seemingly oblivious to the fact that one of the cushions appeared to be smouldering. In the corner diagonally opposite the one I had been occupying, there was a knot of bodies around what appeared to be a burbling hookah. A crowd was gathered in front of the flatscreen HDTV, playing a drinking game: every time the septugenarian Dick Clark said 'rockin' in the millennium,' whoever failed to shout 'Let's party like it's Nineteen ninety-nine!' had to chug from a fifth of peppermint schnapps. What appeared at first to be a diapered child draped with a New Year banner was drawing with crayons on the wall. Upon closer inspection, I saw he was a dwarf, and his drawing elegantly obscene. From the next room a DAT player blared over the sound of projectile vomiting, and I could feel dancers shaking the floor. The whole building, in fact, seemed to be quaking. None of this, however, managed to wake the mousey woman who had gone to sleep six feet off the floor atop a narrow bookshelf.

I had never understood parties. Overheated or freezing, ear-splitting or deadly silent, boring or overstimulating, crowded or sparsely attended, too much food or too little, liquor-saturated or temperance-bound, they always inhabited one extreme or another. Never had I been to a party that was just plain enjoyable, in a moderate way. It was possible none such existed. Certainly, Ann Marie's end-of-the-century bash was not one.

'Just think,' said Ann Marie herself, as she steered me around a recumbent body wrapped like a fashionable mummy in the curtains I had earlier heard being misappropriated, 'there must be a zillion parties just like this one going on around the world tonight!'

'What an appalling notion.'

'Poop! Gee willikers, where is that Greek guy?' We entered the kitchen just in time to be nearly dually decapitated by a colourful flying plate, which crashed and shattered against the wall alongside the door.

'You bitch!'

'Bastard!'

Ann Marie intervened. 'Jules and Melissa, I'm so hurt! That was a piece of original Fiestaware!'

'Sorry, Ann Marie. But he deserved it. I caught him with that slut Oona in the bathroom!'

'I told you, she only asked me to help her zip her dress—'

'And what was it doing unzipped in the first place, may I ask?'

'Now, now,' said Ann Marie, 'why don't you two kiss and make up? You don't want to start the next thousand years off with a silly ol' spat, do you?'

Convinced that she had done all she could to effect a reconciliation, Ann Marie turned away from the glowering couple. Spotting a jug of Smirnoff on the counter, she snatched it up. Setting her own drink down next to an unclaimed lipstick-smeared glass, she splashed a few inches of vodka for herself and me.

'Here you go! Now, if only — oh, there he is!' She dragged me over to a man sitting alone on a countertop.

If you took a composite of Keith Richards at the nadir of his heroin addiction and Charles Bukowski on a six-month bender and started to morph his body into that of Miles Davis just before he died, but stopped with the transformation half complete, you might end up with someone who looked like this guy. He was dressed in sandals and an outfit that resembled blue satin pyjamas, and he was eating from a bunch of grapes with languid disdain. 'Dissipated' was the most charitable word whose dictionary entry he might illustrate.

Ann Marie accosted him with, 'Hell-low! I'd like you to meet someone. This is Loren. Loren, meet — oh, I've forgotten your name!'

Chewing a grape with enervated precision, the man said, 'Bacchus.'

I could almost hear the wind the allusion made, passing over Ann Marie's head. 'Well, Mister Backus, you and Loren have a nice talk. I've got to go mingle.'

Ann Marie left. A pool of silence seemed to surround Bacchus and me, strangely isolating us. I tried to think of something to say, and some reason to say it. The habits of sociability die hard. Finally, I opted for easy sarcasm. 'What happened to the figure, man? Aren't you supposed to be carrying a few more pounds? And what about the ivy wreath? Couldn't get to the florist's tonight? Wait a minute, let me guess. Al-anon, World Gym, Ralph Lauren, and you're a new man.'

I knocked back my drink, watching him out of the bottom of my eyes, waiting for his reaction to the needling. Bacchus finished chewing, regarding me with neither overt hostility nor friendliness. When he had extracted the last atom of taste from the fruit, he spoke.

'You from fucking Disney, or what?'

It took me a few seconds to get it. Then I burst out laughing.

'Yeah,' continued Bacchus, 'I came that close to slapping them with a lawsuit when that fucking cartoon came out. Made me look like a real asshole. The cute donkey, the pratfalls, scared of lightning, for Hera's sake, as if Zeus and I weren't as tight as your mama's twat. But then I figured an out-of-court settlement would be best. I still get thirty per cent on every tape sale.'

'That's cool,' I said, taking one of his grapes and flicking it across the room. 'Keeps you in produce.' The vodka had gone through my empty stomach and straight to my head. Suddenly, it seemed good to be drunk, for what I still intended to do. I made a move towards the Smirnoff for a refill, but Bacchus stopped me.

'Here, let me.'

I stuck my glass out, not knowing what to expect, and he held his right palm over it. Wine gurgled out, as if from a vinous stigmata.

I pretended not to be astonished. 'Hose up the sleeve?'

Bacchus shrugged. 'If you wish.'

I tasted the wine. Cool breezes on a green hillside, ocean spray and hot sunlight, a shaded stream under ancient oaks. That was the vintage.

My head was as light as a Wordsworthian cloud. Bacchus's voice seemed to come from a neighbouring solar system. 'You know, you can call them anything you want. Parties, revels, carnivals, orgies, saturnalia, mardi gras — Hades! Call 'em Bacchanalia, if I can toot my own horn. But all festivities have a certain logic. I could write a fucking book on the dynamics of fun. And one chapter would be all about cases like you.'

I sipped more of the incredible wine. 'And what exactly am I?'

'The spectre at the feast. The suicide. Hanged man and fool.'

I tried not to shiver. 'What if I am? You gonna try to talk me out of my plans?'

Bacchus held both hands up, palms out. I couldn't see any tubes — or holes, for that matter.

'By no means. I just offer my Olympian perceptions, for what they're worth.'

I was suddenly sick of talking. Sick of living. Midnight was fifteen minutes away, and I just wanted everything over with. 'Don't you have someplace else to go?' I said.

Bacchus laughed. 'I am everywhere already.'

I was turning away, but that stopped me. 'Huh?'

Leaning forward as if to confide a secret, the strange man said, 'Every party that ever was or is or will be is connected. Same with every war or every fuck. Or so Mars and Venus tell me. You just have to know how to get from one to another.'

'And how would you do such a thing?'

'In my case, I am simply called, manifesting simultaneously, every place at once. Gods are like that. You see, I am the original party vibe, a permanent, omnipresent wavefront that collapses into physicality wherever conditions are right. But if you wanted to try it, you'd need some props.'

'Props?'

Bacchus skinned back the sleeve on his right arm. The veins in his wrist were not blue, but royal purple, and there was definitely no tube down his clothing. He held up his empty hand in an affected magician's pose. I never looked away, but somehow, with a mere twitch, he summoned up an object. It was a paper-and-plastic party horn, with trailing Cellophane streamers around the bell.

'One blast on this, and you're instantly elsewhere, dispersed randomly along the party matrix.'

'Randomly?'

Another shrug. 'Nature of the beast. Some drunken scientist named Heisenberg tried explaining it to me once, but I didn't dig it. Stochastic, probalistic, chaotic — made less sense than Socrates. Oh, I should mention something else. Wherever you find yourself, you're limited to the psychophysical boundaries of the party. Whatever gathering you pop up in, you can't just step out of it into, say, Armistice Day New York.'

'How come?'

'Outside the special party environment, you'd be a temporal-spatial intruder. Your unnatural presence would cause the instant conversion of your whole mass to energy. Make Hiroshima look like a firecracker.'

'Forget it,' I said. 'Not interested.'

Bacchus tucked the horn in my jacket pocket. 'You never know.'

Despite myself, I found myself saying, 'You mentioned "props", plural—'

Bacchus grinned, and twitched his hand again. A polka-dotted conical party hat appeared. Before I could stop him, he had placed it on my head, snapping the rubber string maliciously under my chin. 'Lets you speak and understand all languages. And then there's this.' He materialised a ziploc bag full of multicoloured confetti. 'Sprinkle a little of this on someone, and they'll accompany you when you blow the horn.' He dropped the confetti into my other pocket. 'Now, you'd better get going. It's almost midnight.'

So saying, Bacchus spun me around and booted me in the rump. I went down to my knees. And when I picked myself up, he was gone, as if he had never been.

But I was still wearing the party hat, and my hands found the other 'props' in my pockets.

Screw all his bullshit! Nothing in my pitiful life had changed. I made for the patio door.

None of Ann Marie's jabbering or insensate guests tried to stop me, and Ann Marie herself was nowhere to be seen.

As was only natural, considering the chill and darkness, the small balcony was empty. I shut the glass door behind me, a barrier to all warmth and human noise.

The narrow flat railing was bitter cold beneath my hands as I clambered on top of it. Below me the city spread out like a Tiffany show-window. Wind plucked at my sleeves, beckoning. My eyes began to tear.

I leaned forward, then hesitated. Was this really my only way out?

Hands in my back shoved me over. 'See you later!' I heard Bacchus yell.

I fell about twelve storeys before I got the horn out and up to my lips. I closed my eyes and blew like Gabriel, releasing a long sour BLAT!

The tremendous passage of the icy wind past my plummeting body stopped. All sense of falling ceased. I seemed to be sitting in a large comfortable padded armchair. The noise of rattling crockery dancing on a wooden tabletop came to my ears. Someone was huffing and puffing. Another someone was grunting. A third someone was squeaking. Then the grunting someone spoke. Shouted, rather, in a high-pitched unhuman voice. 'Put some butter 'round his ears!'

I opened my eyes. A large tree overspread the tea-party-bedizened table, casting an emerald umbrage. I could smell growing grass and warm scones. The Mad Hatter held the Dormouse by his ankles, while the March Hare was pushing on the pitiful rodent's shoulders, trying to cram him into a teapot. Alice, of course, had just left.

Abandoning his efforts, the Mad Hatter lowered the Dormouse's legs to the table, and the Dormouse lay there with his head in the pot, his squeaks gradually subsiding, to be replaced by snores.

The Mad Hatter removed his topper and scratched his sparsely haired scalp. I could see the dark line of sweat around his hatband. '"Put some butter 'round his ears"? Why, whatever for? We're not going to eat him, are we?'

The March Hare wrinkled his nose in disgust, quivering his whiskers. 'Dolt! Naturally not. You can only eat Dormice in months that end with an 'O', and this is May!'

Restoring his hat to his head, the Mad Hatter said, 'As I recall, you were the one who formerly advised me to add some butter to the works of my watch, and we all know how that turned out. Why should this time be any different?'

'You must admit, the time your watch keeps with butter in the works is much different than the time it kept before.'

The Mad Hatter removed his watch from his pocket and gazed dolefully at it, before soaking it in his teacup.

'True, quite true. Although it's still right twice a day, the days seem so much longer!'

'I only suggested the butter this time,' stipulated the March Hare, 'with an eye towards slipperiness.'

'You said, "ears", not "eye". It was the Dormouse's ears that needed buttering, you claimed. I recall it quite distinctly, for it gave me such a disturbing pause as I never experienced before, nor ever hope to again.'

The March Hare grew huffy. 'I said no such thing! I merely claimed that our somnambulent friend had got some butter in his eye, and it needed wiping.'

'What a fib!'

'God's truth!'

'Fib!'

'Truth!'

From inside the teapot came a muffled voice. 'Why not ask the gentleman wearing the dunce cap to settle the matter?'

The March Hare and the Mad Hatter both turned towards me.

I tried to shrink into the chair, but there was no DRINK ME bottle handy. What in sweet Jesus's name had I got myself into? God damn that Bacchus!

'What a capital idea!' exclaimed the Mad Hatter. 'There's no one more impartial than someone who has no idea of what's going on!'

Squinting one eye at me, the March Hare said, 'I question his qualifications. He looks as if he's searching for something. How can a man with a mission possibly help us?'

'We already tried a miss with a mansion, and she was utterly useless.'

The March Hare clapped his paws together. 'That's it! He's looking for Alice!'

The Dormouse, with one paw on the pottery spout and one on the handle, succeeded in removing the teapot from his head. 'I think not. He's merely looking for a lass—'

'Oh, well, in that case, there's always the Queen.'

'Or the Duchess,' added the March Hare. 'Neither one is married.'

'What of the King?'

'The King has nothing to do with the Duchess. That's merely a nasty rumour started by the Knave.'

'The King wouldn't object, then, if this fellow wished to marry the Queen?'

'Why should he? A husband has to do whatever his wife wants, especially if he's as powerful as the King.'

'Then it's agreed? Our friend with the sugarloaf cap is to marry the Queen today?'

'By all means.'

'Excelsior!'

Joining hands, the Hare and Hatter began to dance and sing.

> 'We're going to a wedding!
> It shall be very gay!
> We'll save the groom's beheading
> For another summer day!'

Meanwhile, the Dormouse had walked across the table and stepped down into my lap. Involuntarily, I flinched away from his furry weight. But, restraining myself, I allowed him to curl up and go to sleep.

I didn't dare do anything in this hallucination. There was no telling how I might make it worse. In any case, I fully expected to impact the pavement below Ann Marie's apartment any second now, once this Ambrose-Bierce moment of frenzied delusional brain activity was over.

Finishing their capers, the two strange creatures arranged themselves on either side of me. 'Have some wine?' asked the March Hare.

'Thanks, but I've had enough. Would you answer a question for me though?'

'Only if you ask one.'

'Assuming that what Bacchus told me was true, how is it that I've ended up in a fictional party instead of a real one?'

'Fictional? Who says we're fictional? That's a tall story someone's shortchanged you with! Here, does this feel fictional?' The March Hare inclined his head and made me stroke one long, plush ear.

'No,' I was forced to admit, 'it doesn't—'

'And what of poor Dormouse? If you were fictional, as you fictitiously maintain, would it be possible for him to eat that confetti in your pocket, as he is now so raptly doing?'

I looked down, alarmed. Although his eyes were still closed, the Dormouse had somehow burrowed into my pocket, gnawed a hole in the ziploc of transport-confetti, and was now chewing a mouthful.

'Hey!' I shot to my feet, dumping the Dormouse on to the ground. He lay on his back, still somnolently chewing.

Suddenly, my arms were pinioned with surprising strength by the Mad Hatter. 'That's no way to treat someone you've just poisoned!'

'Off with his head!'

The Queen and all her court had arrived. I was somehow gratified to see that their playing-card bodies had a narrow third dimension to them. It made the whole thing so much more plausible.

The masked executioner advanced on me. He held not an axe, but a butter-knife he had appropriated from the table. 'I'm so sorry we shan't be getting married now,' said the Queen. 'But I can't possibly marry a murderer unless he's paid for his crimes by dying.'

I felt the blade of the knife laid against my throat. Jerking violently forward, I tossed the Mad Hatter over my shoulders. He flew among the playing-card figures, flattening a swathe through their ranks. I found Bacchus's horn and brought it to my lips. I heard the March Hare exclaim, 'How splendid! A fanfare for his own throat-slitting—'

And then I was gone.

By the light of two flaring cressets that cast back the night, I saw that there was a sign over the door of the marble mansion that read:

ANY SLAVE LEAVING THE HOUSE WITHOUT HIS MASTER'S
PERMISSION WILL RECEIVE ONE HUNDRED LASHES

'Ah, Latin,' said a drowsy voice from the vicinity of my knees. 'How I wish I could read that marvellous language! Unfortunately, during my school-days I developed the habit of dropping off to sleep whenever the Master began to declaim Caesar. Even now, the simplest Wee Willie Winkie sends me to the Land of Nod straight away.' I looked down. Standing on his hind legs, the Dormouse began to lick a paw and drag it over one rounded, unbuttered ear.

I couldn't believe my eyes. 'What are you doing here?'

'Why, grooming myself. I'm positively slathered with soggy tea leaves! I'm terribly sorry if I've offended you. Is it considered ill-mannered to groom oneself in public where you come from?'

Obviously, Bacchus's transport-confetti worked as advertised. I had been hoping to leave all traces of the Mad Tea Party far behind me. Plainly, however, the Dormouse and I were now permanently linked.

'Where's the Latin?' I asked.

'Why, on the sign, of course.'

'That's English.'

'I beg your pardon. I'm English, and I like to fancy I'd recognise a compatriot if I chanced on one. No, that's Latin, or I'm not a member of the *Gliridae*.'

Stretching its string, I lifted the party hat without removing it. The sign was Latin.

I snapped the hat back. The sign was English.

'Well, I'll be damned—'

Suddenly, my awful fate dawned on me in its full magnitude. Any lingering drunkenness in my veins burned off faster than gunpowder, and I felt an immense weight bow me down.

I was damned.

Never would I see my home era again, except perhaps in passing. The random path through time and space of my horn-assisted materialisations ensured that. And the temporary nature of the parties I was now forced to inhabit demanded that I perform frequent disorienting transitions. How long did the average revel last? Eight hours? A day, tops? I suspected that for me to linger beyond a party's natural end would be as fatal as attempting to step outside it while it was in progress. No, at the first hint of a party's imminent breakup, the first 'It's getting late, we must be going, thanks, it's been great fun,' I'd have to sound my trump and disappear.

I hated parties! And now I was doomed to spend the rest of my unnatural existence attending them, a Flying Dutchman of the social circuit. I had traded a quick and relatively painless — albeit messy — death for a lifetime of canapés and cocktails, tiny toothpick-pierced hotdogs and mindless chatter, loutish frat brawls and stuffy White House dinners, gallery openings and bar mitzvahs.

Almost, I turned and ran. How painful could it be to become an instant nova?

Voices approaching down the street stopped me. I had forgotten the existence of other people. My fiery demise would surely wipe out thousands of innocents. While I was quite content to go, I had no desire to exit as a mass murderer.

Damn that Bacchus!

'Oh,' yawned the Dormouse, 'all this Latin is as good as a rum toddy for scattering sand in one's eyes.'

Somehow, the Dormouse suddenly seemed like a familiar comforting presence in the face of these unknown people arriving, and I wanted him awake. 'No, don't go to sleep now!'

'I'm — afraid — I can't — help—'

Curling into a ball, the Dormouse filled the air with rodential snores. Hastily, I picked him up and stepped back into the shadows, praying I wouldn't move beyond the party's invisible sphere.

For good or ill, I didn't explode.

The noisy visitors stepped on to the mansion's wide columned porch. They were all dressed in splendid coloured belted togas, save the slaves, whose clothing was drabber and more uniform. The citizens among them had obviously been drinking for some time, and were plainly several trireme-sheets to the wind.

A large man resembling Zero Mostel said loudly, 'Ah, Trimalchio! You're a rich and ignorant ex-slave with no more grace than a camelopard, but we'll drink your Falernian anyway!'

'Hush, Glyco, our host will hear you!' advised an elderly woman wearing too much make-up for any era.

'What do I care! I'd say it right to his poxed face!'

'Still, for my sake—'

'All right, all right!'

Now a young woman, seemingly unaccompanied, spoke. 'The rest of you may as well go inside. I have a last detail to attend to.'

Glyco laughed. 'Fitting a new pessary up your lovely quim, I daresay! The work of one of Priapus's priestesses is never done!'

Even the object of Glyco's crude jest joined in the raucous laughter, though there was an undertone of distaste in her chuckles. She swatted him with a bundle of herbs she carried and said, 'Quartilla excuses your impious jest, Glyco. But I cannot swear that my god is as forgiving. Priapus does not take kindly such insults.'

Glyco immediately paled. 'Please, Quartilla, I meant no offence! Would — would a small donation of one hundred sesterces to the temple perhaps serve to amend . . . ?'

'Two hundred is more likely to soothe Olympian ire.'

'Very well,' grumbled Glyco, 'I'll send a slave by in the morning.'

A hulking man wearing a sword began to bang on the door. He was as ugly as ditchwater and as scarred as the carving tree at your local lover's lane. Drink had transformed what I could sense was innate belligerence into eager malevolence.

'Open up, for Achilles' sake! Hermeros, the life of the party is here!'

The door swung open, and a wizened porter in green livery was framed. 'No need to shout, citizens, the meal's only just commenced. Come in, quickly now, before the night air gives me my death. Right foot first, mind!' The party-goers entered, all carefully stepping over the threshold on the proper foot.

Left alone on the stoop, Quartilla looked carefully about, as if cautious of being observed. Muffling the Dormouse's snores against my chest, I held my breath, fearful that she would spot me. Lit by the torches, she seemed to have stepped fresh from an Alma-Tadema canvas, a Pre-Raphaelite goddess, raven-haired, samite-gowned. As I savoured her delicate beauty, she lit her posy from one of the torches, filling the air with fragrant smoke. Tossing the burning herbs to the stones, she lifted her skirts and squatted over the small bonfire. The sound of her piss quenching the little fire filled the air. 'By Priapus and Hecate, Mithra and Eileithyia, I command the demon to appear now!'

A queer impulse urged me to step forward, and I did.

Quartilla shrieked and lost her balance, tumbling over backwards, her skirts billowing around her waist. Cradling the Dormouse in one arm, I extended a hand to help her up. Somewhat fearfully, she took it. When she was standing, I said, 'Here I am. What do you want?'

The priestess's eyes were large with awe. 'I can't believe this, it's like a dream come true! I should have known it would happen on the night before my final exam! Though I have been trying to summon up a demon for ages ... But anyway, here you are, just like that, familiar and all. Why, there wasn't even any smoke or thunder.'

'Smoke and thunder are out of fashion where I come from, except in balancing the imperial debt, in which case we also employ mirrors.'

'Well, it's not as if I'm complaining, you understand. You're quite impressive as you are, what with your strange attire and all. Is that a gallows rope round your neck? Never mind, you needn't say, if it embarrasses you. One thing, though — I wasn't aware demons needed to shave as mortal men do.'

'You caught me on an off week. My wife left me.'

A gleam appeared in Quartilla's eyes. 'Ah, naturally. Every incubus must be mated with a succubus—'

'That she was,' I agreed.

Quartilla grabbed my hand again. 'You must come back to temple with me! Once Albucia, the head priestess, sees you, I'll surely be promoted! Mum and Dad will be so proud!'

She tried to tug me off the porch, and I quickly disengaged. ''Fraid not, priestess. I have to attend this party. Or some other.'

Quartilla placed her thumb beneath her pert chin and her forefinger at the corner of her mouth. She looked absolutely charming. 'You're under a geas, I take it.'

'Yes. One of Bacchus's, curse him.'

'Oh, him! It's not wise to flout the wishes of Enorches, the Betesticled One. I advise you to comply with whatever compulsion he has put on you.'

'As if I have a choice.'

'Well, what about after the party? Could you come then?'

I hated to disappoint her. 'We'll see.'

She lit up like Greek Fire. 'Wonderful! I'll stay right by your side all night! And so as not to divulge your true identity, I'll claim you as one of my umbrae, an uninvited tag-along guest.' Squiring Quartilla for the evening did not seem like such an awful prospect, so I nodded my consent. 'How shall I call you? "Demon" will certainly not do—'

'Loren.'

'An uncouth name. How about Laurentius?'

'Good enough.'

Satisfied with my new nomenclature, Quartilla adjusted the lines of her skirt with a deft tug and knocked on the door of Trimalchio's big house. The same wrinkled servant appeared in no time and let us in.

A magpie in a golden cage hanging near the entrance shrieked hello. Ahead of us stretched a long colonnade painted with colourful frescoes. 'Do you note the bald and querulous old man who recurs in each scene? That's the image of our host.'

'Did he really fight in the Trojan War and visit paradise with Mercury?'

Quartilla shrugged charmingly. 'When you're rich enough, you may have painted whatever flattering fancy you wish.'

The porter had retreated to a cubbyhole near the door and was busy shelling peas into a silver basin. Meanwhile, an epicene figure had stepped forward. 'The eunuch will show you to the feast,' said the porter. 'By the way, is that beast trained not to befoul my master's fine carpets?'

I had almost forgotten I was carrying the snoozing Dormouse. 'He's quite intelligent, although he does drip tea now and then.'

'Well, don't let him drip on the brocades.'

We followed the eunuch down the hall, and soon entered — right foot first — an expansive dining room. The large crowded room was well lit by several oil-fixtures descending from the ceiling. Three large couches were arranged in a U-shape around a central table, and dozens of other smaller lounges and chairs were scattered about. People milled around, laughing, chattering, drinking and eating small elegant snacks.

As soon as we stepped in, we were besieged by servants. Lissom boys poured ice-water over our hands; the runoff was captured in golden bowls upheld by others. Then our hands were gently dried for us. (I was forced to drape the Dormouse over one shoulder.)

I felt my shoes being tugged off. 'Hey—!' Attendants were removing Quartilla's sandals also. 'It's only the pedicure, Laurentius. Don't they have pedicures in Hades?'

'Not at parties.'

Like a starved alley-cat adopted by Rockefellers, Quartilla was luxuriating under the attention. 'It's one of the essentials of civilisation. Ah, it seems like a lustrum since I last attended a good party!'

I cut the embarrassing procedure short. 'Come on, let's meet our host.'

Both of us now barefoot, we advanced across the carpeted room. I could see Quartilla was irked at having her pedicure interrupted. 'Are all demons so impetuous and impatient?'

'Only those who have lost their wives, their jobs and their homes, and been thwarted in their suicide attempts.'

'Oh.'

We arrived at what Quartilla whispered to me was the Upper Couch. Recumbent at one end, wrapped in a red felt scarf against a visible case of sniffles, was Trimalchio. The murals had exaggerated any of his minor graces. Lying next to the millionaire was Hermeros: the breast of his toga was adorned with the tissuey shells of a dozen shrimps he had consumed, and he gripped a giant flagon of wine in one meaty paw. As we stood there, he emitted an enormous belch, followed by a 100-watt leer at Quartilla.

'Ah, my favourite priestess,' lisped Trimalchio, 'how nice of you to come. I trust your mistress, Albucia, is well . . . ?'

'Thank you for inviting me, honorable sir. Yes, my mistress fares well, although she is somewhat weary from servicing so many soldiers of late, as are all we maidens of Priapus. You know what the average Legionary freshly returned from the provinces is like—'

At this point, Hermeros made a grab at Quartilla's haunch, which she deftly side-stepped. 'Come here, you wench! I'll show you what kind of bronze balls swing under a real soldier staff!'

'Then again,' said Quartilla drily, 'it does not always require service in the deserts of Syria to render one witless. Sometimes, simple inbreeding will suffice.'

There was a bustle behind us which caused Trimalchio to quickly lose interest in us. Before I could be introduced, he picked up a purple-striped tasselled napkin and, tucking it beneath his scarf, said, 'Glad to hear it. Sit now, and take your pleasures.'

We moved to empty spaces at the Middle Couch, and I gratefully set the snoozing Dormouse down. He had been getting quite heavy.

The dish which had diverted Trimalchio's salivating attention from us was being lowered to the central table by four waiters. The door-sized platter was framed with the inlaid signs of the Zodiac, each of which held its symbolically appropriate food. A metal dome in the middle of the platter was soon lifted to reveal several plump fowls, fish arranged in a trough of sauce as if swimming, and a hare with pigeon wings affixed to its shoulders to resemble Pegasus. Also occupying the board were two or three amorphous objects which I did not recognise.

Quartilla gripped my arm and shrieked gleefully. 'Oh, Laurentius! My favourite dish! Fresh sow's udder!'

All the fear, excitement, tension and despair of the crazy night and the past week congealed into one greasy knot in my throat. I felt my gorge rising unstoppably, like an express train in my throat. I tried to get to my feet, but couldn't make it. I averted my head — and found a servant waiting with a copper receptacle ready. Then I heaved for what seemed like a day.

As I sagged back on to the couch, drained and weak, a round of applause filled the room. Trimalchio's voice carried above the diminishing clapping. 'Quartilla's foreign guest takes first honours! Bestow the laurels upon him!'

A slave advanced and dropped a floral wreath over my head and around my neck. Quartilla bestowed a peck on my cheek. 'Well done, Laurentius. That was truly a demonic regurgitation for so early in the feast.'

I accepted a damp scented cloth from yet another slave and wiped my mouth. 'Thank you. I haven't done anything like that since college.'

'Are you ready for some udder now?'

Suppressing a mild gagging, I replied, 'No, please, you indulge yourself. I believe I'll just have something to drink—'

'Mead for our champion, Laurentius!' commanded Quartilla, before spearing and slicing a teat.

I rinsed my mouth with the mead, and then lay back as a spectator to the party. After all, how often did one get to attend a real Roman orgy?

My expectations, however, were greater than the reality. If this was the height of the legendary decadence of Rome, than the twentieth century had them beat hollow. All anybody seemed interested in doing was gorging themselves on the various exotic dishes and gossiping. (Quartilla kept up with the best of the diners, in a somewhat appalling display of bone-stripping, lip-smacking, finger-licking avidity.) On the whole, I had been to wilder Rotary Club dinners. The height of excitement came when an argument flared between a husband and wife. She threw a plate at him, he ducked, and it narrowly missed Trimalchio.

'You bitch!'

'Bastard!'

Trimalchio intervened. 'Julius and Melissa, I'm so hurt! That was a piece of original Corinthian!'

'I'm sorry, Trimalchio. But he deserved it. I caught him with that slut Oenothea in the privy!'

Singers sang ('"Tis a ditty from the Asafoetida Man,' Quartilla informed me), dancers danced and jugglers juggled. After the course which consisted of a roasted whole boar stuffed with live thrushes, a pair of rowdy dishevelled jesters took the stage.

'My name is Haiga, and my comrade here is called Hatta.'

'He's a lying Thracian!'

'Now, what makes you say such a cruel thing, Hatta?'

'You said I was called Hatta.'

'Is that not your name?'

'Of course it's my name!'

'Then what's the problem?'

'My name is not what I'm called.'

'Oh, I see. What are you called, then?'

'Mad!'

The audience cracked up. 'A paradox worthy of Zeno!' complimented Trimalchio, tossing some coins at the performers.

Throughout the evening, I had sustained a virtually unrelenting barrage of glares and growls from Hermeros, who plainly resented my proximity to Quartilla. Whenever she leaned towards me, it provoked him to near-madness. Several times I braced myself for a lunge that he fortunately never quite carried through, restrained perhaps by the setting.

The night wore on in a blizzard of food and drink. Every dish seemed more elaborate than the last, announced by Trimalchio with boorish delight. I drank cup after cup of mead, until my vision and hearing grew fuzzy as the logic of the neural network that had stolen — would steal — my job two thousand years from now.

147

Somehow, it seemed like a good idea to lay my head in Quartilla's lap and go to sleep, whatever Hermeros might do. But that stupid hat of mine. I removed it and put it on the head of the Dormouse, where it wouldn't get lost. All the chatter became a senseless babble, which lulled me to a hazy sleep . . .

I came to a start when the Dormouse screamed. On the table was the latest offering from Trimalchio's kitchens: nestled in a candied glaze were little rodents one-tenth the size of — but otherwise identical to — my personal Dormouse.

The Dormouse was jabbering in Latin. I snatched the hat off his head and put it on. Now I could understand both his English and the Latin of the others.

'What month is it? What month is it?' the Dormouse was demanding.

'Why, tis the month of Quintilus,' answered Quartilla hesitantly when I asked.

I told the Dormouse.

'But that doesn't end in an "O!"' he wailed. 'Oh, how could they do such a cruel thing to my cousins, without even waiting till October!'

'October doesn't end with an "O" either.'

'But at least it begins with one!'

The whole room had gone quiet while the Dormouse and I conversed. Several people were making horned-finger gestures at me, against the evil eye. Then Hermeros, standing somewhat unsteadily, broke the silence.

'He's a magician, an evil magician! That's the only explanation of how someone so puny could have enraptured the priestess so. He must be slain to free her!' Hefting his sword, Hermeros stumbled menacingly towards me.

I fumbled for the packet of transport-confetti, found it and managed to shake some on Quartilla, out of the hole the Dormouse had nibbled. Then I got the horn to my lips.

'He attempts to summon the aid of spirits!' yelled Hermeros, and threw himself clumsily at our couch. As I gave a mighty blast on the party horn, I saw a single dot of confetti fall from Quartilla's shoulder on to Hermeros.

Shit, I thought.

The sun was so bright in comparison to the oil lamps at Trimalchio's, I couldn't see for a moment. I could only hope that Hermeros — had he indeed accompanied us — was suffering from the same disadvantage.

As I did not immediately feel a sword piercing my queasy guts, I assumed the bad-tempered soldier was squinting and rubbing his eyes as fiercely as I. As the sun-dazzles cleared from my vision, the pellucid notes of an electric guitar sounded from some distance away, and I realised from other familiar noises that a constant stream of people was flowing around and past our little tableau.

Finally, I could see.

Quartilla was turning around in slow circles of slack-jawed amazement. Hermeros was dragging a clumsy hand slowly over his apish incredulous mug, the point of his blade resting on the ground. The Dormouse was unconcernedly asleep at my feet, the sad fate of his cousins forgotten. We were in some modern city, standing at the gates of some park. Throngs of people, mostly young, were ambling past us and on to the grassy grounds. One of them, as he passed, tossed a newspaper in a trash can, and I claimed it. It was the *San Francisco Oracle*, and its banner headline read: FIRST HUMAN BE-IN TODAY!

It was 1967, ten years before I had been — or would be — born. The Summer of Love.

Quartilla had stopped turning, and now beamed at me. 'Laurentius, how marvellous! You have transported us to your Underworld home!'

'Close enough, give or take a decade or two and the width of a continent.'

'Little did I ever suspect that the realm of Pluto held such wonders! Just wait until I report these marvellous adventures to Albucia!'

Instantly, I felt remorseful for having dragged this poor girl from her natural time and place. What had made me permanently wrench her from her home, other than greed for her beautiful company? And how could I ever tell her what I had done?

'Ah, yes, well, you see, Quartilla — gack!'

Hermeros's swordpoint was nicking my throat. I swallowed tentatively, and my Adam's apple measured the steel in micrometres. 'You fiend!' spat the soldier. 'You vile fiend! Return us to Rome immediately, or I'll run you through!'

'Now listen, Hermeros, it's not as easy as you might think—'

The blade pushed deeper. 'No excuses! Do it!'

'I can't!'

Hermeros must have concealed in his back one of those buttons that Ann Marie had. His expression went instantly from mere anger to volcanic rage. 'Then I'm damned, and you're dead!'

I closed my eyes and tried to pray.

'Hey, man, quit goofin' around!'

'Yeah, brother. Be cool!'

I opened my eyes. Two strange figures flanked Hermeros.

Both men had hair down to their navels or thereabouts, and flowers and peace signs painted on their faces. One wore a top hat, and the other flaunted a headband to which was affixed a droopy pair of cloth rabbit ears. The guy with the hat was dressed in a ruffled white shirt and denim bell-bottoms, while the other sported a fur vest over his hairy bare chest and tight green velvet trousers.

'You could really hurt someone with that pigsticker,' admonished Top Hat.

'Don't you know it's a day for groovin' in the sun?' enquired Rabbit Ears.

The sight of the hippies seemed to have discombobulated Hermeros. When at last he could speak he said, 'I have seen Druids naked and painted blue, and lice-ridden Syrian anchorites blistering under the sun. But I'll sell my own mother into slavery if I've ever seen two such misbegotten hellspawn as these ones you have summoned, sorcerer.' Stiffening his resolve, Hermeros readjusted his sword for a thrust. 'Though they rend me into pieces, I shall yet have my revenge!'

Top Hat turned to me. 'What did he say, man?'

'He's very pleased to meet you, but he still intends to kill me.'

Rabbit Ears clucked his tongue. 'Major uncool.'

'Bad vibes.'

'Bringdown city.'

'Total bummer.'

Putting two fingers in his mouth, Rabbit Ears produced a loud whistle.

Out of the crowd materialised a brace of enormous Hell's Angels, filthy, bearded and leather-clad. They pinioned Hermeros's arms before he could react. I gulped gratefully. Thinking fast, I said, 'He's a little high. Could you just hold him for a while, guys, until he comes down? And, oh, don't take him out of the park, will you?' The last thing I wanted was to destroy San Francisco on such a happy historic day.

'Sure, man,' grunted one of the Angels. 'That's what we're here for.' Then they marched the struggling Hermeros off.

I knew the respite was only temporary. Linked to me by the confetti, Hermeros would remain my problem. Still, it felt good to be rid of him, even for a short while.

Quartilla had watched the whole affair with pale-faced consternation. Now she said, 'You have mighty servitors here, Laurentius. I am astonished I could summon a demon as powerful as you.'

'Looks count for a lot,' I said.

The Priapic priestess blushed. 'No one has complimented me in so long. It's just wham-bam-thank-you-goddess from most men I meet.'

'Well, you don't have to worry about that from me.' Mostly because we'll never have any privacy, I added mentally.

There came a gentle coughing. I turned towards the hippies, who were smiling bemusedly. 'You cats gonna join the party now?' asked Top Hat.

'What else?' I replied.

'Far out!' exclaimed Rabbit Ears. 'I knew you were dressed up to get down!'

I suddenly realised what I looked like. Barefoot, wearing a crumpled garland, stubble-faced and vomit-bespattered, accompanied by a gal wrapped in a bedsheet. Yet somehow I fitted right in.

'I don't believe we've swapped handles yet,' said Top Hat. 'My name is Fletcher Platt, and my friend here is Lionel Stokely David van Camp, heir to the canned vegetable fortune, and otherwise known as LSD.' Fletcher took off his top hat and bowed to Quartilla, while LSD kissed her hand.

'I'm Loren, and this is, um, Quartilla.'

'Cool. What's the story with the rat?'

I had forgotten the Dormouse. 'He's — I mean, it's, uh — a capybara! That's it, a capybara! World's largest rodent. Comes from South America.'

The hippies regarded the snoring Dormouse dubiously. 'Shouldn't it be, like, on a leash, man?' asked LSD.

'No, he — it's quite domesticated.'

'Groovy. Well, what are we waiting for? Let's make the scene!'

So we made the scene.

Meandering through the rapidly filling park, Dormouse cradled against me, I relished the illusion of freedom. Unlike claustrophobia-inducing indoor parties, the largescale Be-in, with its fresh air, sun and sky, seemed like Heaven.

We bought hotdogs from a vendor (Quartilla bit into hers tentatively, then ate with gusto, while the Dormouse consumed most of mine in his sleep), and made our way towards Hippie Hill, where we could command a view of the stage. On the way, I kept an eye peeled for Bacchus. Surely he would materialise at such a major bash as this? If I could only lay my hands on him, perhaps there was a chance I could undo what he had done to me. But there were simply too many people. I estimated the crowd at several thousand, and not one that I could see was dispensing wine from his palm.

At the top of the hill, we flopped on the grass. Below us, a band was wailing.

'Who's that?' I asked.

'Man, where have you been!' said Fletcher. 'Don't you recognise Quicksilver Messenger Service?'

I shook my head in amazement. 'What history. It's like being at Woodstock.'

'History? "Woodstack?" Man, you're some wiggy cat!'

Quartilla seemed captivated by the music, so I explained to her who was playing. But in Latin, it came out funny. 'Mercury's Heralds? What an honour!' She began to sway with the tune.

I lay back on the grass. Lord knew where I would end up after this. If only I could relax for a moment ... As if reading my thoughts, LSD hove into view. He was brandishing a joint. 'Care for a toke?'

'Mega-awesome, dude.'

'Huh?'

'Uh, right on!'

Pretty soon, after the third joint had circulated among us, the day turned transparent, and all my cares seemed to melt away.

Quartilla giggled. 'I feel like the Delphic Oracle.'

'Hey, man,' exclaimed LSD, 'I understood that! This dope is bringing back my high-school Latin!'

'Even the Caterpillar, curmudgeon that he was, let me sample his pipe now and then.'

Dormouse was awake, leaning on both elbows on my thigh. Fletcher and LSD had turned to stone at the first word out of the Dormouse. Their eyes were big as Mad Tea Party saucers.

LSD was the first to recover. Oh-so-slowly he extended his hand holding the joint to the Dormouse, who took it, puffed deeply, then handed it back. 'Thank you, sir. Did I ever mention that you resemble a friend of mine?'

LSD took a long drag on the roach. 'Heavy, man. Beyond heavy. What was that phrase you used before, man?'

'Mega-awesome?'

'You got it!'

LSD lit a new joint off the old one, and now the five of us partook.

The day wore on peacefully. Someone came by handing out free cold beers from a cooler. Another someone laid a gift on us: a can of compressed air with a horn attached. Fletcher and LSD took turns sending out blasts of sound until they grew bored.

As the afternoon began to shade into night and the Be-in began to show signs of winding down, I grew melancholy, as did the others.

'Man, don't you wish a day like this could go on for ever?' asked Fletcher, in what he falsely assumed was a rhetorical mode.

I was still a little high. 'You'd like life to be one big party?'

'Well, hell, man — who wouldn't?' I took the confetti out of my pocket. 'I've got the power to grant your wish, boys. I sprinkle you with this magic pixie dust' — I suited actions to words — 'and the next time I blow this horn' — I showed them the horn — 'your endless party begins.'

The hippies chuckled. 'Whatever turns you on, man.'

'You'll see how—' I started to say, when I felt cold steel in my back.

'Now I have you, sorcerer!' said Hermeros.

I made to raise the horn to my lips, but a jab from the blade stopped me.

'Don't try it!'

Fletcher stepped forward. 'Here, let me.'

He took the horn from my hand and jammed it into the nozzle of the air can. Then he mashed the button down.

The magic horn blared without cease and the universe exploded. Like a film run at a zillion frames per second, all the parties of history began to rush by. I was dancing on the *Titanic*, I was sharing a picnic with two Frenchmen and a naked woman, I was a champagne-guzzling spectator at a Napoleonic battlefield, I was boogieing at Club 54, I was in a temple in Egypt, a yurt in Mongolia, a ballroom in Russia. And that was the first picosecond.

Summoning up every ounce of will, I tried to turn around. It was like wading through treacle. I could only move in those brief nanoseconds when I flashed through a gaudy party.

Like stone eroding, I pivoted to confront Hermeros. It took ten million, million parties, but at last I was facing him.

At that instant, the horn stopped. Fletcher must have managed to lift his finger.

We were surrounded by a ring of dinosaurs. T. Rexes, I believe. And they were dancing, shaking the earth. Partying, to be precise.

Hermeros was stunned, but I had no mercy. 'That ain't no way to have fun,' I advised him. Then I gave him a tremendous shove, propelling him beyond the circle of beasts.

At the same time, I yelled to Fletcher, 'Hit it!' The horn sounded, just in time.

The actinic radiation from Hermeros's explosion chased us through a thousand frames, forcing us to close our eyes. But it never quite caught us. From First Be-in to Great Die-off. *Mea culpa*, man.

Silence. Blessed silence. The can must have run out of air.

I opened one eye timidly, then the other. Fletcher was holding the shredded remnants of the magic horn, which had disintegrated under the prolonged blast. And, I realised with a shock, we were in Ann Marie's apartment, with the Millennial New Year's Eve party seemingly still in full swing.

I collapsed into a chair. 'Straight back to my old problems. Bummer, man.'

Ann Marie bustled up, perky as ever. 'Loren! I'm so glad you could make it!'

'Don't play games with me, Ann Marie. You don't know what I've been through.'

'Well, how could I? I haven't seen you in twenty years, ever since that night you cut out so rudely after worrying me nearly to death!'

'Twenty—?' I looked more closely at my hostess. Sure enough, there were lots of brand-new lines on her face. So I wasn't in my starting place after all. Which meant that I was still a potentially explosive intruder, with no means of escape. As soon as this party was over, I and my companions would go up with enough force to split the earth.

I hung my head. 'I'm so sorry, everyone. I really am.'

'What are you whining about now?' said Ann Marie. 'I swear, Loren — you're probably the only person in the world who's not having fun these days!'

'How's that?'

'Well, you know. Ever since the neural whatsits took over all work and government, it's been one big party!' I looked up. 'You're telling me than no one has to work any more . . . ?'

'Of course not! It's just play, play, play, from sun-up to sun-down, anywhere on the globe you go!'

I turned to Fletcher and LSD, who had been standing curiously by. 'Guys, here's that endless party I promised. Sorry the ride was a little bumpy.'

'Cool.'

'Groovy.'

'Where's the drugs?'

Ann Marie took one hippie on each arm. 'Right this way. And Loren, try to have fun! By the way, boys, I love your costumes!' For the first time since we had met, Quartilla and I were alone. If you could count being adjacent to a sweaty game of Naked Co-Ed Twister alone. I took her hands and gazed into her eyes.

'Bacchus be praised,' was all I could finally say.

'Yes. And I'd be happy to show you how.'

And as we headed for the bedroom, I heard the Dormouse exclaim, 'I say, is that a hookah I hear burbling?'

Steve Aylett

'GIGANTIC'

Strange aircraft arrived with the sky that morning, moving blood-slow. And Professor Skychum was forced from the limelight at the very instant his ranted warnings became most poignant. 'They're already here!'

Skychum had once been so straight you could use him to aim down, an astrophysicist to the heart. No interest in politics — to him Marx and Rand were the same because he went by pant size. Then one afternoon he had a vision which he would not shut up about.

The millennium was the dull rage that year and nutters were in demand to punctuate the mock-emotional retrospectives filling the countdown weeks. The media considered that Skychum fitted the bill — in fact they wanted him to wear one.

And the stuff he talked about. There were weaknesses in his presentation, as he insisted that the whole idea occurred to him upon seeing Scrappy Doo's mutant head for the first time. 'That dog is a hydrocephalitic!' he gasped, leaning forward in such a way, and with so precise an appalled squint to the eyes, that he inadvertently pierced the constrictive walls of localised spacetime. A flare of interface static and he was seeing the whole deal like a lava-streamed landscape. He realised he was looking at the psychic holoshape of recent history, sickly and corrosive. Creeping green flows fed through darkness. These volatile glow trails hurt with incompletion. They converged upon a cess pit, a supersick build-up of denied guilt. This dumping ground was of such toxicity it had begun to implode, turning void-black at its core.

Like a fractal, detail reflected the whole. Skychum saw at once the entire design and the subatomic data. Zooming in, he found that a poison line leading from two locations nevertheless flowed from a single event — Pearl Harbor. One source was the Japanese government, the other was Roosevelt's order to ignore all warnings of the attack. The sick stream was made up of 4,575 minced human bodies. In a fast zoom-out, this strand of history disappeared into the density of surrounding detail, which in turn resolved into a minor nerve in a spiral lost on the surface of a larger flow of glowing psychic pollution. A billion such trickles crept in every tendril of the hyperdense sludge migration, all rumbling towards this multidimensional landfill of dismissed abomination. And how he wished that were all.

Future attempts to reproduce his accidental etheric manoeuvre resulted in the spectacle of this old codger rocking back and forth with a look of appalled astonishment on his face, an idiosyncratic and media-friendly image which spliced easily into MTV along with those colourised clips of the goofing Einstein. And he had the kind of head propeller hats were invented for.

Skychum went wherever he'd be heard. No reputable journal would publish his paper *On Your Own Doorstep: Hyperdimensional Placement of Denied Responsibility*. One editor stated simply: 'Anyone who talks about herding behaviour's a no-no.' Another stopped him in the street and sneered a series of instructions which were inaudible above the midtown traffic, then spat a foaming full-stop at the sidewalk. Chat shows, on the other hand, would play a spooky theramin fugue when he was introduced. First time was an eye-opener. 'Fruitcake corner — this guy's got the Seventh Seal gaffa-taped to his ass and claims he'll scare up an apocalypse out of a clear blue sky. Come all the way here from New York City — Dr Theo Skychum, welcome.' Polite applause and already some sniggers. The host was on garrulous overload, headed for his end like a belly-laughing Wall of Death rider. How he'd got here was anybody's guess. 'Doctor Skychum, you assert that come the millennium, extraterrestrials will monopolise the colonic irrigation industry — how do you support that?'

Amid audience hilarity Skychum stammered that that wasn't his theory at all. The gravity of his demeanour made it all the more of a crack-up. Then the host erupted into a bongo frenzy, hammering away at two toy flying saucers. Skychum was baffled.

He found that some guests were regulars who rolled off the charmed banter with ease.

'Well see here, Ray, this life story of yours appears to have been carved from a potato.'

'I know, Bill, but that's the way I like it.'

'You said you had a little exclusive for us tonight, what's that about?'

'Credit it or not, Bill, I'm an otter.'

'Thought so, Ray.'

It blew by on an ill, hysterical wind and Skychum couldn't get with the programme. He'd start in with some lighthearted quip about bug-eyed men and end up bellowing 'Idiots! Discarding your own foundation! Oppression evolves like everything else!'

Even on serious shows he was systematically misunderstood. The current affairs show *The Unpalatable Truth* were expressing hour-long surprise at the existence of anti-government survivalists. This was the eighty-seventh time they'd done this and Skychum's exasperated and finally sobbing repetition of the phrase 'even a *child* knows' was interpreted as an attempt to steal everyone's faint thunder. And when his tear-rashed face filled the screen, blurring in and out as he asked 'Does the obvious have a reachable bottom?', he was condemned for making a mockery of media debate. A televangelist accused him of 'godless snoopery of the upper grief' and, when Skychum told him to simmer down, cursed him with some vague future aggravation. The whole thing was a dismal mess, smeared beyond salvation. Skychum's vision receded as though abashed.

There was no shortage of replacements. One guy insisted the

161

millennium bug meant virtual sex dolls would give users the brush-off for being over a hundred years old and skint. Another claimed he spoke regularly to the ghost of Abe Lincoln. 'My communications with this lisping blowhead yield no wisdom at all,' he said. 'But I'm happy.' Then he sneezed like a cropduster, festooning the host with phlegm.

The commentators deemed radical were those going only so far as to question what was being celebrated. Skychum himself found he wanted to walk away. But even he had to admit the turn was a big deal, humanity having survived so long and learnt so little — there was a defiant rebelliousness about it that put a scampish grin on everyone's face. For once people were bound with a genuine sense of kick-ass accomplishment and self-congratulatory cool. Skychum began at last to wish he was among them. But just as he felt his revelation slipping away, it would seem to him that the mischievous glints in people's eyes were redshifted to the power of the Earth itself if viewed from a civilised planet. And his brush with perspective would return with the intensity of a fever dream.

Floating through psychic contamination above a billion converging vitriol channels, towards that massive rumbling cataract of discarded corruption. Drawing near, Skychum had seen that ranged around the cauldroning pit, like steel nuts around a wheel hub, were tiny glinting objects. They were hung perfectly motionless at the rim of the slow vortex. These sentinels gave him the heeby-jeebies, but he zoomed in on the detail. There against the God-high waterfall of volatility. Spaceships.

Ludicrous. There they were.

'If we dealt honestly, maturely with our horrors,' he told the purple-haired clown hosting a public access slot, 'instead of evading, rejecting and forgetting, the energy of these events would be naturally re-absorbed. But as it is we have treated it as we treat our nuclear waste — and where we have dumped it, it is not wanted. The most recent waste will be the first to return.'

'Last in, first out eh,' said the clown sombrely.

'Precisely,' said Skychum.

'Well, I wish I could help you,' stated the clown with offhand sincerity. 'But I'm just a clown.'

This is what he was reduced to. Had any of it happened? Was he mad?

A matter of days before the ball dropped in Times Square and Skychum was holed up alone, blinds drawn, bottles empty. He lay on his back, dwarfed by indifference. So much for kicking the hive. The authorities hadn't even bothered to demonise him. It was clear he'd had a florid breakdown, taking it to heart and the public. Could he leave, start a clean life? Everything was strange, undead and dented. He saw again, ghosting across his ceiling, a hundred thousand Guatemalan civilians murdered by US-backed troops. He'd confirmed this afterwards, but how could he have known it before the vision? He only watched CNN. In a strong convulsion of logic, Skychum sat up.

At that moment, the phone rang. A TV guy accusing him of dereliction of banality — laughing that he had a chance to redeem himself and trumpet some bull for the masses. Skychum agreed, too inspired to protest.

It was called *The Crackpot Arena* and it gathered the cream of the foil hat crowd to shoot the rarefied breeze in the hours leading up to the turn. This interlocking perdition of pan-moronic pundits and macabre gripers was helped and hindered by forgotten medication and the pencil-breaking perfectionism of the director. One nutter would be crowned King of the Freaks at the top hour. The criteria were extremity and zero shame at the lectern. Be ridiculed or dubbed the royal target of ridicule — Skychum marvelled at the custom joinery of this conceit. And he was probably in with a chance. In the bizarre stakes, what could be more improbable than justice?

The host's eyes were like raisins and existed to generously block-ade his brainlobes. As each guest surfaced from the cracker-barrel he fielded them with a patronising show of interest.

A man holding a twig spoke of the millennium. 'All I can reveal,' he said, meting out his words like a bait trail, 'is that it will be discouraging. And very, very costly.'

'For me?' asked the host, and the audience roared.

'For me,' said the man, and they were in the aisles.

'Make a habit of monkey antics,' declared another guest. 'Pleasure employs muscles of enlightenment.' Then he led in a screaming chimp, assured everyone its name was Ramone, pushed it down a slide and said 'There you go.' Skychum told him he was playing a dangerous game.

A sag-eyed old man pronounced his judgement. 'The dawn of the beard was the dawn of modern civilisation.'

'In what way?'

'In that time spent growing a beard is time wasted. Now curb this strange melancholy — let us burn our legs with these matches and shout loud.'

'I . . . I'm sorry . . . what—?'

And the codger was dancing a strange jig on the table, cackling from a dry throat.

'One conk on the head and he'll stop dancing,' whispered someone behind the cameras.

Another suspect was the ringmaster of the Lobster Circus, who lashed at a wagon-ring of these unresponsive creatures as though at the advancing spawn of the devil. 'The time *will* come,' he announced, 'when these mothers will be *silent*.' And at that he laid the whip into a lobster positioned side-on to him, breaking it in half.

A little girl read a poem:

> behind answers are hoverflies
> properly modest,
> but they will do anything
> for me

One guy made the stone-faced assertion that belching was an actual language. Another displayed a fossilised eightball of mammoth dung and said it was 'simply biding its time'. Another stated merely that he had within his chest a 'flaming heart' and expected this to settle or negate all other concerns.

Then it was straight in with Skychum, known to the host as a heavy-hitter among those who rolled up with their lies at a moment's notice. The host's face was an emulsioned wall as he listened to the older man describe some grandiose reckoning. 'Nobody's free until everyone is, right?' was the standard he reached for in reply.

'Until *someone* is.'

'Airless Martians still gasping in a town of smashed geodesics,' he stated, and gave no clue as to his question. After wringing the laughs out of Skychum's perplexed silence, he continued. 'These Martians — what do they have against us?'

'Not Martians — metaversal beings in a hyperspace we are using as a skeleton cupboard. Horror past its sell-by date is dismissed with the claim that a lesson is learnt, and the sell-by interval is shortening to minutes.'

'I don't understand,' said the host with a kind of defiance.

'The media believe in resolution at all costs, but that's only human.' Once again Skychum's sepulchral style was doing the trick — there was a lot of sniggering as he scowled like a chef. 'Dismissal's easier than learning.'

'So you're calling down this evangelical carnage.'

'*I'm* not—'

'In simple terms, for the layman' — the eyebrows of irony flipped to such a blur they vanished — 'how could all these bodies be floating out in "hyper" space?'

'Every form which has contained life has its equivalent echo in the super-etheric — if forced back into the physical, these etheric echoes will assume physical shape.'

'Woh!' shouted the host, delighted, and the audience exploded with applause — this was exactly the kind of wacko bullshit they'd come to hear. 'And why should they arrive at this particular time?'

'They have become synchronised to our culture, those who took on the task — it is appropriate, poetic!'

The audience whooped, flushed with the nut's sincerity.

'The great thing about being ignored is that you can speak the truth with impunity.'

'But I call you a fraud, Dr Skychum. These verbal manipulations cause a hairline agony in the honest man. Expressions of the grave should rival the public? I don't think so. Where's the light and shade?'

Skychum leaned forward, shaking with emotion. 'You slur me for one who is bitter and raging at the world. But you mustn't kick a man when he's down, and so I regard the world.' Then Ramone the chimp sprang on to his head, shrieking and flailing.

'Dr Skychum,' said the host. 'If you're right, *I'm* a monkey.'

The ringmaster of the Lobster Circus was declared the winner. The man with the flaming heart died of a coronary and the man with the dung fossil threw it into the audience and stormed off. A throne shaped like the half-shells of a giant nut was set up for the crowning ceremony. Skychum felt light, relieved. He had acquitted himself with honour. He enjoyed the jelly and ice-cream feast set up for the contestants backstage. Even the chimp's food-flinging antics made him smile. He approached the winner with goodwill. 'Congratulations sir. Those lobsters of yours are a brutal threat to mankind.'

The winner looked mournfully up at him. 'I love them,' he whispered, and was swept away backwards by the make-up crew.

At the moment of the turn, Skychum left the studio building by a side entrance, hands deep in his coat pockets. Under a slouch hat which obscured his sky, he moved off down a narrow street roofed completely by the landscape of a spacecraft's undercarriage.

During the last hour, as dullards were press-ganged on to ferris wheels and true celebrants arrested in amplified streets, hundreds of multidimensional ships had hoved near, denial-allow shields up. Uncloaking, they had appeared in the upper atmosphere like new moons. Now they hove into position over every capital city in the world, impossible to evade. Fifteen miles wide, these immense overshadow machines rumbled across the sky like a coffin lid drawing slowly shut. New York was being blotted out by a floating city whose petalled geometry was only suggested by sections visible above the canyon streets. Grey hieroglyphics on the underside were actually spires, bulkheads and structures of skyscraping size. Its central eye, a mile-wide concavity deep in shadow, settled over uptown as the hovering landscape thundered to a stop and others took up position over London, Beijing, Berlin, Nairobi, Los Angeles, Kabul, Paris, Zurich, Baghdad, Moscow, Tokyo and every other conurbation with cause to be a little edgy. One nestled low over the White House like an inverted cathedral. In the early light they were silent, unchanging fixtures. Solid and subject to the sun.

The President, hair like a dirty iceberg, slapped on a middling smile and talked about caution and opportunity. Everywhere nerves were clouded around with awe and high suspension. Traffic stopped. Fanatics partied. The old man's name was remembered if not his line — one girl held a sign aloft saying I'M A SKY CHUM. Cities waited under dumb, heavy air.

Over the White House, a screeching noise erupted. The central eye of the ship was opening. Striations like silver insect wings cracked, massive steel doors grinding downward.

The same was happening throughout the world, a silver flower opening down over Parliament, Whitehall and the dead Thames; over the old Reichstag building, the World Bank, the Beijing Politburo.

The DC saucer eye was open, the bellow of its mechanism echoing away. Onlookers craned to see up inside.

For the space of two heartbeats, everything stopped. Then a tiny tear dropped out of the eye, splashing on the White House roof.

And then another, falling like a light fleck of snow.

These were corpses, these two — human corpses, followed by more in a shower which grew heavier by the moment, some crashing

167

now through the roof, some rolling to land in the drive, bouncing to hit the lawn, bursting to paint the porticoes. And then the eye began gushing.

Everywhere the eyes were gushing. With a strange, continuous, multiphonic squall, the ragged dead rained from the sky. Sixty-eight forgotten pensioners buried in a mass grave in 1995 were dumped over the Chicago Social Services. Hundreds of blacks murdered in police cells hit the roof of Scotland Yard. Thousands of slaughtered East Timorese were dumped over the Assembly buildings in Jakarta. Thousands killed in the test bombings at Hiroshima and Nagasaki began raining over the Pentagon. Thousands tortured to death showered Abuja. Thousands of Sudanese slaves were dumped over Khartoum. The border-dwelling Khmer Rouge found themselves cemented into a mile-high gut slurry of three million Cambodians. Thousands of hill tribesmen were dropped over the Bangladeshi parliament and the World Bank, the latter now swamped irretrievably under corpses of every hue. Berlin was almost instantly clotted, its streets packed wall to wall with victims. Beijing was swamped with tank fodder and girl babies.

The Pentagon well filled quickly to overflowing, blowing the building outwards as surely as a terrorist bomb. Pearl Harbor dupes fell on Tokyo and Washington in equal share. The streets of America flooded with Japanese, Greeks, Koreans, Vietnamese, Cambodians, Indonesians, Dominicans, Libyans, Timorese, Central Americans and Americans, all beclouded in a pink mist of Dresden blood. London was a flowing sewer — then the bodies started falling. Parliament splintered like a matchstick model. In the Strand the living ran from a rolling wall of the dead. A king tide of hole-eyed German, Indian, African, Irish and English civilians surged over and against buildings which boomed flat under the pressure. Cars were batted along, flipped and submerged. The Thames flooded its banks, displaced by cadavers.

No longer preserved by denial, they started to sludge. Carpet-bombing gore spattered the suburbs, followed by human slurry tumbling down the streets like lava. Cheap human fallout from pain ignored and war extended for profit. The first wave. So far only sixty years' worth — yet, tilling like bulldozed trash, it spread across the map like red inkblots destined to touch and merge.

Skychum had taken the 8.20 Amtrak north from Grand Central — it had a policy of not stopping for bodies. Grim, he viewed the raining horizon — dust motes in a shaft of light — and presently, he spoke.

'Many happy returns.'

Bill Drummond

'LET'S GRIND'
or
'How K2 Plant Hire Ltd
Went To Work'

Extracts from Drummond's Log, 31 December 1999

'That's just plain evil. Why in God's name would you want to destroy Stonehenge?' — is an approximation of the standard answer either Jimmy or I get whenever we let it slip that the removal of the stones is the last great undone contract of K2 Plant Hire.

It's tea time, my place, and I'm waiting for Jimmy to turn up with the gear.

We have had the notion for the best part of ten years that something had to be done about Stonehenge. Either somebody had to fix it up or the whole thing should be scrapped as unworkable. I could easily launch into an attack on heritage culture, but that is best left to the broadsheet journalists who know how to put a rational argument together.

I think we are drawn to the stones not because of some sort of new pagan yearning in our souls, but more because they seem to symbolise something for us that lives on these isles. A continuity that has a stronger and deeper pull than the Union flag, our royal family, our mother of parliaments, our victories in war, our language, our sterling currency or even our pop music. They haven't been rammed down our throats at school. They aren't on the coins in our pockets. They don't try to tell us what to do, or make us feel guilty. They are just there, from generation to generation.

173

Back when we did the Timelords thing in the late eighties and were flush with cash, we looked into hiring a massive helicopter and lifting the fallen stones – mending the Henge, getting it working again. We then learned that all the air space down there was military, and we couldn't get any civilian pilots to do the job with us. So we had our photograph taken with Gary Glitter in front of the fallen stones, then went off to the Sierra Nevada and blew all our cash on making a mystical road movie instead.

Next. After we knocked the KLF on the head, Jimmy spent about a year doing a series of large paintings depicting apocalyptic scenes involving ourselves, the destruction of Stonehenge, the unleashing of dark forces and the death of thousands. All a bit childish and comic horror, but incredibly well executed. I liked them. Then he destroyed the lot by sanding the paint off the canvases, carefully sweeping up the dust and keeping it in a series of jam jars. One jam jar for each painting. Why? Best not ask. We all deal with our moments of doubt in different ways.

Next. One night in February 1993, Jimmy and I were walking in an easterly direction along the A303, away from Stonehenge. We had been doing some nocturnal research at the stones and were now deep into a rambling conversation, out of which the idea of the K Foundation evolved.

Next. November 1995. Jimmy, Gimpo and me were in Glasgow with our film *Watch the K Foundation Burn a Million Quid*. We were supposed to be showing it to prisoners and Buddhist monks and Rangers supporters and all sorts of other people, site-specific style, but it was pointed out to us by a man that our efforts were a waste of time. Me and Jimmy agreed with him, and jacked in being trustees of our bogus art foundation. Instead, we decided to become K2 Plant Hire. (At that point in time, being the owner of a plant hire company seemed to be the ultimate ambition of any proper man.) We set to work immediately and started to design our calendars. Decided that all our plant would be painted yellow and black. And we imagined what the inside of our hut would look like. We then did some other stuff in Scotland and Gimpo got pissed off with us and left us stranded in a transport café. K2 Plant Hire has waited patiently over the passing years for its first major contract.

Next. Some time in early 1997 Sarah Champion, editor of the cash-in-on-Irvine-Welsh book *Disco Biscuits*, contacted me. Was I up for contributing to her next anthology of short stories, *Disco 2000*? She explained the theme of the book, a collection of stories all taking place on New Year's Eve 1999. I like Sarah. I was up for it. I had an idea that I would do a bogus 'Drummond's Log' about what me and Jimmy got up to on that date, thus realising our joint ambition of destroying Stonehenge through the safe medium of fiction. I was also into the idea that once it had been written as a partly fictitious story in 1997, it would then give us the impetus to go and do the real thing on the given date. Somehow the story would be a contract. If we didn't do it, it would undermine the whole 'Drummond's Log' thing. I would never believe myself again. I don't care if *you* don't believe me, but ...

Before I got the story written, though, I was committed to getting some things done. If this meant I didn't meet Sarah's print deadline, so be it.

Then on Thursday 15 May 1997 Gimpo and I met up at the BRS truck hire place at the back of King's Cross Station. You know, the area where all the prostitutes used to hang out. We hired a seven-tonner. Big enough. The two of us drove through London, stopping off at a cashpoint to pick up the grand in cash that we needed to do the job. On to the M4, then down it for a few miles before doubling back on ourselves. Parked up in the service station and waited for Jimmy in the café. He came. We ate breakfast before unloading the chains, the blocks and tackle and the rest of the gear from the back of Jimmy's van into the back of the truck. Loaded. The three of us climbed into the front of the truck and headed for the M25.

Jimmy and I had been working together for the last ten years, and seeing as we are in an age of anniversary fever, we thought we should celebrate our ten-year partnership of sorts. Which is what we were doing, that May morning. Some time in the early nineties our interest in sheep had waned, to be replaced by an infatuation with the cow. We had as yet done nothing to express this interest in the idea of a cow. The fact that Damien Hirst won tabloid fame with his mother and daughter divided thing had kind of put a stop to things. Added to that, when Jimmy accidentally caused a cow to miscarry while testing his advanced acoustic armament equipment and got splashed across the media and branded as a cow killer, it seemed to make any of our joint interest in exploring the meaning of the cow redundant. But the cow came back, and refused to go away. We had to do something. We did.

So we got on to the M25 at the M4 intersection and headed south, anti-clockwise. We were looking for pylons, or if there weren't any good-looking pylons visible to the passing M25 motorist, we wanted a stout oak tree with a good strong horizontal branch fifteen feet clear of the ground. We wanted a good lynching tree. Like the ones you see in those old black and white photographs; Ku Klux Klan members in the foreground, the boughs behind them laden with their strange fruit.

We had seen the right tree in our imaginations and were positive it was going to be easy to find. It wasn't. There was none. As for the pylons ... The whole pylon thing had started when we had been driving up the M6 through Birmingham and there were loads of these great squat pylons glowering over the weary landscape, tempting young boys to come and climb, heavy with their thousands of volts of instant death. Strung together with cables to snare and fry migrating swans. I suppose each of us had always been into pylons, what lad isn't? But it was there and then that we began to share our vision of what could be done with them.

Jimmy and I were being open-minded. Strong oaks or squat pylons — either would do, as long as they were clearly visible from the M25 and we could get the truck up to them. We drove the southern arc under the belly of London. Nothing. At some point it started pissing down, but that just added to the perfect gloom. We stopped at Clackett services and we all played on Road Rage, a brand-new arcade game. Drank a bowl of soup. Gimpo told us what Blair would be putting in the Queen's Speech.

We drove under the Dartford Tunnel and up into Essex. This felt more like it. West Thurrock marshes. Plenty of pylons, keeping guard over a crumbling industrial landscape. We came off the motorway and started to explore. Industrial estates, run-down chemical plants, disused oil refineries, feral buddleia breaking through everywhere, and us in our truck, looking for the right place. Then we came across a massive entertainment complex. Cinemas, shopping mall, discos. We drove slowly past and watched, like paedophiles outside a school gate. A police car pulled us over and asked what we were looking for. Gimpo answered: location hunting for a film about the end of civilisation, starring Sean Connery. They asked for tickets to the premiere and wished us well.

Then we caught sight of the perfect pylon. It was perched on top of a dirty chalk cliff. No bluebirds. The cliff ran alongside a busy dual carriageway, the pylon was in a position to gaze across the above described landscape of multiplexes and industrial wasteland. Perfect. It took us some time to find an access path to the pylon. We were going to need bolt cutters to liberate the gate from the padlock to get the truck down. We parked up the truck and walked down to the pylon to join it in surveying the scene. Its high-voltage cables were buzzing in the late afternoon drizzle. We reckoned if we got the truck down under the pylon and climbed on the roof, we could get the chains over the lowest horizontal girders. The only problem seemed to be: how long would it take us to do the job, and how visible were we from the dual carriageway below? We had spotted the cop car that had pulled us up a number of times by now. They seemed to be on a constant patrol of the area, a perfect place for joyriders.

We left the pylon, satisfied we had found the perfect site. We would be back later that night with bolt cutters. And loaded with meat.

Heading north on the M25, still anti-clockwise, I used Gimpo's mobile to phone the brothers. The job's on, I told them, be there in an hour. They ran a small backstreet business, about sixty miles north of London. For their protection I can't be any more specific than that. Most of my dealings had been with the younger brother; he seemed the less paranoid of the two. He told me they would do the job about thirty minutes before we got there. He didn't want rigor mortis to set in before we got loaded up. But thirty minutes was time enough for him to get things cleaned up. He then took pride in telling me that he had brought his 2.2 rifle in and was going to use that. It would make a far smaller hole than the bolt gun they usually used. It would be a neater job, far less leakage.

We stopped off in the small market town of Tring to buy bolt cutters, a pair of brown card parcel labels and a ball of twine. The next thirty miles were cross country. We got to the brothers' place some time after seven. It was officially closed. The brothers were there, and the job had been done. The bodies were stacked in the back of their blood-proof truck. The first thing that drew my attention was their cunts; both of them were gaping open. Big enough to slide your arm into without touching the sides. There was this sort of semi-translucent jelly stuff that was seeping out. I was filled with the same indefinable fear that I'd felt as a nineteen-year-old lad, when cleaning out similar parts of the dead women whose bodies I laid out on the hospital ward where I worked.

I was able to push the terror out of my mind. Only then did I notice they were black and white Friesian, huge udders, perfect. A dead cow is so much bigger than you imagine. I know this will sound trite: there is something so undeniably final about a dead body, animal or human. Only that morning, these two cows had been chewing the cud in their field, enjoying the sun's warming rays and waiting to be relieved of their milk. Somewhere else a mobile phone had rung, deals had been done, sums agreed and their fate sealed.

The brothers were uneasy. Mad Cow Disease had swept the nation over the previous year. All cattle slaughtered had to be accounted for; spinal cords and brains were collected by the authorities on a daily basis, counted, ticked off and taken to be incinerated at designated sites. No beasts were allowed to stray out of the chain. BSE had become the Aids of the nineties, it was going to be the thing that killed us all.

We had tried to tell the brothers the truth. What we told them went something like this: we were going to take the two cows off to some private land in Essex, where we had permission from the landowner to string them up from the bough of a large oak tree. We were then going to have the scene photographed at dawn, after which we would have the carcasses cut down and brought back to their place to be dealt with in the proper way. Except our plans had changed, we were no longer going to bring them back for them to dispose of, but we had made arrangements with a local Essex knacker's yard to do the job. We had already dealt with the questions of who we were and why we were doing this by explaining we were a pair of those modern artist types that like to do stupid things in the hope it shocked somebody and got publicity. This they understood, had seen it on TV, knew that was what artists had to do these days to make a living. And anyway they liked the colour of our money.

They wanted to know the name of the knacker's yard in Essex. We couldn't remember. They wanted our assurance that whatever happened, Farmer Jones, who had owned the cows until that very day and was a long-standing and trusted customer, would not open the *Daily Telegraph* tomorrow morning to see his Daisy and Buttercup strung up in some disgusting stunt. We gave them our assurance, knowing that if Daisy and Buttercup did make the front cover of the *Daily Telegraph*, it would not be until the morning after next.

One of the brothers took it upon himself to take a knife and cut an ear off each of our cows. Each of the severed ears had a tag that could identify the beasts as easily as a car number plate. Both brothers knew they were too far into this to get out now.

Jimmy got changed into his wellies, waterproof overalls and

acid-resistant gloves. Gimpo was already clambering over the beasts, trying to work out the best way to get the chains around them before winching them across into the back of our truck. Buttercup's eyes were open. They were big, a dark and very deep blue, the eyelashes were as big as a cartoon cow's. She looked very friendly. She smelled of fresh hay and warm milk. Blood dribbled from her nostrils. Gimpo had the chains fixed and we started the long, slow process of winching her over. Milk squirted from her udders, slurry from her arse, and she coughed up a fist-sized lump of congealed blood.

Jimmy and I tried to make ourselves useful, but Gimpo was in control (as ever). It took us the best part of an hour to get them in our truck. There was blood and shit everywhere. The brothers hosed everything down. It was only then that they told us that the beasts' guts would swell up to twice their normal size overnight, that the innards would probably be forced out of their arses. That the law of the land states that all carcasses must be dealt with and parts disposed of within twenty-four hours of slaughter. Things can quickly become dangerously toxic, and be a severe health hazard to anybody coming into contact with them.

We counted the crisp new fifty quids out on the bonnet of their van and bunged in a few extra for the farmer. Blood money. No invoices were written, no surnames known. We bade our farewells, and the three of us drove off with our heavy load. Silence in the cab as awful repercussions slurried around our as yet BSE-free brains.

We stopped off at my place. A farmhouse. Gimpo played with my daughter, Bluebell. She is only just over two, already wants to marry Gimpo, and often asks for Gimpo to live with us, insisting he could sleep in the attic. I collected eggs from the chicken house and made us all scrambled eggs for supper. Jimmy and my girlfriend caught up with gossip and compared pharmaceutical notes. Gimpo had to read Bluebell a bedtime story before we left. It was dark.

We drove across country again. I felt the weight of our load as we took each bend on the lanes. We joined the M25 just north of Watford and headed south for Essex.

The bolt cutters went through the hardened steel like a Stanley through a cheek. The gate opened and we bumped the two hundred yards down the rough track to our chosen pylon. Below us were the lights of the dual carriageway. The Warner Brothers multiplex was entertaining the Essex men and Essex girls. The Deep Pan Pizza was packed. The police were busy with the joyriders and Gimpo was up on the roof of the truck pulling on chains.

Jimmy and I had our felt-tip pens in hand. Each of us writing the same two words on our separate cardboard parcel labels. The labels were to be tied around our cargo's necks.

For the previous few years, I had relished the idea of stringing up a beast like this, with no further explanation than a plain cardboard label with the two words 'FUCKING COW'. There were times when I was driving along in my truck, cocooned from the rest of the world, and I would laugh and laugh and laugh in an almost maniacal state, just thinking of it.

FUCKING COW.

FUCKING COW.

FUCKING COW.

Louder and louder.

(Of course, the reason for wanting to have just two cows and not the full twenty-three, or the more economical one, was not just to have one each but to proclaim, as loudly and as silently as we could, 'Mu Mu'.)

I can't remember if either of us got the two words written before we not only confronted ourselves with the fact that we couldn't go through with it, but admitted it to each other. Who said what first I can't remember. But it was agreed that this was the end of the road; we had got to this brick wall. We had been able to burn a million quid of our own money, but we could not do this. Were we worried for the health and safety of the local government workers who would come out to clear the whole thing up? Or were we just too horrified about whatever this statement said about our own dismembered psyches?

Contrary to what we said to the brothers, there had been no plans to tell the media or even have the event officially witnessed or photographed, although one can never stop Gimpo bringing along his video camera, so he must have evidence of our sad failure somewhere. We had just wanted the two cows to be discovered, the way that a dog in a ditch or a body in a canal would be — anonymous, horrible, true — and for people to make of it what they would. We didn't want anybody tracing the act back to us.

We helped Gimpo to pack the chains. We drove off in silence.

The next morning I took the bloated and stiffened Daisy and Buttercup back to the brothers. Although they had hoped never to see my face again, they were mightily relieved to see the two now worthless carcasses and hear that they had not taken part in any art prank, scam or pop publicity stunt. After a few more crisp notes changed hands, they were willing to dispose of the bodies in a clean and legal way.

Some weeks later Jimmy and I got talking about Stonehenge and its clearance as a K2 Plant Hire Ltd millennial gift to the nation, and we admitted that it could no longer be part of the master plan. If we couldn't get it together to string up a couple of dead cows, there was no way we would ever do the stones.

Something had ended.

Time shifted and we ended up celebrating our tenth anniversary in a different way. What started as Jeremy Deller's Acid Brass project evolved into our 2K 'Fuck the Millennium' project. It was some way through this mammoth recording that I got home one Sunday night to find an answerphone message from the skinhead, novelist and thinker Stewart Home, telling me the Rollright Stones were up for sale. Being a keen ley liner, he was afraid they might fall into the hands of the New Age fascists. He thought Jimmy and I should buy them and put them to good use.

I forgot to tell Jimmy this for a couple of days. We were too consumed with the prospect of fucking the millennium and getting our electric wheelchairs. When I did, it was with no thought of us buying the things, more out of politeness to Stewart Home. Another couple of days passed, with us doing whatever it is that gets done in a recording studio. Then Jimmy said, 'We've got fifty thousand left in the K2 Plant Hire account. It seems fitting that we should buy the Rollright Stones and clear the account.' I liked his logic. He had already been working on some drawings of what we should do with them. It involved a huge drilling rig, like a traditional Texas oil one. We would use it to drill down into the crust of the Earth and extract the mystical powers of Avalon and sell them, or something like that. Both the great and the stupid thing about Jimmy's ideas is that they are usually wildly impractical, thus protecting him from ever having to realise them and face the consequences.

I was quite happy for us to get a K2 Plant Hire JCB in, dig up the stones and cart them off to a lime works. There, they could grind them down to a fine powder and, using the powder and whatever other substance would do the job, remake all the stones in pristine rectangular shapes. Stewart Home had faxed me a photo of the stones. I could see they were in a shocking state, all worn away by the weather, with bits of lichen and moss growing on them. They looked like they were trying to blend in with nature. Obviously, nobody was looking after them.

It was partly the fault of the original contractors who constructed the site. They used limestone, which, as anybody who knows anything about the building trade or geology is aware, doesn't last more than half a dozen millennia if exposed to the elements. At least the blokes that built Stonehenge knew to get some imported hard rock, and not the local soft shit from Salisbury Plain.

But out of respect to the geezers who made them in the first place, and as a millennium gift to the nation, K2 Plant Hire Ltd would replace the stones in perfect working order. A precise circle, each stone of equal size and equidistant from each other.

Then we could all relax, safe in the knowledge that they would last, if not an eternity, then at least as long as the monoliths in *2001*. And we would provide good car parking facilities. Yeah, I know you're thinking I'm just trying to be knowingly stupid in an attempt at humour, but this is what we were thinking and the logic we were using.

It was on getting the particulars that we discovered it wasn't the actual stones that were for sale, just the land they crumbled on. The stones were the property of English Heritage or something. On purchasing the land, we would have no right to improve the stones and make them our millennial gift to the nation.

Initially we just gave up on the idea, knowing that we hadn't got what it took for all that illegal cow lynching, Stonehenge clearance stuff. But after we did our 2K 'Fuck the Millennium' performance at the Barbican in September of that year (1997), Jimmy and I couldn't face going to the after-show 'do' and all those 'why?' questions, so we drove up the M40, turned off at Ardley and found the Rollright Stones.

We were horrified. They were in worse condition than we had ever imagined. Something had to be done. We knew that the responsibility once again fell on our shoulders. We also knew the perfect night to do it, a night when the rest of the world would be otherwise occupied. As for the fucking cows, whatever problem that was in my psyche seemed to have been sorted out. Stonehenge would have to wait; one thing at a time.

There's a knock at the door, it must be Jimmy. It is. The week before Christmas he did one of those JCB crash courses. He has just driven up from Devon in the one he got in an auction down there. Gimpo has finally passed his HGV Grade A, and will be driving the ten tonner. Time for one more cup of tea, and then a night's work for K2 Plant Hire Ltd to be done.

Martin Millar

'RADIANT FLOWER OF THE DIVINE
HEAVENS'

This is a story about my friend Radiant Flower of the Divine Heavens. It is not the only story I could tell about Radiant Flower. There are plenty of good ones to choose from. The incident where she broke a pot plant over the head of Crag Master of the Planets and then chased him through the streets with a whip is always entertaining. Their relationship was always stormy. The time where she helped out her friend Hawthorn with a photo shoot for his magazine *Squeegee*, a publication dedicated to the pleasures of messy sex, by posing naked in a bath of strawberry ice cream has gone down in folklore in certain circles. The pictures still change hands for high prices among messy sex devotees.

I have never actually met anyone who admits to being a devotee of messy sex, and is unable to be aroused unless they and their partners are covered in mud, tomato sauce or some other goo, but there are apparently enough of them to keep a magazine going. Fair enough. Each to their own.

Radiant Flower of the Divine Heavens is happy enough that her photo shoot went well.

'I don't like the magazine too much but I was pleased to help out my friend Hawthorn. He always has terrible trouble coming up with new ideas,' she says. 'And I felt that if I had to writhe around among some sort of foodstuff, then strawberry ice cream was a good one to choose. I wouldn't have helped him with one of his baked bean spectaculars.'

I understand that the models in the baked bean spectaculars fall far short of Radiant Flower's marvellous beauty, which is hardly surprising. Few people can approach the golden-haired and black-clad Radiant Flower of the Divine Heavens in terms of beauty. It is breathtaking, often stopping people dead in their tracks: sometimes it produces strange results; on one occasion at a party in a dungeon next to the river a man in black leather hood and a PVC kilt, overcome with passion, threw himself at her feet and told her that although he appreciated he wasn't looking the part right now, he was in fact the son of the richest oil billionaire in Texas and if she would come back to Dallas with him he would give her a few oil wells and a private jet and anything else she cared to mention. When Radiant Flower declined, he grabbed up a big Gothic candlestick and started beating himself over the head with it.

This only confirmed Radiant Flower's belief that she had been right to refuse, although she supposed that she could have done with an oil well. She was quite happy in her small flat in South London but while she was certainly the queen of any fetish club she surveyed she was far from rich. Radiant Flower of the Divine Heavens only managed to appear at every event looking so spectacular thanks to a great deal of care, attention and ingenuity on her part

But I have chosen this story to tell as it seems most appropriate to the moment, being related to me by Radiant Flower in the women's toilet at the Millennium Bondage Ball on the night of 31 December 1999. It concerns her millennium bloom. This a small plant which, according to Radiant Flower, will flower only once every thousand years, at the start of a new millennium.

I have been dubious about this ever since she first mentioned it, but as I don't really know anything about plants, I can't say that it is untrue. I've known about the plant problem for a few months, since Radiant Flower of the Divine Heavens first started complaining that her millennium bloom was not doing at all well.

'Its leaves are turning brown and it's starting to sag. It's a disaster.'

'Is it of great sentimental value?'

'No.'

'Then why is it a disaster? It's only a pot plant.'

'Only a pot plant? I stole this cutting at considerable risk to myself from the private gardens of Garth the Mystic Plant Collector.'

'Considerable risk? You told me he was tied up on a bed at the time.'

'He was. But it was still a considerable risk. I mean, I had to enter into a relationship with Garth the Mystic Plant Collector to get into that position in the first place and you know what a weirdo he is. Anything could have happened. He wanted to rub my body with melon juice. Horrible sticky stuff. He couldn't understand why I wasn't keen. He said he thought I'd be well up for it after these strawberry ice cream pictures in *Squeegee* magazine. You know, ever since then people have been making me an awful lot of strange food related offers.'

She pauses as some people squeezed by. I'm queuing in the women's toilets with Radiant Flower of the Divine Heavens as the men's toilets are at this moment no place for a peaceful person to be due to a violent altercation between a very large man dressed as the Emperor Nero and an equally large transvestite in a frightening red wig. It seems best to just avoid the situation.

Now you might expect that Radiant Flower of the Divine Heavens, a kindly woman, would be concerned about the welfare of a plant but you wouldn't necessarily think she would get so upset about it. The importance of the matter is that it concerns Radiant Flower's Feng Shui. This is the ancient Chinese art of manipulating your living space in order to help your life go well. Radiant Flower is very keen on Feng Shui. She claims that Mao Tse-tung managed to seize power in China largely because of the excellent Feng Shui of his mother's grave. As Radiant Flower's mother is alive and well and living in Somerset she does not yet have to worry about this, but she worries a great deal about the Feng Shui of her living space. Her small flat is festooned with wooden chimes, metal chimes, mirrors, plants and various other things, all intended to circulate the energy freely around and make things go well for her. Things generally do go fairly well for her. But the thing that is going to make things go really well is the millennium plant. She has it in the south, which is her fame point, and once it flowers, apparently the sky will be the limit as far as fame is concerned.

'So it was all Crag, Master of the Planet's fault really. If I hadn't been obliged to break my pot plant over his head I'd never have had an empty space in the south and needed to replace it.'

Still, following the example of Mao Tse-tung, the resourceful Radiant Flower had turned adversity into victory with the purloining of the millennium bloom.

'That millennium plant will do wonders for me,' claims Radiant Flower. 'Much better Feng Shui than the old plant. Provided it flowers on cue.'

Of course if it doesn't flower, it's not so good. If it was to die it would be something of a disaster and Radiant Flower soon convinced herself that if it was to die she might as well pack her bags and go and get a job as a barmaid in her native Somerset.

Radiant Flower of the Divine Heavens is very beautiful, very intelligent and very talented. So it is no surprise to me that she is often depressed, anxious and unhappy about the strangest of things. I would in fact be surprised if she wasn't because I have noticed that the more beautiful, intelligent and talented women are, the more they get depressed and anxious. Why this is, I'm not sure. I suppose it produces stress that is difficult to manage. Radiant Flower was always in the grip of some useless therapist or other. Putting her trust in a plant was in some ways a step forward.

Although Radiant Flower's recent spells of anxiety have been non-specific — unlike the times she would phone at four in the morning and demand to know if she really existed or was just a figment of someone's imagination — I strongly suspect that she is concerned at the guest appearance Venus Beauticia is to make at the Millennium Bondage Ball. Venus Beauticia is the Bondage Queen of San Francisco. Various fantastic descriptions of her beauty and allure have also circulated in the news group. While Radiant Flower of the Divine Heavens would not publicly admit to anything as trivial as feelings of rivalry with another fetish queen, I strongly suspect that she is worried about being overshadowed. A dead millennium plant in her fame point certainly won't help.

Radiant Flower had appealed for help with her plant by posting a message in the Alt. Sex Fetish UK news group, this being an Internet discussion group to which she subscribed. Hardly the sort of thing the massed ranks of Alt. Sex Fetishists would want to be bothering themselves with, I would have thought, but I suppose it was all right coming from Radiant Flower, as she is a famous person among their ranks, and the most beautiful, so can get away with virtually anything. It might have been easier just to ask around, but she claims not to know anyone who knows anything about plants, apart from Garth the Mystic Plant Collector, and she can hardly apply to him, as she stole the cutting from him in the first place, and in quite an underhand manner.

'Isn't there an Internet news group dedicated to plant welfare?'

'Probably. But I couldn't find it. I get bored looking for new things and then my computer crashes. It only works properly when I'm interested. Anyway, I did get some helpful suggestions.'

Radiant Flower of the Divine Heavens makes some tiny adjustments to her already fabulous make-up. She has not mentioned Venus Beauticia all night but I still believe she's worried about her arrival.

Some yells of pain come from a cubicle in the toilet. This seems to me a little out of order, people indulging in private sex practices while other people are waiting to go in, but after a little while two young women, one naked and the other in a shiny cat suit emerge grinning rather sheepishly and explain to the interested Radiant Flower of the Divine Heavens that they were just sniffing a little cocaine and one of them sneezed and blew some powder into the other's eye, which was quite painful. It seems to be taking effect anyway, although they don't recommend it as a means of ingestion. They offer some to Radiant Flower, and she accepts.

Well when Radiant Flower posted her appeal for help she had various replies but none of them was much use. The members of Alt. Sex Fetish UK were willing to help but none of them seemed to have much of an idea apart from feeding the plant Baby Bio and giving it plenty of light.

'Not good enough,' thought Radiant Flower. 'This is a very special plant. It might not like Baby Bio and plenty of light.'

Incidentally, I once accepted a lift from a man who told me that Baby Bio was the only known product ever to receive a 100 per cent score in consumer recognition tests. I thought that was interesting.

There was one more helpful sounding suggestion. Unfortunately it came from Gamin.

'And Gamin is high up the list of people I never want to meet.'

Radiant Flower of the Divine Heavens had never met Gamin and had no wish to. The problem was, after discovering the Alt. Sex Fetish UK news group on his computer, and reading various reports of Radiant Flower's activities like flying off to New York to be special guest at bondage parties, or having entire editions of fetish magazines devoted to her incredible collection of black leather bodices, he seemed to have become obsessed with her. Now he was posting messages to her every day, and sending her countless e-mails telling her she was the most fabulous creature in the universe and would she like to meet him for a cup of tea some time.

'How did he get your e-mail number?'

'I don't know. Perhaps he's a computer wizard. Although as he tells me that he works every morning in a small wholefood co-op in Brixton it seems unlikely. Still who knows, he might get a lot of time to read up on the subject in between measuring out cupfuls of green lentils. And he watches daytime television every afternoon. He tells me about the programmes, in between sending me poems and stuff. Apparently the cookery programmes are his favourite. Last week he sent me a recipe for roasted parsnips with thyme, tarragon and garlic.'

'How was it?'

Radiant Flower doesn't know. Even though it came from a daytime cookery programme it was way beyond her culinary skills. Actually she doesn't have any culinary skills. This was partly the reason for the ending of her relationship with Crag, Master of the Planets, because in what I always think is one of the weirdest things I have ever heard, he actually complained to her because she could never cook a meal. How Crag, Master of the Planets, ever got it into his head that this was an appropriate thing to say to Radiant Flower of the Divine Heavens I will never know. It just goes to show how oddly conventional some people can be, even when they go around dressed in leather all the time and spend their lives at fetish clubs and bondage parties. From what I understand of the ensuing scene, he was lucky to escape with his life.

Radiant Flower of the Divine Heavens had been avoiding Gamin, refusing to answer his messages and making sure she didn't appear at any place he was likely to be. And so it might have gone on had he not outmanoeuvred her by sending back the only likely sounding reply to her cry for help.

'Working among organic vegetables all day,' he mailed her, 'I have a good knowledge of exotic plant life. Also my sister is studying botany at university and is just back from a field trip to the East. She tells me that she has a simple recipe for an holistic oriental fertiliser which nourishes both the body and spirit of the plant. She got it from a famous Feng Shui gardener in Hong Kong.'

This of course left Radiant Flower with no option but to meet Gamin, although she had sworn to herself many times that she would never so much as exchange a word with a man who sent her three poems and a recipe for stuffed aubergines all in one day.

Reports filter through that the altercation between the man dressed as Nero and the large transvestite has now come to an end. Everyone is relieved, as these fetish events are generally very polite and peaceful affairs. Well I suppose being whipped or branded is not exactly peaceful, but such things only happen to enthusiastic volunteers.

'Radiant Flower I've been looking for you.'

It's Hawthorn, editor of *Squeegee*. He gives Radiant Flower a bottle of beer and a bottle of water and she drinks them both quickly.

'How's the magazine?'

He shrugs. 'Okay. Except I'm in trouble with the proprietor for having too many baked bean photo shoots. He says the readers don't like too much repetition. The January 2000 edition is meant to be a squelchy spectacular but it's hard coming up with new ideas. We've got a good story where a woman is preparing a picnic for a boy scout troop and she accidentally gets jam all over her and then the boy scouts come in and have to help her get the jam off, but apart from that it's looking fairly bleak. Sometimes I wish I'd never taken this job. I was quite happy at Lambeth Council.'

He tells Radiant Flower that he is still getting enthusiastic mail about the strawberry ice cream pictures.

'*Squeegee US* wants to buy them and they've offered us loads of money for more pictures of you.'

Radiant Flower of the Divine Heavens says she'll think about it. Hawthorn's mobile phone rings and he goes off somewhere quiet.

Although the men's toilets have now calmed down I remain where I am as I want to hear the rest of Radiant Flower's story.

Her eyes are dark and they shine brightly. This is partly down to their natural beauty, partly down to her fine make-up, and partly down to cocaine. After some more adjustments to her make-up and a little teasing of her dazzling hair, and a brief interruption from some friends of hers who admire her stiletto-heeled boots and offer her some ecstasy, which she accepts, she carries on.

'Well I had no choice but to meet Gamin and get hold of the holistic fertiliser. It's not every day someone offers you such a thing. Gamin wanted us to go out somewhere but I declined. I fully expected him to turn out to be an axe-wielding maniac and said I'd meet him at midday in the library. It seemed safest. Libraries are very calming. I've often felt better in them when I was feeling anxious.'

She pauses. The large man dressed as Nero, or to give him his full title, Nero Claudius Caesar looks in, waves his hand benevolently as if blessing the crowd, then departs. Radiant Flower of the Divine Heavens frowns.

'That's who invited Venus Beauticia over from San Francisco. He doesn't like me because I fucked his slave and wouldn't fuck him. I suppose it was a breach of etiquette. Are you interested that it's the start of a new millennium?'

'No. Not at all.'

'Neither am I. I don't like New Year's Eve. Any New Year's Eve, new millennium or not. It's always dull.'

To Radiant Flower's surprise, Gamin had turned out to be young, moderately attractive, and not obviously insane. He did watch too much television but as radiant Flower herself was not above slumping on a couch in front of the television for sixteen hours at a time when the outside world seemed too unbearable, she couldn't really hold that against him. In fact, had she just met him under some more normal circumstances, she felt that she may quite have liked him. It was just unfortunate that he had bombarded her with poems and messages and thereby become annoying. Which just goes to show that even if the person you want to meet is a fetish queen, famed for her marvellous beauty, a simple hello is as good a way to start as any.

Radiant Flower lost no time in learning the secret of the holistic fertiliser.

'What happened then?'

'I bought the ingredients and made some then I put it on the plant. It worked well. There was an immediate improvement.'

'What about Gamin?'

She shrugs, which I take to mean that Radiant Flower had no interest in pursuing the relationship. I can't blame her. Just because you rescue someone's plant doesn't mean they have to sleep with you. I can see that Gamin must be disappointed, though Radiant Flower possibly does not. She is not heartless, but gets far too much attention to worry over every single person who would like to sleep with her.

'Do you think the plant will flower on cue?'

She nods. 'I brought it with me. Gamin is looking after it in the cloakroom for me. I'm expecting it to flower when the clock strikes twelve.'

On cue a young man arrives. Radiant Flower introduces us. It's Gamin. He looks at me suspiciously for a moment then turns to Radiant Flower of the Divine Heavens. Speaking to her, he looks very like a young man desperately in love.

'I just came to tell you the plant is safe. And I think it's getting ready to flower.'

'Good,' says the fetish queen.

'And I brought you a drink.'

'Thank you.'

'And the pills you asked for.'

'Thank you.'

He waits expectantly.

'I'll come and look at the plant in a while,' says Radiant Flower, eventually, and waves her hand, dismissing him.

He goes away looking disappointed, getting tangled up in the process with a middle-aged couple who are coming in, both similarly dressed in leather body suits. The man is wearing a gag. His partner removes the gag and they sit down in a friendly manner to smoke a joint. They offer it to Radiant Flower, and she accepts. When the joint is finished the woman puts the gag back in, carefully, and they depart happily together.

'I like them,' says Radiant Flower of the Divine Heavens. 'They work in the library.'

It is close to midnight. Almost the start of the new millennium. Someone mentions to Radiant Flower that Venus Beauticia has arrived. Radiant Flower does not respond.

'How does she look?' I ask.

'Like a gooddess,' is the reply.

'Can't people think of anything better to say than that?' mutters Radiant Flower. 'I'm sick of hearing the word goddess.'

It seems like time to leave the toilet. It's almost midnight. I hope no strangers try to kiss me. I hate that.

'Are you coming?'

Radiant Flower of the Divine Heavens doesn't move. She doesn't seem to hear me. Her pale features have no expression. Slowly this changes to one of anxiety. She puts her hand to her face. I know she is again troubled by the feeling she doesn't exist.

She withdraws her hand, and looks at it. Radiant Flower used to have rings piercing her long nails but gave it up when it became too popular.

We depart into the main hall. Radiant Flower of the Divine Heavens is a small step away from a major bout of anxiety. An attack of the weirds, she calls it.

Radiant Flower has many friends and countless acquaintances who greet her as she passes, shouting above the music. She barely acknowledges them but takes bottles of beer from their hands and drinks them quickly. Radiant Flower drinks a lot of beer although as she smokes joints and cigarettes and rarely eats, she stays thin.

The crowds part in front of her and there is Venus Beauticia, sitting comfortably in the lap of Emperor Nero. Around her is a great crowd of admirers. Standing right beside her is a young man in very new-looking leather jeans and a shiny black plastic waistcoat. He looks familiar. I can't quite place him. For some reason he looks very pleased with himself. Perhaps he's just pleased to be beside Venus Beauticia who is certainly very, very beautiful. Her eyes are large and dark and her hair is deep black and massively thick. I see by my watch that it is quarter to twelve. As happens every New Year, I get the strong feeling that it would have been better to stay home and read a book

Radiant Flower of the Divine Heavens holds out her hand in a friendly manner to greet Venus Beauticia. Venus ignores the proffered hand.

'You must be the ice-cream lady,' she says.

I notice that Crag, Master of the Planets, Radiant Flower's one-time boyfriend is in close attendance, with muscles like cannonballs and a huge spiked collar round his neck. And I remember who the young man by Venus's side is. It's Gamin. He has gone over to the enemy. Obviously his devotion to Radiant Flower did not withstand her summary rejection of him. He stares at Radiant Flower, and his eyes are very hostile.

Crag reaches forward and hands something to Venus Beauticia. A small plant. It has on it the beginnings of a flower. Venus drops it on the floor and grinds it under her heel. People gasp. It is widely known how important the millennium bloom is to Radiant Flower. It lies there on the floor, mangled and broken among the black spiky heels of the onlookers. Radiant Flower of the Divine Heavens stoops to pick it up. She stares at it briefly. It is obviously never going to recover. Anything ground beneath the heel of Venus Beauticia stays ground.

'And don't come back looking for another one,' says Garth, Mystic Plant Keeper, appearing from among the throng. Her enemies have formed a conspiracy against her.

I am troubled. Radiant Flower of the Divine Heavens was already in a shaky state. I wouldn't want to see her ground down along with her plant.

Radiant Flower looks at Venus Beauticia. She smiles. 'How nice to meet you. I must say, you are far more beautiful than even the wildest descriptions of your greatest fans. But you should have kept the plant. I brought it here as a present for you.'

'As a present?' says Venus, suspiciously.

'Yes, as a present. If correctly positioned in your home it would have greatly boosted your fame and reputation. As I obviously have no need of such a thing, I thought I would give it to you.'

Radiant Flower of the Divine Heavens strolls off, having had, I would say, much the better of the exchange.

Later I congratulate her on her handling of the situation.

'Of course you are right, Radiant Flower. You don't need a special plant to give you fame. I expect any old bit of shrubbery will be just as good.'

She looks at me with amazement.

'Are you mad? That was just for show. I was relying on that millennium bloom. I'm devastated. Who would have thought that Gamin would show such treachery? I can't believe it.'

'You completely ignored him after he told you he loved you.'

'So? I do that all the time. I don't expect people to go and be unpleasant to me just because I ignore them.'

Four young men in black leather straps come and greet Radiant Flower. They give her beer, and some unknown substance to inhale, which she accepts. Hawthorn struggles through the crowd to speak to her, still clutching his phone. 'The Americans will pay eight thousand dollars for pictures of you falling into a vat of uncooked salami,' he says.

'Certainly not. I'm a vegetarian.'

'They'll negotiate on a vegetable substitute.'

Radiant Flower promises to think about it, although I know she has decided against it.

'Incidentally, Garth the Mystic Plant Keeper asked me to tell you he'll give you another millennium bloom if you want. And Gamin's looking everywhere for you.'

Gamin appears, looking very miserable. For some reason he now looks preposterous in his unfamiliar fetish clothing. He apologises profusely to Radiant Flower of the Divine Heavens and tells her he still loves her. Radiant Flower dismisses him with some contempt. I see things are returning to normal. Radiant Flower's anxiety is melting away.

'You may be right,' she says to me. 'I expect any old plant

would do for my fame point. I'll take a cutting from the hedge.'

The bells ring out for new year and the start of the new millennium. Pandemonium breaks loose. Celebratory whippings happen spontaneously in every corner. Despite my best efforts to avoid it I am kissed by several strangers.

Helen Mead

'GAME ON'

Nick's freaking out. Even in paradise. Maybe especially in paradise. We've been wined, dined and are now settled possibly more comfortably than anyone, anywhere else on this planet. The perfect party. Fresh drinks in our hands, bodies sinking into inflatable cushions that blow the sun loungers beyond Superhuman-size. Comfy. Nothing to do but sip tequila from tall, iced glasses filled with red fruit juices and observe. Relax. People are beached all around. Draping their appropriately hardly-covered tan and glittering forms on fellow loungers; spreading out in loose intermingling groups on the tables and chairs set in spirals from the terraced bars of the hotel's restaurant, circulating down to the sea. Conversation. Dancing. Laughter. Music. The space under Orion's belt pumped rigid with a pure shot of sexual energy, the mantra of drums mimicking rushing heartbeats. Two more of our girlfriends are swimming around somewhere amid this atmosphere of drunken pleasure. It makes me think of Rome. Of orgies. Of the end of an empire. The buzz is deafening. It is deafening Nick.

'I should never have come,' says Nick. He wants out. Out of these visuals. New Year's Eve 1999. I never expected it to be easy. When has any New Year's Eve ever been easy? But half way across the world from Trafalgar Square and its Norwegian Spruce, sitting on a beach bordered by palm trees hung with fairy lights, and the Gulf Of Thailand should be escape enough.

Our host is chopping out a kilo block of grass on the table in front of him to the heavy, heaving rhythm of hedonism emanating from the island's soil. Piles of magic mushrooms lay already divided into 'dose' portions to the side of him. Long-stemmed with golden caps. I wonder if Nick's going to chill: give in to it — the continuum reality. Year 2000. Time's not going to run out; not tonight. Even the 24/7 sandwiches at Bangkok airport were screaming 'what's the big deal?' with their best before 3/I/3543 sell-by dates. It's all an illusion. An egotistical prime-time Western psyche-out. A pre-set time tomb. Obsolete programming conspiring mass social crises. An ingrained Christian deadline, a prophecy of Armageddon. Forget it. It's just another day in space.

Magz comes bursting through the bodies grinning from ear to ear, and lands on the end of my lounger. There's something magical about Magz. You catch glimpses of it: when she chants to send the rain back up to the heavens, or, investigating the reef earlier, looking every bit a mermaid as she played with the angel fish in their nursery pools as the sun ebbed — as our last twentieth century sun set. Westie weaves along after her in a 'modest little after-dinner number', of black silk and copper thread, a boy with an impish grin revealing a third front tooth, already by the hand.

'So what are we doing first, taking the 'shrooms or making a huge spliff?' Magz's question punctuates the atmosphere. Just a huge exclamation. On for the mission.

We all look at Nick. It was the night of the Millenniumeers: one for all and all for ...

'Or,' she pauses, for effect. 'Would you like to start off with some pure Californian MDMA?' Shrieking with delight Magz pulls out a smuggled Kinder Egg from under her dress.

Nick smiles and licks the tip of his little finger in anticipation of the powder. Game on.

The decision had been made for me. For all of us. We'd all

landed here by chance. A random grouping. We'd never been away together before. Just danced together, then chilled together – pulling the strands of innumerable disjointed weekends, framed by London's skyline and basements, into a nocturnal friendship.

I'd planned — well, more dreamed — since it had been announced at Berlin's Love Parade that summer, to go to the party at the Pyramids. The great tribal gathering. Hundreds of thousands had been pouring into Egypt for weeks by air, sea, land, any way they could. Creating their own temporary Bedouin court. By the time I was ready to set out from my work-a-day life (in a progressive architects' co-operative, where we were always trying to make major changes, but rarely even got to lay the foundations), the state had stamped its last official entry visa and the only way left to get in was an illegal border crossing.

Nick hadn't fancied a romantic holiday in Bali soaking up the rays of Gamelan since he'd split up with his boyfriend. Westie was already out East, taking a sabbatical from her Ministry of Defence job, doing a bit of social bar-flying for humanity's sake. This trip had been Magz's call: her best-friend Bailey, was invited to spin at this party on Koh Chang at the last minute by Domenico, a promoter he'd worked with for years in Rimini, Italy's Costa Del Dance. Practically damned by the Pope in the early nineties as hell on earth, the area's notorious reputation went international. What better recommendations, endorsement or PR could a promoter hope for? *People love to sin* ...

This island between the coasts of Thailand and Cambodia was Domenico's customary winter retreat. This year, bolstered by huge summer profits despite — or more probably due to — the well-publicised £3.6 million he'd spent on extending his club Arcadia to include a replica of the Sistine Chapel he decided to book the entire hotel (and with it the east side of the island) for the month, and then throw the most exclusive party there to pay for it. Domenico's appetite for debauchery and chaos appeared to expand exponentially with his wealth, the party was yet another way to satisfy this hunger. Tickets were limited and their price-tag exorbitant. Somehow this seemed to make the proposition more attractive to Domenico's clientèle. The Italian was definitely Lord of his own dance, and apparently he could lead them anywhere.

Bailey was up for the trip but hadn't fancied the journey unaccompanied. 'No problem. Bring your people,' said Domenico. So we were his entourage, and currently the host's best friends for the night — entertaining us while Bailey was playing with everybody else on the decks.

Domenico is beautiful. Mesmerisingly so. Fifty and complete. My mum likes commenting that people get the face they deserve when they're forty, there's no hiding your real self after that. If that's the case Domenico's already died and gone to Heaven. Constantly stolen glances by the endless procession of bodies bound for the dance floor feed the golden glow of his earthen skin. Face-to-face with the centre of the intrigue, the bizarre stories circulating around and about him, dissolve into novelty. I guess this was the *art* of his art. The projection and suspension of his own reality.

I'd visited Thailand before but had never heard of Koh Chang. It wasn't surprising. Nobody had. Domenico had found his own little Bermuda Triangle. There were hardly any Thais here at the moment — he'd brought his own staff from his summer residence who spoke to each other and their boss in nothing but Italian. Domenico said the ambitious beach boys who usually hawked or kow-towed to us *Farangs*, were glad to get away. There had been no natural, indigenous population for years, the spiritually-superstitious believing the island cursed by the souls of drowned pirates and more recently, just sensibly avoiding the attacks and raids from their Cambodian neighbours. The kidnapping of some Australians by Cambodian bandidos had also managed to keep the soil unpolluted by tourists. It was purely the most curious of travellers that found their way now. And the pirates. There were always pirates . . .

'There's always a price,' says Westie, making a point, as she lowers her nostril to greet the MDMA powder on the table. 'We have to pay to be alive.' This line of reasoning is to make sure he's done bad-tripping us. Westie has no patience. Especially not tonight. Can't be bothered with Nick's arguments. Nick's introversion. She believes that life is for living, not dissecting. A lesson she'd had to learn literally. At twenty, in her first year at college, she discovered chlamydia. A sexual infection which had kick-started cervical cancer that threatened to eat up her womb. No time to be hysterical. The operation left her without a scar and on HRT. This, was the basis for her theory on life. This was her price. Half Nick's age, she had assumed a maternal role, scolding him like a naughty little boy. Nick liked that. He hadn't had much of that.

Nick had started living early. Every wave that came along — he caught. His parents were in the services so the twelve year old's summer holidays from public school in Sussex were spent fictionally at a friend's parents, while he hitched his way to the Isle Of Wight for the festival.

That was the first time he felt that feeling — that particular mass psychosis that makes you feel you belong, that you can change things — even the status quo. It was Jimi Hendrix who hypnotised him, inspired him. He dropped LSD for the first time and ended his initiation drinking Rise 'n' Shine as the sun broke through into the tent where he was being watched over empathetically by a young woman who'd left her family to study Buddhism in London. He too made a break for freedom and watched Mick Jagger release thousands of butterflies in Hyde Park in memory of Brian Jones marvelling at the words of Shelley that spilled from his lips.

Bowie embraced his androgyny, punk his anger, his repression. The eighties nearly killed him. He'd evolved into a dreamer. A romantic. An idealist. His heroes were his aspirational reality. He wasn't ready for the true meaning of Thatcherism. He wasn't ready for them and us. The divide. The record stuck. Acid house saved him. Ecstasy healed him. There were no more heroes ... just us.

Just the taking part. Now every man and every woman could be a star.

But his belief tonight of all nights was shallow. Caught in a loop. Unable to evolve and move on. The question was there. Fixed in the most ancient, primal part of his brain. 'Why does nothing ever really change?' He didn't want to leave the party — it wasn't that. He didn't see the point any longer. He'd lost his faith. He wanted to stop the world and get off. Nick was Peter Pan — he refused to grow old. Yet it was Domenico who appeared truly ageless.

Nobody knew the truth about Domenico. Unless the truth was he threw the best parties. Maybe that was the only truth needed to put ourselves into his hands. Club gossip composed a minimal score of his life: born on the southern tip of his country where they still spoke Greek; stories of his summer vacations spent lying on the side of Eolie's volcano, skin painted blue from head to toe; of arcane ritual; the absence of lovers, devotees both male and female made stories of having no tales to tell. Almost as notorious, his mother was rumoured to be a twentieth century Josephine, a card sharp, her favourite twist, poker – currently her passport through China.

'Here Mona!' Domenico passes a perfectly rolled grass spliff around the circle for me to light, his arm gently brushing Nick's shoulder. It was one of Domenico's four-paper specials. Confidently spun with an extra-thin, extra-long roach to keep the smoke cool. With a twist in its tail; tapering down to pure grass so that it was a treat to be handed even the roach. Etiquette and consideration were paramount to his style. 'A real-life Mr Doasyouwouldbedoneby,' I giggle to myself, exhaling the blue, hazy smoke, making a mental check to return the favour later.

I watch a smoke ring float from my mouth. Expanding and contracting. And think of my boyfriend lying in bed, post-a different sort of loved-up, puffing rings like a steam train to entertain me, keeping our spirits connected after our bodies have parted. It was just a fluke when the smoke obeyed my mouth. He taught me to cheat. To make them to order. Linking into his reality, I send another five clones through the ever-widening mother hole — wondering what sort of time he's having, whether he made it to the pyramids. I sense he has ... I'm drifting, watching dimension drift within dimension within dimension ...

'Hey Mona!' I fell down to earth. Back into my beach Babylon. My E had kicked in. Either that or the mushrooms. Or both. I felt my heart quicken. My attitude shift. I made earthly contact, Nick smiled. 'Fancy a stroll?' We set off down to the sea, towards the rippling phosphorescence. The sand eating up the space between our toes, massaging our soles, gently exfoliating our heels. The surface of the planet pushing up to meet us, encouraging us to make an impression. For a change, it didn't feel like we were treading on it, treading it down. I became very conscious of my clothes. These usual comforters felt strange, unnecessary.

Tripping, definitely tripping. Nick was cool. One step ahead. More in control of his trip. Watching over mine. Taking me into a nice space. Guiding it. Keeping me on track. There was nothing for putting Nick's head back on course like having someone to look after. He was back in his element now. Dipping in and out of the rock pools — watching baby crabs scatter in the front and to the side of us. Knowledge hits me. I'm having fun. More than that: I'm happy. It's going to be a great New Year's Eve. A great New Year. A great beginning. The thought makes me feel even happier. Another dimension loop. I give Nick a spontaneous hug. Take a time-check. We started early this evening. We were on Equatorial time and entering the Interzone without even realising it. No watch could measure this time: the time of memories, of hopes.

The sun had set exactly twelve hours after it had arisen at six thirty, in perfect time to Domenico's first trick. The colonial style veranda where we sat sipping gin fizzes like Old World ex-pats, was transformed into Ibiza's Café Del Mar with José slipping disc after disc into the backbone of our memory. Reminding us why we were here. Recapping on our lives for us. Prodding us with whatever triggers we needed. As the trays of La Bamba — the Café Del Mar house special of iced brandy in thick chocolate milk — were handed among us, our night-lives started flashing before our eyes, triggered by our ears, like freeze-frames caught in the strobes. When all that remained of the sun was a blood red kiss staining the horizon, Domenico stood and proposed a toast 'To music, the food of life,' the words rippled through us and on cue José projected the mood into the future spinning in virgin trax. 'Play on!'

That's when I'd first thought of Rome. 'Play on.' The words of the emperor, the roar echoing back from the crowd, the ancient duel of life and death being played out in the Coliseum below him. The power. The price ...

Domenico was making a round of the tables — the perfect host. A true chameleon. Falling in with any table effortlessly. Adopting whichever persona his guests wished him to provide: profound, witty, sage or fool. Maintaining the energy. Nothing ever looks this seemless without intense effort. He greets us last — I've no idea whether with the same or different line he's used before but I wonder. He talks about London, about Bailey, about 'our island', 'our freedom'. Total freedom. We can do whatever we like: limited only by ourselves. We can be back in the Garden of Eden — it wouldn't be too hard to imagine, not here. Heaven on earth if we decide to paint it that way. It was a delicious thought to flirt with. This entire island, a canvas; shaded, toned, suggested by Domenico's brush. It was true we were entering a new reality. Albeit, for the meantime, a controlled one. But for how long? This performance was just the setting of a scene. The triggered visions of our past, the flesh but not the plot. It wasn't the future. That was up to us ...

'Time to die.' Domenico answered my thoughts. He didn't speak. His eyes talked — reflected mine. A mirage of images. And I felt him see them too. Or suggest them. I thought of

Blade Runner. Rutger Hauer on the rooftop of a decaying city, drenched by a rain that was too late to wash it clean but not too late to drown his tears. I understood the meaning of this scene differently now. It wasn't really an ending. And the realisation immediately lodged itself at the back of my subconscious, in the deep end with Nick's freak out.

Dinner was served. Plate after plate arrived at the tables. Domenico stayed as we ate. Light dishes he explained to lift our evening. Local oysters and imported champagne for our libido; Miso soups and Nori rolls, loaded with an earlier seaweed crop, instant B12 shots for *joi de vivre*; lobsters with garlic to purify our blood; sashimi on a bed of grated burdock and mooli radish — green tea ices with a hint of bergamot to cleanse our palates. Nothing on our plates had been long dead: you could sense the energy, almost imbibe their last heartbeat; taste the flavours of the sea that gave them life. Desert evokes the aromas of the land — mango and banana in coconut cream and finally, fresh durian. A large, prickly fruit the size of a football. One of the East's most notorious exports — just its smell got it banned. And what a fragrance. As Domenico cut through the rind it tickled our nostrils with reminders of English summer fruits: raspberries and white strawberries — tantalising. As he passed the fruit round for us all to take segments, the real odour it was masking cut through. A foul stream of incontinence, of death. Domenico smiled as he swallowed — we were scrupulously British, at least away from home and in his company, we all followed suit.

'Mona, remember you're tripping!' For a while I have the agility of a mountain goat. Far above the shore line — scaling the cliff face — everything's a long way down. Including Nick. 'Mona it's too dangerous. Come down, I can't follow anymore.' I freeze. Gripped by the sensation of a mirror shattering in my brain. Of the pixels reforming. Of resistance. Of not wanting to come back. Not yet. It's cool in there. Safe. The bump of my conscious as I come back down. Finding myself back in the same clumsy, limited body. When I land I'm resentful.

'I'd have been all right.'

I mean to go on. To complete the mission. Until I try to move. Little rocks glance off bigger stones under my feet — no longer navigating a safe path just skirting peril — either way, up or down. 'What was the mission? Beats me.' I realise how dark it is, the snake-mouth of a long, trailing cloud taking a bite out of the just full moon. 'Move girl.' I listen to the internal dialogue and lower myself as quickly as I can to safety, feeling in more danger now — conscious.

'Time to rejoin civilisation,' says Nick joined to a ledge by his back like a tower-block jumper. I follow his gaze, looking down at the party and over to the hotel, through its domed glass roof at the illuminated figures inside — looking into their lives. A surreal scientist's exotic culture in a petri dish, mutating and evolving before my eyes. Stopping at the edge of the bodies: blocked by the dance's intensity, I wonder at the physical force that's being generated. Impenetrable. Lighting one of the Blue Peter's I'd slipped safely into a Camel lights packet earlier, I inhale deeply and observe from the sidelines. Distanced. Removed. Watching even myself. Spying in on Mona.

The smoke filled Mona's lungs to capacity. Already stoned she rolled the smoke out like sea mist low over her body. Empty she wanted more. She checked herself. 'I must be really flying.' It was an early morning MDMA feeling. A watermark moment — when the usual coarseness and heat of the smoke became imperceptible. When your lungs disappear. An invisible interface between the inhalation and the blood. Automatically, she checked the length of the body of the spliff for holes anyway, before taking another deep pull. It was like a popper's rush. The next set of waves when they hit her. Engulfed her. Swallowed her whole. Folding her into itself like the eye of a hurricane.

The drums called. She recognised the rhythm. Bailey had

moved from the decks to percussion. Automatically Mona plunged through the wall of flesh into the muscle of the crowd and moved her hips in the direction of the heart of it all. Climbing up on the wooden platform that mimicked a ra-ra skirt around his 360 degree stage she saw Magz and Nick and Westie all movin' on up. Automatically responding to the vibe. He was calling them. His familiars. All caught up in their own trips all evening – there had been no time for this. They'd all been too busy, happy finding themselves to find each other. This was Bailey's special code. Bringing them together with that fascinating rhythm. It meant something more. A conclusion. Experiencing the rollercoaster of the century's last minutes. Hips almost down to the floor. The hem of Mona's A-line mini-dress dusting the wooden boards as the girls found each other for the midnight play-off. Nick was all camp, queenie appreciation — as the girls fused in motion, leading the dance floor with their own instinctive dance. Bailey's fingers on the tautly stretched skins translated directly into the way they moved. Osmosis. The dance was his. A visual expression of his play. Actors under his direction. It was familiar — mapped onto every strand of human DNA. Warmth, comfort and happiness radiated from it. Fusing, they found their own path. Grounded in one another. Firmly moored but further out than they'd ever been. In the grip of the music, the drugs, the pull of the planet.

Feeling the touch of downy, silken skin, Mona distantly noticed the hands that comfortably circled her waist. 'How long had they been there?' It felt like for ever. Mona opened her eyes. Face to face. Eye to eye. With another girl. Long treacle curls. Rich tan. Sweat beads lacing her top lip. Rich brown eyes. A loose flowing veil of a dress. No shoes. Painted feet. No words but 'Isabella'. Bodies moving in perfect time to each other. A reflection. A known quantity. Further into the trance.

Bailey stares as the dance leaves his hands and enters a new level as Mona's body stretches downwards and meets Isabella's fingers on their way up. A flash of blue light crashes through

Mona's cranium the same picosecond as she feels the flesh of lips that whisper 'Le petit mort.'

Time to die ... The words spiral out at me, expelling me. The loop's turned full circle. The party opens and closes around me. It's definitive. I don't feel part of the action anymore. Or any need to be. A substituted player. The game's out of control. I want to find Domenico. Complete my promise to myself and return his compliment — a perfect spliff from back in trip-world. I want to connect the two realities. Make them one. Make them whole. But I can't see him. Anywhere. I get angry with myself. Where could he be? Then comes the answer. Where would you go to watch the first sunrise?

I look east. Across the gentle rise of the beach. Towards the light that's as much a part of us as the dark. To the cliffs I'd tried to climb earlier. At the top — an evergreen and two sky-blue flags stream in the breeze on either side of a Buddha-shaped silhouette that can only belong to Domenico. I stop and take in the image for a while, feeling echoes of my earlier mission: 'That's where I was trying to get to — that's where my trip was leading me.' Up there. Out there.

Now I can see a clear path up to the headland. There's no danger this time. I walk up easily, happily, into the light. He's built this moment in time for us. Given us something most people can't even dream of. I can feel it enrich every part of me. Ringing deep inside. Amplifying. Merging with the sound of a bell. A giant copper cup the size of a fruitbowl is resting on a gold silken cushion in front of his knees. Domenico's hand comes down and gently strikes the bell again in such a way that it's reverberations get stronger as they flow, resonant and low, coming to rest in my heart. Another twenty or thirty seconds silence and he sounds it again. Calling.

His eyes are fixed on the horizon. Meditating in the first rays — golden in the light of a new dawn. The emblem on the flags is clear now. Set free in the sky. Cranes — heads centred in a circle of wings. The recognition makes me smile. Reminds me again of my mother. She always told me that cranes personified everything that motherhood should be about. When there was no food they would pick off their own flesh to feed their babies. Sacrificing themselves to sustain the future. She said they could teach the majority of humans a thing or two. The vibration changes. Imperceptibly. Takes on Domenico's voice. A seemless chant looping back on itself. Growing in volume. In his hands he holds a scroll, turning it very, very carefully with the tips of his fingers. My footsteps break his spell. He turns to his right and for the second time on this rock I freeze. Spellbound. I see Nick kneeling on the other side of him, resting on his heels. Ceremoniously, Domenico places the scroll in a silk bag and passes it to Nick. He looks beautiful. Ageless. Like he's finally found out who he really is. One and the same, Nick and Domenico's expressions reflect each other. Open. Infinite.

'This is yours,' says Domenico voice lower than silence. Nick stares at the gift in his hands as tears stream down his face.

'What is it?' I ask feeling ignorant again. Then I see the joy in his smile. 'A second chance,' says Nick. Cleansed. Reborn. His skin a veil of golden tears. The colour of enlightenment.

Courttia Newland

'PIECE OF MY MIND'

They met up outside Belsize House around seven that evening. The estate was dark by that time, and the night wind cold enough to have them all muttering curses and complaints about the weather, just like they did every winter. A thin, smoky kind of fog was drifting across the adventure playground towards their block, like a shapeless spirit wandering through an empty house, desperate for someone to haunt. The streets were filled with a constant flow of designer-dressed ravers, their faces alight in anticipation of the forthcoming celebrations.

Though most of them acted like ravers normally do before a good night out, others seemed subdued and tense. These party-goers walked silently with their people passing around champagne bottles and weed spliffs, numbed by the historic event due to take place in less than five hours' time. Livelier people blew whistles and foghorns, or shouted seasonal greetings with a frenzied kind of glee; heading for the 'new' end of Greenside, where a street party to celebrate its official opening was being held. Couples kissed and touched warmly, as if every look or stroke would be their last.

The group of youths outside Belsize would look up occasionally, but took no more notice than that, their faces unimpressed by the scenes going on all around them. There were fifteen of them — nine boys and six girls who'd agreed The Rose Garden in Croydon was the club to be at, as it boasted an impressive four floors of Garage, Hip Hop, R&B, and Drum 'n' Bass. None of them intended getting to the venue before eleven — but as they hung around the block most evenings anyway, it was inevitable they'd eventually meet up for a pre-rave drink, and smoke.

They crowded together on the pavement, spotlit by the yellow glow of the block's landing lights, gazing unseeingly in the direction of the adventure playground. Most of the group were silent. Sissy hung on to Valentine in the tight possessive manner new lovers often acquire, and he responded in kind — both of them completely unaffected by the presence of the others. Orin watched his sister and smoked cigarettes hard, while his best friend Malcolm stood by his side, catching quiet jokes with Alex Carter (who was fast becoming the estate's Top Boy). Carolyn was singing the latest offering from The Box, with Lilah, Siân and Sophie accompanying her with harmonies that were surprisingly good. Benji was yakking it up loudly with Robby over his latest female conquest, as Ryan took a last blast on his zook, before sending it over to Ray.

Little Stacey stood with his hands in his pockets, his face tight, contemplative and thoughtful, as if a million and one dark thoughts were flashing through his brain. He stood watching the fog come closer, mulling over his life, and wondering what route it would take after midnight; when he and the rest of the world stepped boldly into the next century. He didn't mind admitting it, but he was shitting himself. Everyone, everywhere had a theory on what came next, and none of the theories sounded promising. His mother thought the end of the world was coming. Benji reckoned computers were set to take over the world, like Skynet did in *Terminator*. His cousin Nadia said right-wing fascists would start the ultimate world war, and black people's lives in England would become twice as hard. Even at sixteen, Stacey thought his life had been hard enough; he didn't know if he could handle it getting any worse.

His nerves twanged like guitar strings every time he thought about the millennium. His fear was so sharp it seemed to pierce his insides.

Ray nudged his elbow idly. Stacey looked down, then pinched the remainder of the spliff from his friend's fingers, and put it to his own lips silently. Ray moved his shoulders and arms to an imaginary beat, then bounced on his toes and grinned at the others.

'Can't wait t'get out dere tonight star,' he told them truthfully. Ryan lifted an eyebrow.

'Yeah man, should be all right y'nuh. Rose Garden's doin' it — las' time I reach dere I chirp bere gyal. Hol' all t'ree, four digits, y'get me.'

'Believe!' Benji shouted over from where he'd been listening.

'Pure yatty was at the Garden las' time I was dere too. Lookin' to smash it tonight as well blood, done know!'

The youths said nothing in reply to this; the girls because they were fed up of Benji's constant bragging — the boys because they knew he was right. Stacey clutched his sides and shivered.

'Gonna be cold out tonight star.'

'I ain' watchin' dat!' Carolyn piped up. She was sixteen and very beautiful. 'I'm jus' lookin' to smoke an' drink, an' have the bes' time I can. It's gonna be a dark rave tonight man!'

Stacey threw the roach away and hugged himself grimly. 'Looks like it's gonna snow,' he grumbled in a deep voice.

'Fuck you talkin' about man, it ain' snowed for about four or five years!' Ray argued hotly. 'You ain' seein' no snow tonight star!'

'It snowed las' year man, you know it did!' Stacey retorted. 'We was sittin' right here when it did as well!'

'Dat weren't snow,' Benji sneered. 'Proper snow's meant to settle man; dat shit jus' dissolved on the pavement one time, y'get me.' He laughed in Stacey's face and popped his bottle of orange Hooch. ''Bout snow . . .'

Stacey kissed his teeth.

'Yeah, well the only reason the snow don't seckle is 'cos of all dat global warmin' shit. It's already gettin' like the Tropics in dis country, wid all dem mad up insects and bugs flyin' about the place

every summer, and no snow every winter. I'm sick of it man —
I jus' wish I could get out o' dis place ...'

Stacey kissed his teeth angrily, then sighed and turned his
attention back to the rolling, swirling fog. The others studied
him in silence, then looked at one another and shrugged. Siân,
a petite, spectacle wearing Chinese girl, turned to the youth with
a frown. 'Whassup wid you den?'

He hugged himself tighter, then sighed once more and let go.
'Nuttin' man, I'm okay ...'

'You sure?' Lilah joined in. ''Cos you sure don't look okay ...'

'Innit though,' Siân agreed.

'He's safe man, jus' 'llow the brer nuh,' Benji roared at the girls.
He was one of those people that always had to speak ten times
louder than anyone else. 'He done tell yuh he's cool, so stop fussin'
over 'im ...'

'Ah fuck off Benji,' Lilah snapped all at once, rounding on the
youth in a flash.

'Stacey's supposed to be yuh bredrin an' you can't even see when
summick's bunnin' 'im. You're rubbish man. Yuh mout's too damn
big anyway, yuh talkin' loud but you ain' sayin' jack shit ...'

'Yeah yeah, an I ain' the only big mout' person around 'ere,
y'get me?' Benji retorted snidely. 'Mus' be all dat hood yuh takin'
dese days, innit Li?' Benji opened his mouth and moved his jaw
up and down to illustrate his point. There was a roar of laughter
from the youths. Ryan started singing Arkinele's 'Put it in your
mouth', which made them crack up even more. Lilah gave Benji
a look that would have turned Medusa to stone, but stayed quiet,
knowing she'd lost. Ryan beatboxed the remainder of the hip-hop
classic, then looked up as something caught his eye. He pointed
at the adventure playground.

'Raa ...'

Apart from Stacey (who was now staring sulkily at the road),
they all looked that way. A hooded figure was straddling the high
playground wall, just in the process of climbing on to the street
side; as they watched, he threw his left leg over and let himself

fall to the pavement, then looked in their direction and raised a fist. Ryan squinted.

''Oozat?'

Little Stacey looked up, his expression full of boredom — then he suddenly smiled as he recognised the person bouncing their way. He nodded and held out his fist as the figure reached them.

'Whassup Nemo? Wha' gwaan?'

The youth called Nemo touched fists with Little Stacey, then the rest of the young men in turn. His hooded Nike top was splattered with paints of all colours, and his army fatigue trousers were in much the same state. The small rucksack on his back rattled with his every movement, and was as battered and paint-covered as the rest of him.

'Safe man. Jus' hard at work y'get me? You man ravin' tonight den?' They all nodded eagerly.

'Where yuh goin'?'

'Rose Garden innit. Gonna be ram star, everyone's on it tonight.' Little Stacey looked happy about the prospect of raving for the first time that evening, even though it had largely been his idea, and he'd got hold of the stolen MasterCard they'd used to book the tickets. Nemo raised an eyebrow, his young-old face intense and serious.

'Yeah man, Rose Garden's a cold venue blood — yuh due to 'ave a good time dere.'

'So what, are you goin' out den Nemo?' Sissy asked, from where she was cuddled up with Val. Nemo shook his head with a faint smile.

'Nah man, I passed dem stages dere long time, y'get me, I ain' even on the ravin' no more. I'm into the Art man.'

Little Stacey smiled at that, like a proud parent listening to his child recite the alphabet. The others frowned at one another, then looked at Nemo strangely, as if he'd said he was into devil worship.

'What, you writin' tonight blood?' Stacey asked.

Nemo looked around, seemingly unsure of whether to expose

his plans to them or not. He blinked, cleared his throat, then spoke slowly.

'Yeah man ... I got a idea dat's jus' ... it's the lick man, I'm showin' you now ... I affa get it up man ...'

Now the youths were interested. They moved a little closer to the hooded young man, curious as to what could be more important than raving on New Year's Eve. Especially this New Year's Eve. Orin sparked up another cigarette and gestured at Nemo.

'A piece? Or jus' a throw up?'

Nemo sneered.

'Throw up? Come on, you know I ain' on dat shit man, bere big tings ah run fuh Nemo, y'get me? An' as fuh tonight ... Star, tonight I wanna do the biggest piece I've ever done, dedicated to the millennium.'

'What's it gonna say?' Nemo grinned at the youths, then tapped his nose three times. 'Wait an' see star, you affa wait an see. I can't be exposin' my plan of action till the right time. Lemme jus' say dis — my millennium piece is not only gonna be the biggest and best form of artwork dis estate has ever seen — it's also gonna be strategically placed somewhere it can't be missed.'

'Like ...?' Stacey prompted eagerly.

'I can't tell you dat either,' Nemo admitted lamely.

The youths groaned.

'Why not?' Malcolm asked.

Nemo looked into their stern faces sheepishly. ''Cos I can't risk even one person knowin' what I'm up to, jus' in case the word gets about. Idle gossip could get me nicked mate.'

'C'mon man,' Little Stacey pressed, not at all convinced by his friend's speech. 'Dis is the man's dem yuh talkin' to blood ...'

'An' the girls ...' Carolyn broke in. No one took any notice.

'What, you reckon man's gonna be grassin' you up?' the small youth concluded.

'Course not ... But it's bes' if I jus' hol' it down for now. Believe me, after tonight everyting's gonna be revealed — there's no way you're gonna be able to miss it. What, you can't wait one day blood?'

There was a general collective grumble from everyone. Nemo shrugged. 'Anyhow, I gotta shif' man, nuff tings to do an' dat. You man gonna be about later?'

'Yeah man,' Stacey told him, 'At least till about ten, half ten. Come check me in my drum if we ain' out here innit. We can bun a Millennium spliff together, y'get me?'

'All right spee,' Nemo replied, doing the rounds with his fist again. 'I'll buck every man up later, yeah?'

'Yeah man, good luck wid dat suttin' deh,' Orin mumbled, over his friends' chorus of farewells. Nemo nodded in acknowledgement, then turned and walked towards his home in Bartholomew House. Orin watched him leave, then shook his head.

'Graffiti,' he spat snidely, 'I thought man stopped doin' dem tings from way back, y'get me?'

'Nah man,' Little Stacey countered, a knowing, proud look all over his face. 'Nuff man's still at it star, an' I tell you dis — if Nemo says he's gonna do a Millennium piece ... it's definitely gonna be suttin' worth seein' ...'

While on his way home he eased his marker from his pocket and inscribed his name upon various walls, on numerous occasions — smiling grimly and shaking his head whenever he saw the tags Xendo, and Boozy, which adorned almost as many walls as his. He used thick, looping, swirling letters, linked together for easier execution, intricate enough to make them illegible to the untrained eye. Although everyone knew him as Nemo and he still wrote the name when it suited him, his latest tag was Omen '99 — which he'd been using for the last six months; and, of course, was really Nemo backwards. A friend once said they'd gone for a piss in a cubicle at a Leicester Square Burger King, and had seen the tag high above their heads, scrawled across the cistern in red spray paint. Nemo loved it when people told him things like that.

Other times he wrote Risk, though he hadn't used that name for about a year or so — and only the hardcore grafitti-heads knew him as such. He'd been seriously writing since he was twelve; now, at twenty-three, he was as hooked and obsessed as any normal human being with a healthy hobby. Ever since he'd seen the film *Wild Style*, Nemo wanted to do what the New York graffiti artists did best — tags, massive throw-ups, top to bottom whole cars . . . Obviously, train yards weren't as accessible as in the States, but together with a crew of seven like-minded individuals known as ICV (Inner City Vandals) Nemo had done his best to paint every train, wall-space and public building with his crews' name. By the time he'd reached his nineteenth birthday, ICV had disbanded for almost three months, due to in-house wrangles and arguments. Ever since then, Nemo worked alone — which had been scary at first, but something he'd grown to love and cherish.

A sudden noise from behind made him jump as he was putting the second nine on his tag — he turned quick as he could to see a tall, middle-aged-looking black man crossing the road opposite him, his head fully turned Nemo's way. Nemo jumped and made his Edding disappear, before shoving his hands into his pockets and turning on his heel. The black man continued watching him, then smiled as he saw the youth acting the innocent.

'Yuh safe star!' he shouted, waving a little before turning and walking away. Nemo followed slowly, a tiny grin on his face, feeling fine. Not everybody, it seemed, hated graffiti artists. In fact, he could take that incident as a good omen for tonight's venture.

The man walked past the youths' block, and on towards the 'new' end of Greenside, swinging a plastic bag in a relaxed manner. Nemo crossed the road outside Bartholomew, and saw a crew of girls leaned up against the swing doors at the entrance way. He groaned inwardly, his feet moving slower through no conscious decision of his own.

Vanessa, the tallest and prettiest of the group of four, detached herself from them and approached with a smile that could melt the coldest heart.

'Hey Nemo,' she trilled, sauntering his way sexily. 'What's goin' on in your world?'

'Ah, same ol' shit,' the graffiti artist replied brusquely, with an uncaring shrug of his shoulders. 'Jus' out dere bombin' the place up, you know the flex . . .'

He stopped by the block's entrance, sizing up her and her friends with a non-committal eye. Vanessa and her best friend Barbara (called Boozy by everyone that knew her), came from Cunningham House, the most recently built block on Greenside. Vanessa was a walnut-coloured, athletic-looking girl, nineteen years old, and academically smart, as well as streetwise. She'd moved on to the estate with her disabled sister a mere three months ago, and was studying A-level Art with the idea of becoming a fashion designer at some stage. Both she and Boozy were mad on graffiti, and inevitably became drawn to Nemo, one of the most prolific writers in the West London area. Nemo was flattered by the attention, but something about the intensity of her obvious attraction sparked the loner's instinct in his brain, and made him want to run for cover. Cute and fun-loving, Boozy meanwhile had become cool with him – they'd formed a comfortable platonic friendship, based on their mutual love of the Art.

Vanessa screwed up her face at his last words, and put her hands on her hips menacingly. 'How come you never call me an' Bee when you go bombin'? We wanna get our tags up as well.'

Vanessa was the owner of the tag Xendo, while Boozy simply wrote her nickname. They constantly bombarded Nemo with requests to be taught how to piece; but he'd refused, saying it wasn't a skill that could be taught. His attempts to put them off hadn't worked. Yet.

'Ah, 'llow me man, I ain' got time t'be lettin' everybody know every single move I make. It's not as if I plan it or anythin' anyway, I jus' do it when I feel like doin' it.'

'Well you should feel like lettin' us know,' Boozy retorted casually. 'Anyway, we saw dat ting you done in the industrial estate on Mobley Way. It was good. How d'you expect us to get dat good by ourselves? We need you to help us.'

The girls' demands were getting on his nerves. He hated being pressured, too – especially by these wannabe writers, who seemed to have made pressuring him a way of life. He screwed up his face and flared his nose. 'I don't expect you to do nuthin' ...'

Something in Vanessa snapped and she rounded on him in anger.

'How come you're always goin' on so renk?' she suddenly spat, her face turning dark and thunderous. 'What've we done to cause you to go on like dat?'

Nemo looked at both girls silently, not knowing the real answer to Vanessa's question. He kissed his teeth and decided he couldn't take it any longer.

'Fuck it man, I can't handle dis ...'

He pushed past them agitatedly and nodded curtly at the other two girls, Melinda and Kate, before heading for the lifts without looking back. A great deal of curses followed him. Once inside and heading towards the eleventh floor, he made to lean his head against the lift's wall, then realised what he was doing and jumped quickly.

Well, you coulda handled dat better, he told himself, glancing up at the digital numbers flashing by the lift ceiling. He hated snapping at people like that, but it was uncontrollable most of the time — a reaction he found hard to contain. Vanessa wasn't that bad really, and she didn't deserve his rough treatment; but he was a solitary person and he detested people invading his space. Even now, so soon after having a go at her, he felt like apologising — but somehow he just couldn't; his mind and mouth wouldn't let him, he knew that already.

His floor was dark and grimy. Nemo paid it no mind as he let himself into his flat, flicking on the light switch and slamming his door shut behind him. He lived alone, but had previously shared the two-bedroom flat with his Gran, who'd died almost a year ago. Since then, the council grudgingly turned the place over to him. The living room and kitchen remained as his grandmother had left them; but as Nemo got closer to his bedroom, little ballpoint tags began to appear on places like the toilet door, and the wallpaper beside it – legacies to fellow graffiti artists who had visited his home. His bedroom door was covered in so many tags, it was impossible to see any trace of the white emulsion that had covered it before. Nemo shrugged his bag from his back and grasped it in his left hand, while turning the door handle and letting himself into the room — which over the years, had become more like a shrine to the pagan god of graff.

A huge spray-painted mural covered the whole of the largest wall, boasting the legend 'I love graff'. Behind the words was a six foot high cherub standing by a brick wall, dressed only in a fig leaf, and holding a can idly. The cherub had just finished spraying an enormous love-heart; the quiver on his back was filled with cans instead of arrows. On the opposite wall, a large white sheet was tacked to the ceiling, covered in a wildstyle piece — City Fever — which Nemo had done years ago. His TV and video perched precariously on a chair mid-centre of the room. His bed was a mattress on the floor; a floor which was covered in nozzles, and bits of paper, and pens, and spraycans, and magazines ...

A small desk and chair in the corner was the only neat spot in the room. A mug containing an array of pens sat on this, underneath a shelf packed tight with books and his sketches. Spread across the tiny desk was an A3 sheet of paper bearing a mosaic of colours and forms. Nemo approached this with a proud gleam in his eye, dropping his bag on the floor and pulling back his hood, taking in every line, every letter ... This was his masterpiece. His dream. His crowning achievement. This was his millennium piece.

Over three months, eight sheets of A3, and four boxes of coloured pencils had gone into this titanic example of artwork. The words Happy New Year 2000 exploded across the paper, while a huge muscular figure of a black man stretched his arms out wide behind them, fingers on either side of the sentence, as if he was squeezing the letters together. Even though his hands were full, the figure still had the time and presence of mind to be puffing on a fat head, which was glowing and smoking like a forest blaze. Beneath his jean clad thighs, the man's legs faded into a tableau of dancing, raving figures, of all ages, sexes and races.

No one had seen his work. It had been a top-secret design, told to none of the other hundred odd artists he knew, never even mentioned before today. God alone knew why he'd told Little Stacey and his crew of his intentions. He guessed it was because he admired the youth — he was clever, and funny, with a canny intuition wiser than his years and a healthy interest in the Art. Nemo had taken the seventeen-year-old out bombin' with him on a few occasions, and for the first time in ages, he'd felt comfortable with the company of a partner in crime. It was too early to say whether he was good enough to start grabbing the spraycan, but from what he'd seen of Little Stacey's pencil work, he had the potential to be a devastating graffiti artist.

Grudgingly, Nemo admitted to himself he was lonely. Since his Gran had died the flat had become forever cold, and way too quiet; plus he still felt her spirit moving through the house, watching over him. It didn't make him feel scared or anything, but to be frank and up-front, sometimes he ached for the sound of another voice. Preferably a female one. It was almost a new century for fuck's sake — and right about now he lived alone, worked alone, and played alone. Nemo needed a companion. Only he was too stubborn and shy to do anything about it.

The youth looked at his watch. Noting the time, he moved to his bed, stretching across to snap on the portable radio. Midnight FM (the estate's former pirate radio station) had been granted a three-month licence which ran a month into the New Year. Hip hop immediately filled Nemo's room. There were beats and a bassline for a second, then the tune got pulled up as the MC's voice interrupted, making him smile. He reached for his ashtray and found a half-smoked spliff, then fired it up eagerly.

'Pull dat one back my DJ, 'cos you know dat's the article ... Midnight FM rinsin' tonight wid the tunes of yesteryear, the soun's from way back. Dat one dere was the man Busta, Busta Rhymes for dat ass, "Everyt'ing Remains Raw ..." Dat's how we stay on Midnight R-A-W, so selekta drop the tune for da ol' skool massive an' crew . . .' The tune fired up and the beats rolled in, as crisp and tight as Nemo remembered it. Putting his loneliness to the back of his mind, he nodded his head, drew the spliff hard, and closed his eyes, relishing the fact that his moment had very nearly arrived.

Little Stacey was getting ready to go raving at a very restrained pace — he showered slowly, he creamed slowly, he got dressed extremely slowly; by the time he was looking at himself in his bedroom mirror proudly, he still didn't know if he was up for it. He was wearing a sky-blue silk Yves St Laurent shirt, which shimmered in the room's dull light, and a pair of brand new Versace jeans, which had both been bought on the MasterCard. His hair had been freshly cut back in the afternoon. His trainers came straight from the local JD Sports in Hammersmith.

The room was fairly neat and tidy for a seventeen-year-old's. It boasted an expensive and colourfully quilted double bed, an IKEA pine wardrobe with matching dressing table, and a whole Sony Hi Fi/TV/Video set up in one corner. The walls were rag-rolled lilac. A row of trainer and shoe boxes stood piled up on top of the wardrobe, and the half-open door displayed a whole row of shirts, jeans, tops and trousers. His mother never asked him where he'd got the money for all his stuff, as she had her own ways of making ends meet (through a catalogue scam she ran with her workmates). On the whole, the youth had a fairly untroubled home life, apart from a few run-ins with his cat of an older brother.

Stacey was listening to Midnight's hip hop show too, though only on the limits of his sub-conscious thought. He glanced at himself in the mirror again. He looked the lick. So how come everything seemed right — but felt so damn wrong? He sighed and flopped on his bed, just as his bedroom door knocked loudly. He flicked the radio off and the TV on, and yelled without looking.

'Come!'

It was his mother, Gayla, dressed in a skimpy black number that showed off lots of leg, and cleavage. She tottered into the room on high heels, and threw her arms out wide, grinning at him inanely.

'Ta-da!' she sang, in her husky, off-key tones. He stared at her.

'Go on den, wha' d'yuh reckon? Do I look sexy, or do I look sexy?'

Stacey gave her the teeniest of glances, then turned his attention back to the TV. 'Yeah, you look well sexy Mum,' he mumbled. 'You off out wid Lewis den?'

'Uh huh ...' Gayla smiled. 'He's takin' me to dinner, den we're gonna par-tay, I'm tellin' yuh ...'

She danced a few steps, making Stacey laugh and grin at her. Lewis was Sissy and Orin's father, and his mother's man-friend. Gayla had been in a relationship with him for the past two years — they seemed very happy together. Stacey was pleased for his mother, though his older brother Nicky seemed a little put out by the whole thing.

'You still goin' Rose Garden den?' Gayla continued, searching for, then finding, the tail of a spliff in his ashtray. She took it and lit up, dragging hungrily. Stacey paid her no mind, well-used to this by now.

'Yeah man ... I think so ... Uhh ... I dunno though man ...'

She squinted, then scrutinised him closer, finally seeing his morose pose and the foreboding look on his face. 'Are you okay?'

A pause. He thought about it deeply — contemplating acting hard about the whole thing, as he'd done with his friends earlier. Then he remembered he was talking to his mum — and according to her theory they could all be dead and gone by tomorrow. He decided to fess up.

'Ah, I dunno Mum — I jus' feel scared man — scared of what's gonna happen to us tomorrow. Every time I think about it my stomach goes weak. I tried tellin' Rochelle about it but she jus' reckons I'm bein' stoopid an' childish ... But I can't help it. I really think summick bad's gonna happen Mum. An I jus' feel so frightened ...'

The doorbell went. His mum looked reluctantly backwards, then returned her gaze to her son, regret filling her eyes. She walked over to him and put a warm hand on his head. 'It'll be all right Stace, nothin' bad's gonna happen tonight. It's a celebration, a step into a new era ...'

'Dat ain' wha' you was sayin' before!' he retorted. 'You was sayin' the end of the world was comin' an' all dat!'

Gayla shrugged, looking at the bedroom door again. The bell went once more, louder and more insistent. Stacey knew that for now at least, he'd lost his mother's attention. He ignored her hand, staring at the TV screen. Gayla looked torn.

'You know me, I chat the mos' shit innit luv — you should know better than to lissen what I gotta say innit?'

'I suppose,' he grumbled, not caring any more. 'You better go where yuh goin' innit, before Lewis gets mad an' dusses.'

His mother needed no further prompting. 'Okay den, I'm off,' she sang, passing the zook over to him. 'See you later, an' don't worry — dere's not gonna be any disasters or wars or anything; it's jus' another New Year, same as all the others. All right?'

'Yeah man safe. Have a good time, yeah?'

'You too darlin'. Happy millennium.'

'Yeah, happy millennium Mum.'

He let his head flop on to his duvet as his mum left the room, feeling lost and full of hopelessness. No one seemed to understand how he felt.

The front door shut. While his head was down and his eyes were closed, he heard his bedroom door open and footsteps shuffle inside. He stayed where he was, speaking loudly, though his voice was muffled by the covers.

'Can't you fuckin' knock?'

'Shut yuh mout' man. Gimme a spliff.'

'Nah man.'

'What?'

He looked up to see his brother Nicky standing there, large as life, dressed in his canary-yellow Excel suit, and a thin purple bandanna to hold in a head full of wild locks. He took after his father, who wasn't Stacey's, and was big, broad-chested and strong. Nicky was twenty-five, and also a Greenside badman who seemed to live to make his younger brother's life a misery.

'I said I ain' got nuttin' man,' Stacey spat angrily. He really wasn't in the mood to deal with this.

'Don't lie man, I can smell green in 'ere, an' I know you always got star.' Nicky went over to Stacey's cupboard and started pulling on drawers, searching for weed. Little Stacey raised himself off the bed and glared at his brother.

'Get the fuck out my drawers man, don't take 'berties in my room. Go an' fin' yuh owna tings, an' stop troublin' me fuh min'!'

Nicky kissed his teeth and kept on digging.

'You ain' findin' nuthin' in dere anyway, guaranteed.'

Nicky dug some more, opening every drawer, before he eventually saw Stacey was right. Kissing his teeth again, he slammed the drawer shut, then got up and walked across the room.

'Fuckin' sap,' he sneered, before leaving and slamming the bedroom door too.

Stacey rolled his eyes and stuck a finger up at the closed door, then turned over on his back, staring at the ceiling. His head hurt, and he really didn't need his brother making it feel any worse. Maybe everything that was happening was a bad omen for the night. Maybe he shouldn't rave. But then, if he didn't go out, what else could he do? He sure as fuck wasn't going to hang around Greenside waiting to see in the year 2000, that much was for sure. So what could he do?

He contemplated ringing his girl Rochelle and telling her he wasn't coming out tonight. He knew she'd be livid. He knew she wouldn't understand. Rochelle was an ebony-coloured dream, full of curves and soft spots, though as serious and business-minded as any of his friends. They worked well together, their families loved each other, and they both looked good too. She was the rock in his stormy street-life, even though he sometimes wondered which one of them was deeper involved in its complexities.

He got up from the bed, went over to his bedroom door, and turned the lock easily, so Nicky wouldn't hear. Then he crept over to his wardrobe and pulled until it jutted out at an angle to the wall. He bent down and retrieved a thick package wrapped in a towel, then put the package down on the bed. He unwrapped it, then stared as if hypnotised.

There lay half a kilo; and at least twenty prepacked ten-pound bags of weed. Benji had secured some bone, and Orin had Es — between the three of them, they planned to run the whole rave red. Rochelle and the rest of the girls said they didn't mind holding the drugs while the boys got searched by Rose Garden's bouncers, so everything was cool. That was why he couldn't stay home tonight. There was money to be made, as well as fun to be had.

All at once, he heard a light tapping on his door. Alarmed, he jumped up from the bed and stared about the room as if a whole platoon of police officers had burst inside, holding search warrants and sniffer dogs. His eyes grew hard and determined.

'Who is it?' he barked fearfully.

'Nemo man,' the voice came back. 'Come to bun dat millennium ziggy, y'get me.'

Relief made Little Stacey's face young again. He let out a breath of air and relaxed a bit. 'Hol' up!' he yelled at the graffiti artist, picking up one of the ten bags and putting it in his pocket quickly. After that, he wrapped up the weed and pushed it back behind his wardrobe, then he pushed the wardrobe until it clunked against the skirting board. Behind the door, Nemo was sighing exaggeratedly.

'Come on, wha' you doin' in dere star, palmin'?'

'Free dat,' Stacey grumbled in return. He walked over and opened the door. Nemo strolled inside, his rucksack drooping on his back and rattling with the sound of numerous aerosol cans. He looked as if he was wearing at least two jumpers under his hooded top; and a thick scarf was wrapped across his face. The youths clasped hands tightly, then Nemo went back to the door and pushed it shut. When he pulled the scarf away from his mouth and spoke, his voice was a coarse whisper.

'Ay, wha's your brudda goin' on wid Stace? Man was actin' like he wanned to kick off wid me or summick.'

Stacey shrugged.

'Don't watch my brudda man, he jus' smokes too much shit,' he explained casually. He noticed the rucksack and pointed at it. 'All set fuh tonight den?' he smiled.

'Yeah yeah ...' Nemo sat on the bed and beamed back at the youth. 'I can't wait star — I'm gonna make sure dis is the bes' ting I ever did. For real. I got the vibe man, everyt'ing's right ...'

He trailed off, still beaming at nothing. Stacey sat on the bed beside him, feeling a little envious at his friend's good cheer.

'Wanna buil' it?'

'You do it man,' Nemo muttered hoarsely.

'Nah, go on — I can't be bothered.'

'Ahh — all right, gimme the Rizla den.'

Stacey dug in his pocket for the ten drawer, passed everything over, then flicked the radio on again. They sat in silence for a while. There was a freestyle rapping session going on, and they listened intently for at least five minutes.

'Brer's all right y'nuh,' Nemo finally commented, giving the last lick to his spliff. Stacey raised his eyebrows in acknowledgement.

'Yeh man, he soun' ruff ... What time you gettin' started Mo?'

The graffiti artist made a face. 'When I feel like it I suppose. I dunno.'

'I wish I could come out dere wid you.'

Nemo turned to the youth seriously, regarding him through glazed eyes. 'Why don't you? I could do wid a man to help me get along, y'get me? You ain' worked on a piece before 'ave you?'

'Nahh . . .' Little Stacey looked lost for a minute, and slightly bewildered. Then he shook his head, as if he suddenly remembered all he had to do. 'Nahh, I can't do it man. I affa make some carn tonight Mo, I can't go into the nex' Century wid broke pockets, y'unnerstan'?'

'You look like yuh doin' all right,' his friend pointed out. Stacey twitched his nose in the beginnings of a scowl and rubbed his forehead absently.

'Yeah, but I affa maintain star. Keep up the hard work, y'get me? Dese tings don't pay for demselves y'nuh.'

Nemo nodded slowly. 'All right den blood, whatever. But yuh welcome to come wid me if you change you min'.'

'Where you gonna be?'

'You know the big wall dat runs along the side of the BBC, in BBC park?'

There was a moment of silence, before Stacey's eyes went as wide as saucers. Nemo laughed at his expression.

'What?'

Stacey shook his head, then began to join in with the laughter. 'Yes bredrin!' he chuckled, reaching over to touch his fist. 'You definitely ain' rampin' star, honest to God!'

'You know me, man,' Nemo replied modestly.

Little Stacey's Nokia cried out insistently, like a lonely child begging for attention. He rolled over and picked it up swiftly. It dropped out of his hand and on to the floor with a thump.

'Fuck!'

The phone was still ringing. Urgently, he leaned over the bed and grabbed it, stabbing at the send button with a hasty finger.

'Yeah yeah . . . Oh, y'all right babes whassup . . . Huh? Oh, I jus' dropped the bloodclaat phone, dat's all . . . Nah man minor, it's safe . . . Yeh man . . . Anyway, I'm gonna come an' link you up soon, I jus' gotta knock for Ray . . . He's got the rental innit? I'll be about a hour, no more than dat . . . All right babes . . . Soon come . . .' He rang off. Nemo was smiling.

'Rochelle?'

Stacey smiled back and nodded. 'Yeah man. She's sensible man, even gimme some money to help me juggle the green. She's seventeen too, but she's clued up mate.'

'So yuh definitely goin' ravin' tonight den?'

Little Stacey nodded slowly. 'Yeah man, it look so innit? I can't let dem man down tonight man, they're relyin' on me, y'get me?'

'Safe man ...'

Nemo got up from the bed and touched Stacey's fist. 'I'm gonna miss out, but 'ave a good jump up for me anyway, yeah?'

'Done know! If anyt'ing when I'm comin' back from Garden I might pass BBC park y'get me. See wha' gwaan ...'

'Cool. You take care yeah.'

'Yeah man.'

Stacey watched Nemo leave with a small amount of regret in his face. His bad feelings for tonight hadn't diminished any — they'd merely been pushed to the back of his mind by other thoughts. Alone in his room once more, these thoughts attacked his brain mercilessly. Five minutes after Nemo left, he picked up his jacket, keys and One2One, and decided he was going to Ray's right there and then.

It was almost time. Nemo walked as if in a surreal dream world, between the blocks that made up the west side of his estate, and through the streets that were filled with scores and scores of people by now ... The whistles and foghorns had got louder, and some flats, although dark, were blazing with the sounds of music and party-chatter. He could hear louder music coming from the street-party on the east of the estate. Fireworks lit up the sky. High above them, blimps owned by large companies floated like air bubbles, bearing messages welcoming the new century. A huge digital clock atop of Denver House counted down the minutes and seconds until blast off, saying; 10.05: 35 ... 36 ... 37 ...

Nemo ignored it. He didn't really want to know.

People he knew called him; he'd simply wave, exchange greetings, and walk on. Raw excitement filled his whole being. His fingers clenched and unclenched by his sides, stiff with cold, but eager to do work once the time came. His eyes gleamed fanatically.

He was passing the shops when he saw the four girls again — Vanessa, Boozy, Kate and Melinda — drinking from small champagne bottles and smoking cigarettes, as though they'd just come from the off-licence. He felt bad enough to want to walk straight past the lot of them, but suppressed his feelings with an iron-will; instead, he made a direct bee-line for the group. Boozy and the others looked shocked at his movements, while Vanessa turned away, acting as if she hadn't seen him. Nemo walked square into her path, then stopped and stared hard. Vanessa continued to ignore him.

Boozy (his good friend Boozy!), gave him a little reprieve.

'Hey Nemo, whassup?'

'Safe y'nuh. Y' all right Melinda, Kate?'

'Yeeaah,' came the reply. They were too busy watching him and Vanessa to even bother saying anything.

'Oi Vanessa, can I 'ave a word a minute?' he asked, somewhat awkwardly. She crossed her arms and gave him a soul-piercing glare, her top lip pushed out in an angry pout.

'For what?'

'I jus' wanna talk to you man, don' go on like dat.'

Her hands fell by her sides and her head constantly moved in aggressive posture. Her voice was loud and filled with emotion. 'Why shouldn't I go on like dis? You take the piss lettin' off on me like dat for no reason Nemo, I ain' done nothin' to you for you to carry on wid dem fuckries I don' response. An' furthermore you should be grateful dere's someone so interested in you an' what you're doin', instead of actin' like I'm some kinna leech dat's gonna suck yuh talent dry. I can't believe the 'berties you was goin' on wid back dere man, I bin brewin' ever fuckin' since man, you're way out of order star . . .'

Nemo looked at the others, gazed around at the sky a bit, then faced Vanessa full on. 'I know . . .'

She stopped mid-sentence, frowned, then blinked. 'Eh?'

'I said I—' He looked at Boozy again. She seemed stunned, her mouth hanging open; but there was a faint smile around the corners too. Melinda and Kate didn't look that much different. Nemo started again.

'Look, can I jus' talk to you over dere a sec?'

He was pointing at the small park across the road from the shops. Mutely, Vanessa nodded yes, so they turned and walked until they reached the park gates, then turned and stared at each other. Above them, the fireworks screamed and exploded in twos, threes and fours. The variety of colours was endless. The very air was electric, and both of them felt it; there was no doubt about that.

'Did I hear you right?' Vanessa started, her face bemused and unsure.

'Yeah man you did, an' don't go inta one about it, dis is hard enough as it fuckin' is. Basically — I want you to come wid me while I do dis piece tonight — I mean, I'd really like your company. D'wanna come?'

She put her hands on her hips and kissed her teeth. 'Is dat meant to be a apology?'

Nemo sighed. 'C'mon Nessa — I know I was outta order earlier, an' I realise I bin goin' on dark. It's ... It's really hard for me to do shit like dis, so ease me up will yuh?'

'So am I s'pposed t'be sorry for yuh? An' why should I ease you up? Was you easy wid me though?'

More fireworks. This time they were white, like small flashes of lightning which illuminated Vanessa's friends standing across the road from them. A group of boys passed the group, then stopped and started chirping. The girls responded casually, their eyes and attentions on the scenario being acted out in front of them.

'So what, gimme yuh number nuh Melinda.'

'You got a man? I know you got a man innit?'

'I got champers at my drum y'nuh Boozy — come we go an' celebrate the New Year ...'

Eventually, Melinda turned to the boys and addressed them fiercely. 'Will you go away Jason, we ain' goin' nowhere an' drinkin' champers, we're waitin' on our friend den we're goin' to the street-party — all right?'

The youth called Jason pushed his hands into his mac and shook his newly-grown locks. 'All right man, fuck you lot den star,' he growled, before he and his friends bounced off. Boozy just heard this last and turned to see their departing backs.

'Wha' you tellin' us to fuck off for Jason? You think yuh men? You lot ain' nuttin' but boys star, done know. Go home an' play at bein' men!'

One of the youths, a dark stocky guy, made to turn back; but his friends, including Jason, held him by the arm and persuaded him otherwise. There was an aura of displeasure around them as they left. The girls dismissed them and turned back to Vanessa and Nemo, who were still talking.

'So what, are you comin' wid me or what?' Nemo was saying exasperatedly.

The girl rolled her eyes and looked away across the pitch black park. 'See, you can't even ask me properly Nemo — is dat s'pposed to make me wanna go?'

He sighed with venom and folded his arms. 'Nah man, you're s'pposed to come 'cos you wanna come innit,' he hissed at her, feeling foolish even as he said it. 'Lissen man — we're bredrins ain' we?'

'Sometimes — when you ain' in a mood.'

'But we get on don't we? If someone asked you if me an' you got on, what would you say?'

'Nemo ...'

'Nah man, what would you say?'

Her fingers began to play nervously with her bangles; yet again, she couldn't look him in the eye.

'I'd say we got on wouldn't I? What else would I say?'

''Cos we never had a argument before today innit?'

Nemo sounded almost desperate. Funnily enough, Vanessa

found the sight of this didn't give her any pleasure. Still, she had to speak her mind.

'Yeah we've never had a argument before today, but dat don't mean you've ever treated me as a friend Nemo. To tell the truth, you're usually rude, dismissive, opinionated . . .'

Nemo's mouth opened wide in a loud gasp. 'Wha'?'

'It's fuckin' true Nemo, don't gimme dat look, you know I ain' tellin' no lie!'

He stuttered a bit, before he finally managed to find the words that formed his defence. Up until that point, what Vanessa had said stung like a handful of nettles. ''Nessa man, will you 'llow me an' face the fac' dat I'm sorry. Dere yuh go — I'm sorry. I'm fucked up. I'm wrong. Is dat all right now — can we go?'

Long pause. They stared at each other with such an intense and deep gaze, they both got scared and looked away. Nemo felt his stomach churn in a way that he hadn't allowed it in years. It left him feeling hollow, and desperate to see it reflected in Vanessa's eyes again.

Unfortunately she kept her head down, looking at the dirty pavement beneath them. She sighed deeply, in a way that made his heart catch in his throat.

'No it ain' all right, but it don't matter,' she said warily. 'I don't think I've ever seen you dat sorry lookin' in all the time I know you. I s'ppose dat mus' count for summick.'

He rubbed his hooded head and shrugged, a little embarrassed. Vanessa shook hers and took a few, tiny steps towards him.

'Don't you ever take dat hood off? It'd be good to see yuh face sometimes . . .'

He pulled the hood back and let it fall to his shoulders. She smiled, and he began to smile back. They stood like that for quite a while.

Across the road, Melinda and Kate were looking puzzled. 'Wha's goin' on?' Melinda said rapidly, her eyebrows knotted and tense. 'Shall we go over an' tell her we gotta go?'

A slow smile took over Boozy's face, which the girl found

impossible to remove. 'Nah man, leave her star,' she grinned, her eyes never leaving the couple. 'To tell you the trut', I don't think she's goin' anywhere wid us tonight.'

'Damn,' both Melinda and Kate breathed, virtually simultaneously. The three girls looked at one another and cracked up.

The rented Espace shook with the bass. Ray steered the ride fluidly through the traffic-laden streets, a blazing zook in his mouth, and an un-popped can of Red Stripe between his legs; beside him, Little Stacey and his girl Rochelle were both hurriedly building theirs, while behind them, Benji, Robby, Ryan, Orin, Malcolm, Sissy and Valentine, all drank from a multitude of champagne bottles and shouted over the beats. Orin poured a little of his champagne on to the van's carpeted floor. Little Stacey saw him and went mad.

'Oi, Oi, wha' the fuck you doin' man!' he shouted, turning around as much as he could, and holding his half built spliff in one hand. Orin gave him a blank look.

'Wha's up wid you?'

'Don't pour drink on the floor man, dis tings gotta go back tommora!'

'Fuck dat man, I'm pourin' for the mans dat ain' here innit? For Johnny man!' Orin replied, his voice filled with righteous indignation.

'Yeah man,' Ray spoke up. 'For Johnny!'

He drove one-handed for a moment, and turned the ring pull of his Red Stripe to face the steering wheel. He popped it with his first finger, lifted the can up, and poured a splash on to the floor in between his feet. Stacey couldn't be bothered to argue after that. Johnny Winsome had been one of Ray's closest friends; he'd been knocked down by an out-of-control motorcycle on Bush Green eight months ago, and died on the spot. The youths all became silent at the same time — briefly, the music and the Espace's engine were the only sounds in the car.

'Yeah, we miss you blood,' Malcolm suddenly murmured,

echoing everybody's feelings. Valentine nodded, then shrugged and reached for another bottle of champagne.

'Yeah, but don't dead the vibe man! Don't dead the vibe!' he warned them, almost toppling over as the van turned a corner.

'Done know!' Benji yelled, as usual speaking at the top of his voice.

Little Stacey smiled and shook his head — his love for the friends he'd known all his life stirring him as it never had before. He turned back around and winked at Rochelle. She clutched his hand and put her head on his shoulder gently.

And the Espace cruised on.

'You sure yuh all right to jump dat fence?' Nemo asked Vanessa worriedly, around ten minutes after they'd finished their conversation by the other park gates. His voice was hushed and his manner gentle — he'd been acting that way for a while now, and Vanessa wasn't sure if she liked it. Still, she supposed it made a welcome change from his usual brash self. She turned to him with a hint of pride at being able to affect him in that way.

''Course I'll be all right. I ain' a invalid y'know.'

'Yeah I know.'

'Good.'

Another long intense stare. Vanessa broke it off again and turned to the fence, grasping it with both hands and hoisting herself upwards with a faint grunt. She scrabbled and kicked until she was at the top, then swung her tracksuited leg over and sat astride the wall running beside BBC park's gates. Actually, it was called Hammersmith Park, but it wasn't in Hammersmith and no one gave a fuck about its real name anyway. Vanessa looked down on Nemo and stuck her tongue out at him sassily.

'Quick den,' she called with a cocky grin. He nodded and swung the rucksack.

'Catch,' he ordered, before throwing it up to her. She caught it and let herself drop on the other side of the wall.

Nemo followed her swiftly, and within no time they were

both strolling through the darkened park's confines with sturdy, yet quiet steps. They crossed a small stone footbridge which overlooked a black mossy pond, then Vanessa hopped from foot to foot and pointed at a cluster of trees.

'Gotta pee. All dat drink's gone right through me.'

'Cool.'

He waited while she darted off, his stomach tugging with tension. Vanessa was really all right. Now he was looking at her differently, he'd seen an amazing number of things he'd never even noticed about her before — and all of them were good. The way she smiled. The smell of her hair (they'd hugged as a gesture of solidarity back in Greenside — now the scent was lodged in his mind like a corn kernel between teeth). The smooth, rounded curve of her body, apparent even through the baggy tracksuit bottoms she was wearing. It was as if she'd blossomed into a new person right in front of him . . . Nah, fuck that; it was like a veil had been removed from his eyes, and he'd allowed himself to feel what he'd denied for so long. Fuck the self-analysis, he sneered to himself cynically. You're just lonely on New Year's Eve — dat's all.

But it was more than that, and he knew it. His grandmother, God rest her soul, had often commented on his solitary lifestyle; though he'd shrugged it off and claimed he was happy. He wondered if he'd just been fooling himself all that time, and he'd simply been scared of the natural process of bonding with someone. If so, that definitely had to change.

It's nearly the year 2000 — I can't be on my own no more man!

Vanessa was tramping through the trees, coming back towards him with a look of relaxed relief. As she got nearer to him, she reached out and clutched his hand.

'Dere's a whole load o' used condoms in dat little area,' she told him candidly.

He grunted and squeezed the offered hand, accepting it as easily as he'd accepted her statement. They walked that way until they reached the long wall that formed a concrete boundary around the park, then they stared at it, subdued by what they were about to do. On the other side of the wall, towering over them, stood the broad silhouette of the BBC building — the biggest live studio space in Europe. White lights across the side made it look like an alien craft that had just docked. It cast some light on Nemo and Vanessa, but not much.

'Well?' Vanessa said, when she decided they'd stood there long enough. Nemo nodded, let go of her hand, then dropped the rucksack where they stood and studied the wall carefully. After his quiet scrutiny, he dug inside the bag and produced some hefty looking cans.

'Krylons an' Beltons,' Nemo said proudly, throwing one of the cans over to Vanessa. She took it and read the label. 'Bes' paint you can get man, gi' you the livin' colours y'nuh. I'm gonna use a thin cap to sketch the outlines, den a fatter one to fill all dat shit in. Fat caps use up more paint, but deal wid the fill-ins quicker.'

'Okay . . .' the girl said dubiously, coming a little closer. 'What d'you want me to do for now?'

'Uhhh . . .'

The graffiti artist was getting his folded A3 sheet out of his pocket, using it as a sketch for what would eventually end up on the wall. He clicked his pocket Maglight on, and frowned down at it, before he remembered that he'd heard Vanessa speak on the edge of his hearing.

'You can't do nuffin' for now Nessa, besides keep watch. I don't fancy spending New Year in a police cell.'

'Yuh damn right,' she replied, stamping her feet on the grass to keep warm. Nemo gave her a look, but she made a face and shrugged.

'I'm all right, I'll jus' plot here an' let you get on wid it.'

'Okay . . .' he muttered, his voice already distant and far away.

She smiled to herself and sat of the grass with her legs crossed, in a very prim and proper way.

Nemo began. He used long strokes of his arm to paint the outline — Vanessa watched, but the lines meant nothing to her, and she could make no sense of what the youth was doing. Nemo would spray, think, then turn to the A3 and see whether what was on the wall matched up with what he had there. Then he was back to his task — jumping up when he had to, blowing on drips, and using his thumb to ease surplus paint away.

After half an hour of watching and saying almost nothing, Vanessa got up and stood by his side. Nemo was stuck in one of his contemplative moments, rubbing his stubble-covered chin and gazing at the wall. Eventually he looked down on her and smiled.

'Wha d'you reckon?'

'Don't make much sense to me at the moment. But dat looks good,' she replied, inclining her head at his penciled sketch. He winked at her.

'Don't worry yuhself man, it'll come together soon enough,' he promised, with the confidence of a seasoned professional.

'Bettah get on wid it den.'

'Yeah yeah . . .'

The character of the huge muscle-bound man took a bit longer to outline, and a great deal more of Nemo's concentration. He used chalk to do this at first, as it gave more room for mistakes — then when he was happy with what he'd done, he went over this with the spraycan.

'Oh yeah,' Vanessa drawled, peeking over his shoulder at the original. She could finally see where he was going. The piece was slowly taking shape.

Soon, the whole outline was finished, including the ravers and all. It was just before eleven thirty. Nemo coughed and sat by the girl, taking a well earned break. He dug a can of Coke from his bag, then popped it, drunk half, and gave the rest to Vanessa. She took it, then rubbed his thigh with one hand proudly.

'Looks good,' she smiled.

'Cheers man. It'll be better once I get started on the colours an' dat. Den I'll do the highlights an' dedications . . .'

'I hope I get one!'

247

''Course you will ... An' after dat I'll be done.'

She leaned back. Nemo watched, trying to suppress the feelings she was giving him. 'How long d'you reckon dat'll take?'

'Hopefully, not too long.'

'How long's dat?'

'I dunno ... 'bout half hour. We should be finished jus' after twelve.'

'An' wha' we gonna do after dat?' she asked, watching him hard. Nemo laughed, hoping the harsh sound covered his nervousness.

'Whatever you wanna do. I live alone if yuh interested ...'

She gave a wry grin. 'I know dat ... Anyway ...'

As soon as she stopped talking, Nemo knew it was time for trouble. He glanced at her, to see her mouth was open and her eyes were wide.

'Shit Nemo ...'

He turned the way she was facing. Outside the park gates, car headlights could be seen, and the muted barking of dogs was heard, even over the idling sound of the car's engine. One look told him who it was. He got up, reached for her hand, and pulled her to her feet as one of the newcomers fumbled with the keys for the park gates. They had very little time.

'Park policeman. We gotta duss!' he hissed at her, already lamenting the loss of his rucksack — there was no way he was going to slow himself down by going for it or his paint. Any ordinary girl would've frozen, or screamed, or gone into hysterics right there and then — but Vanessa, like it or not, was a Ghetto girl — and little things like running from the police meant nothing to someone who had done it on numerous occasions.

In other words, Vanessa legged it.

They ran towards the other set of park gates, the ones nearest Greenside, as the men behind them began to shout and yell for them to stop; but obviously there was no chance of that. Once there, they threw themselves at it like army cadets on an assault course, as the barking dogs began to get closer and closer. Vanessa got to the top first, and reached out a hand to haul Nemo up.

The dogs, three hungry looking Alsatians, reached the foot of the gates snarling and baring their teeth at the youths.

'Fuck you man!' Nemo yelled, throwing himself over on to the other side. The lights and sounds of partying from Greenside were as welcoming as outstretched arms. He dusted himself off and flipped up his hood.

'We wanna get goin' about swearin' up the place,' Vanessa chided him motherly. Nemo nodded, knowing she was right.

A police car roared past them, then screeched to a stop a hundred metres from where they stood. Nemo felt his stomach plummet. He looked back at the park, to see running figures heading their way. The police car changed gears, and started reversing back to them.

'Fuck. Tings ain' done y'nuh Nessa.'

'Come den.'

They sprinted into Greenside, with the police screaming insults behind them. Past Denver House, past Makenzie, on towards Rockwood ...

When they reached this block Nemo skidded to a halt, a deep and thoughtful look on his face. The bay at the bottom of Rockwood's rubbish chute was standing wide open, with the litter-filled bin pushed inside. He stared at it, entranced by the implications it held. Vanessa looked the same way, then tugged at his hand.

'C'mon ...'

'We better find somewhere to hide ...' Nemo said quickly.

She'd known why he stopped, but still hoped she could change his mind.

'No way! I ain' goin in dere man, you gotta be kiddin'!'

'D'you wanna get shif'?'

'Wha' d'you think?'

It was quiet for now, but who knew how long it would be before sirens invaded the area. Vanessa kissed her teeth. Nemo took that as consent, and darted into the bay with the reluctant girl being pulled along behind him. Once inside, they heaved the door shut as best as they could and stood straight as pool cues, trying not to touch a single thing.

It was disgusting. An unearthly stink pervaded the whole bay, making Vanessa feel sick within two seconds flat. She could honestly kill Nemo. Fuming, she pulled her hand away when he reached for it, and her face had a stubborn, miserable set.

'We'll be out soon enough anyhow,' Nemo whispered. 'The rats probably won't even bother lookin' for us, they got too much to do dis . . .'

The sound of running feet came from outside, then sirens and crackles from police radios. They gave each other resigned looks, then slowly shrank back against the huge bin. There was scratching, then the squeak of some kind of rodent that had joined them.

Vanessa decided she better take Nemo's hand after all.

The Rose Garden was packed. Little Stacey squeezed his way through the people, two cans of Holstein balanced in one hand, two in the other, his eyes scanning the shuffling, moving ravers. The bar behind him was covered in a sea of punters, most of them shouting orders at the staff, and dripping thick sweat droplets on to the beer mats. MCs rode the tunes with a laid-back kind of ease, under the seamless beats that London's top DJs were spinning. Women were pushing their bodies to the limits with sensual, carefree movements. Men either watched them, danced with them, or smoked any one of the many types of drug being consumed inside the venue.

The others were plotted in a dark corner of the hall, already jamming to the sounds of Garage, the floor they'd all decided on. It was half eleven. Stacey gave his girl one of the drinks. He gave the other two to Benji and Ray, while Orin stepped in behind him, his hands just as full as Stacey's had been.

'Hear what now, I'm goin' back f'dat barmaid blood!' he yelled in the youth's ear, making Stacey smile and nod vigorously.

'Yeah man, look like she was on it!'

'F'real she was on it!' Orin babbled. 'Dis time now I ask her where her man was an' she tell me she done wid him two days ago! All her bredrin's are 'ere wid their geezers an' she's on her jones! She reckons she ain' seein' in the New Year like dat! I mus' get a little work tonight star, trus' me!'

'Bes' hol' dat down before some other brer fly in dere den,' his friend warned seriously. 'I see nuff man clockin' dem breas' boy.' Orin popped the can and waggled his thick eyebrows.

'Dat's held man, nuh worry yuhself wi' dat! I'm gonna cotch wid the mans dem, den burs' over dere an' gi' 'er some agony blood! Ain' no way I'm lettin' dat suttin' get 'way tonight!'

'Don't,' Stacey agreed, turning his attention to Rochelle once more. She smiled widely at him, held her arms out and wound her body low, her short skirt riding up high on her thighs. Stacey joined her, close and rhythmic, feeling her heat and loving the look of concentration on her face. They came back up. Rochelle laughed and threw her arms around his neck, pulling him close and burying her head in his neck.

'Fuck you goin' wid all dat wind up dancin'?' he grinned, speaking close into her ear and making her wriggle in a way that excited his lower parts no end.

'Yeah, yuh know yuh love it though innit!' she retorted truthfully.

'Yuh damn right!'

'Never know, play yuh cards right an' yuh might get piece in 'ere tonight,' she said, wriggling away from him and sliding over to where Carolyn, Sissy and the rest of the girls were.

Little Stacey grinned to himself, thinking that the special occasion seemed to have turned everybody into sex freaks. All around Rose Garden's four floors the youths had seen embracing couples; some just kissing and feeling, but others very obviously making love. Even when he took closer note of the darker places in this very lively hall area, he could see shadowy figures that moved from positions that seemed very suspicious. When he turned around Rochelle was back again, forever dancing while she stared at him a little lustfully.

'Gettin' horny are yuh?' she asked, beaming like a minx and inclining her head at one of the more frenzied sets of lovers.

'What, are you or summick?' he returned, part of him half-hoping she was. She giggled and shook her head, her white teeth gleaming.

'Not yet — but at midnight; well, you never know do yuh?'

'Yeah, well jus' make sure you let me know,' he yelled, swaggering away from her while she swiped at his arm and mouthed the word 'silly'.

Stacey left his crew and headed for the flight of stairs that ran outside the hall, looking for a change of scene. Orin caught him up, grabbed his arm, then followed him through as far as the bar.

'How yuh jus' leave yuh girl like dat bredrin?' the older youth wanted to know, his head bopping along to the bass.

'Ah, Rochelle's safe, she don't need to know where I'm goin all the while,' Stacey responded easily. 'She's secure in 'erself blood; I love dat about 'er.'

'You know, dat's a good woman you got dere,' Orin agreed with venom. 'Got a good head on her shoulders too. I'm gonna go see if I can link up a good woman too,' he finished, his eyes back on the bar.

'Yeah yeah. Good luck an' dat star, I know you'll get t'rough,' Stacey replied. Orin was off in two seconds flat. Stacey made for the stairs, embedding himself in the crowd and following their flow.

Soon enough he found himself on the Hip Hop floor. Everyone was jumping wildly, and the basslines were making the walls and door frames shake and vibrate as if they had a life of their own. Just as on the floor he'd left a moment ago, Moschino, Versace, Armani, and Tommy Hilfiger garms ruled, while other less-expensive name brands were scattered loosely among the people. Crews of badmen waded through the dancers with no qualms about how they did it; if anybody complained, a look was all it took to shut them up.

Stacey walked about until he saw a crew of white boys dressed in baggy jeans, T-shirts, and heavy-looking trainers. He approached them and sidled alongside the nearest shiftily.

'Lookin' green?'

The brown-haired youth glanced up, then saw who had spoken and gave his head the tiniest of shakes, before returning his gaze to the floor. Stacey gave the others an enquiring stare — only one, a tall lanky guy, with a reassuring gleam in his eye, could hold his gaze. The Greenside youth gave up. Sometimes it wasn't annoying, shameful, or frustrating when people were so obviously scared of you. Sometimes it was just plain old tiring.

He left the youths, wandering through the crowd once more, and mouthing the word 'Green', every time someone looked his way. He'd only gone six or seven steps when a firm hand grasped his shoulder. Stacey turned to see the lanky white youth he'd just left.

'Whassup blood?'

'Hear what now, did yuh say you 'ad weed mate?' the youth asked eagerly. Little Stacey nodded.

'Yeah man, the lick cross star, boun' to mash you up f'the night, y'get me?'

'Gotta quartz?'

Stacey shook his head sadly.

'Nah man, bere johns is runnin' tonight mate. It's all I come out wid innit.'

'Ah, what.'

The white guy looked pissed off. Stacey studied him a while, thinking. 'Tell you what — I'll gi' yuh three johns for a score five — can't say fairer than dat can yuh mate? They're all two grams, so you ain' losin' out.'

'You can do dat?'

'Yeah man safe. Come we fin' a corner an' we'll sort t'ings out.'

They walked until they found an area where the crowd thinned a little. Stacey got out three bags and passed them over. The white boys gave him a twenty and a ten. Stacey gave him his change with a nod.

'What's yuh name mate?'

'Simon,' the youth replied.

'Where yuh from?'

'Grove.'

'Ladbroke?'

'Arnos.'

'Seen—'

Stacey put the money away, while glancing around to see if anyone had noticed. There were no security guards present, but a worrying-looking knot of teenagers around his age were watching him talk with Simon; none of them were dancing, some were smoking, and all were wearing Rolexs, and at least five hundred pounds' worth of clothes. Stacey wasn't sure about it, but on his manor he'd mark the youths down as earnatons. Out there youts. Street robbers in plain English. He didn't like the way they were staring at him, but he was fucked if he was going to back down. The disquiet in his stomach returned, but double the strength this time. Fuck dem fools, his inner voice told him. You ain' even tooled up ...

But Raymond was. He'd made Siân smuggle a .22 past the bouncers in her knickers — uncomfortable, but very necessary if you were planning to sell drugs in raves these days, as things were getting very hectic. Stacey decided not to push his luck, and go and find his crew before their crew got any ideas. If anything, once he linked them up, he could come back up here and see what the fools in the corner had to say then.

He turned to Simon and touched a fist with him lightly. 'Hear what now blood, I'm missin'. Happy New Year an' all dat, enjoy the green.'

'Nice one mate,' Simon replied, before rejoining his paranoid friends in the middle of the dance floor.

Stacey was off as soon as the youth's back was turned, twisting and turning his way through the crowd, not looking back until he'd reached the bar area. He paused. When he looked back over in the corner, the crew of earners were gone. He cursed himself and wondered what that meant.

'Shit ...'

He wouldn't run. He refused to run. Stubbornly, he leaned over the packed bar trying to get some staff attention. Just as he caught a plump white woman's eye, an arm was thrown around his shoulder and right around his neck. Stacey jumped a little, as he felt the knife-point in his back. Two of the youths pushed past the people on either side of him, inserting themselves roughly in their occupied spaces. Both removed parties thought the better of arguing, and found another spot to stand in. The youth behind Stacey, the one with the knife, leaned over and spoke in his ear coarsely, so only the Greensider could hear.

'Me bredrins dem waan brandy an' coke, so yuh better mek dat t'ree, y'unnerstan'. After dat we're gonna go for a little bop. Talk about all dat wong you got for us, yuh n'mean?'

The woman behind the bar stared at Little Stacey, perhaps guessing something was wrong, but not quite sure. He leaned a little further over the bar, croaked 'T'ree brandy an' cokes,' then hoped and prayed Ray would come and get him out of the very serious shit he'd landed in.

Police cars seemed be everywhere. Vanessa and Nemo crouched beside the huge rubbish bin, waiting for the sirens to die down, just as they'd been waiting for the last thirty minutes — although the minutes had passed like hours to the girl. The stink coming from the bin was terrible. Every so often, there'd be a rattling, clunking sound from high above them, as someone put their night's load of bottles and other rubbish into the chute. The noise would then get louder and louder the closer it got to the ground floor, before falling into the bin with an explosion of glass and rank odours. She clutched Nemo's arm every time this happened, and he'd hold her tightly and shush her, his attentions on the noises of patrolling cars outside.

Eventually, the noises stopped altogether. When five more minutes passed, he nodded at her. They stood up, their knees popping, and pushed their way to the outside world.

The streets were alive with kids running around with their faces painted, looking like pygmy warriors who'd given up on the fighting for now. Their laughter was wild and manic, but for once the adults let them get on with it. Every block seemed to have a party going on. High up on Denver house, the huge digital clock said: 11.59:22 ... 23 ... 24 ...

Vanessa and Nemo looked at each other and grinned.

At a sudden thought, Nemo took his hooded Nike top off, balled it up, and went back to the rubbish bin. When he came back, he took off one of his jumpers and gave it to the girl.

'Jus' in case,' he told her seriously.

'Thank you,' she replied, looking at him with emotion-filled eyes. She put the jumper on and shrugged into it, waving at some kids she knew as she did so. Nemo touched her arm.

'Hey, d'wanna go to the street-party or summick? I can't be bothered to go back to dat piece now, it ain' gonna get done in time anyway. We might as well jam or summick man, I dunno. Everyone'll be dere. All yuh bredrins an' dat.'

Vanessa looked shocked at his words for the second time that night.

'Are you feelin' all right? I thought you'd be brewin' about not finishin' up back dere. In fac', I almost expected you to start chattin' 'bout how you wanned to go back!'

He made a wry face and seemed a little embarrassed. 'Well, I am brewin' about all my Krylons gettin' left in some park for the rads to pick up, but ...'

He moved his head from side to side and shrugged. Vanessa laughed.

'But what, stoopid?'

'Well ... when we was hidin' by dat stinkin' ol' bin I was thinkin' to myself ... You know ...'

'Ah for fuck's sake Nemo spit it out will yuh!'

'Well ... graffiti ain' everythin' is it?'

Vanessa narrowed her eyes at him for a second, hands on hips, trying to hold down her smile. This time, Nemo laughed. She walked up and punched him on the shoulder playfully, then paused to roll the sleeves of his jumper up a little so she could do it again.

'Fuckin' bastard,' she was muttering as she rolled. 'You 'ave me sitting nex' to some stinkin' ol' bin for near enough half an' hour, running from police an' jumpin' walls, jus' to tell me graffiti ain' everythin'?! Watch me an' you when I sort dis poxy jumper out mate, you're gonna get it, I'm tellin' yuh!'

'Jus' cool will yuh,' Nemo chuckled, holding up his hands in surrender. 'I'm jus' sayin' although I love the Art very much, it's not good to be blinkered by the talent you have. Meanin', I finally realised how much I enjoy your company as well. You can't beat me for dat!'

'Can't I?' Vanessa mumbled, advancing on him menacingly. 'All I can smell is stale beer an' babies nappies Nemo, even now ... Somebody has to get it ...'

The sound of loud cheering came from the east side of the estate, as well as the blocks surrounding Vanessa and Nemo. They looked at each other in realisation as the whistles, foghorns and other celebratory noises got more and more intense, making their ears ring, and any attempt to speak inaudible (if they couldn've thought of anything to say). For both of them, it was a moment which was completely theirs — with no distractions from anyone. They gobbled one another up with their eyes, while in the background the crowd had merged into one overpowering voice, which was saying, 'Ten ... nine ... eight ... seven ... six ...'

Neither of them could hold their urges back any more. They rushed at each other; hugging tightly then kissing hard, hands roaming, breathing in and out harshly, oblivious to the little kids Vanessa had waved to earlier. The children laughed and giggled and jumped on the spot, unable to believe their luck. The couple continued their embrace, while the voice of the crowd continued their counting.

'Five ... four ... three ... two ... one!'

The fireworks went off and the whole place went crazy. People could be heard screaming, yelling, cheering ... even crying in delight at being a witness to this marvellous, magical occasion. Nemo hugged Vanessa tighter, feeling glad, so glad that he'd not been alone for this night. Vanessa squeezed him back, while the night became day on Greenside, for the first time in the history of the estate.

Little Stacey had to admit, he hadn't been too aware of how close it was to millennium time, as he was guided steadily through the crowd by the earnaton with the knife and the coarse voice. The guy had a hand on his shoulder and the blade still pushed into his back, as he steered Stacey out of the packed hall area, and on towards the stairs, his friends keeping and eye out for the bouncers all the while. Once on the stairs, Little Stacey hoped he'd see Ray, or Benji, or even Orin; but no one was in sight. The youths pushed him downwards. They spiralled until they got to the bottom, where the men's toilets were. Instinctively, Stacey headed for them knowing this was the kind of place where he would've robbed someone if he was in a group as large as this. They pushed him through the swing doors brutally, while one of them broke off and stood look-out. Then they grabbed him up, threw him into one of the cubicles and ordered every one else out of the place.

One badman refused to move, simply staring at them over the urinal with red, terrible-looking eyes.

'Do yuh ting my youts, nuh bodda yuhself wid we. Do yuh ting.'

The youths decided the guy wasn't worth the hassle, and made a bee-line for Stacey with no delay. The small Greensider held his hands up and surrendered straight away.

'Hear what now, put yuh bora away star, I ain' got nuffin' anyway. You want my green? See it deh.'

He dug for the bags and passed them over, his face tight and angry, but desperate not to show it. Any sign of aggression could get his throat cut, but then if he acted too soft, they might chop him up for the fun of it anyway. It was a thin line, and one that Stacey would've preferred not to tread. He heard the badman zipping up his flies, then his footsteps and the eerie creak of the swing door as he left. He sighed. One of the bigger youths leaned against the cubicle door nonchalantly.

'Wha' about the wong?'

'All right man, gimme a chance man what's up?'

Another youth appeared on the other side of the cubicle door like a genie. He had cat's eyes, and a don't-give-a-fuck manner that Stacey didn't like at all.

'Ay my boy, don't start get feisty an' all dat star, jus' let off, seen. Don't make my bredrin affa do you suttin'.'

Stacey glared at the newcomer, then swallowed his pride, looked down, and reached into his pocket, handing over about a third of the money he'd made that night. The rest was rolled up in a little pouch around his ankle, but what these fools didn't know wouldn't hurt them. The knife-wielding guy snatched the notes from Stacey's grasp, then handed them to his friend to count.

'Thirty, forty, fifty ... What, is dat all you got?'

'Dat ain' all he's got man, my man's bin sellin' green all over tonight, I see 'im in the garage room. Let off on the wong my yout' don't make us affa come an' get it.'

'You know,' one of the others added.

'Fuck you star!' Stacey shot back. 'Dat's all the wong I got man, I ain' got nuffin' else f'you! Jus' cool man, it's New Year's fuckin' Eve ...'

'Think I give a fuck about New Year?' the guy with the cat's eyes exclaimed, before the main door to the toilet slammed open, and four meaty-looking bouncers rushed in.

'Oi, wha' the fuck d'you think you're playin' at? Come 'ere cunt!!'

For Little Stacey, this was the best thing that could've happened to him; and although he couldn't see what was going on, he'd been clubbing enough times to be able to guess. He slammed the cubicle door in the youth's faces, then unbuckled and pulled his jeans down, as the sound of harsh blows resounded in the urinal area. Just to make it look good, he closed his eyes and started to piss, though he was damned if he was going to shit in there. From what the bouncers were saying, it seemed as though the look-out had been caught smoking bone outside — and that in turn had led the men to here.

'Get the fuck off me man, get the fuck off!'

'Suck yuh mudda yuh pussy!'

'Watch dat knife!' There was a scream, then a clatter of metal on tile. Stacey only just held back an urge to laugh.

'Search dat one Dave, dis cunt's got money on 'im.'

'Fuck you man, it ain' mine, it ain' fuckin' mine! Ahhh!'

There were a few more slaps, then laughter.

'Well, well, well, what a surprise . . .'

'Good stuff is it mate?' the bouncers were chiding, like police-men dead sure of a collar. The crack-head youths screamed their innocence.

'Look man, I'm clean, wha's up wid you star!'

'Stop pullin' on my arms man, dis cos' more than your whole wardrobe y'nuh!'

'Check the cubicle, dere's a guy in dere jugglin' man!'

More laughter.

'Yeah, yeah, pull the other one mate . . .'

After a few more horrid-sounding blows, the shouts and protests from the youths faded as they were escorted from the toilet, along with the deep voices of at least two of the bouncers. Even though they seemed disbelieving enough, Stacey knew they'd have to check the youth's claims out, if only to satisfy their own curiosity. He waited open-mouthed, until the cubicle door slammed back open and a skin-headed white guy about three men wide stared down at him through drug-filled eyes. Stacey grabbed for his jeans.

'Raa . . .'

'Get up an' out, come on mate,' the bouncer ordered, not even expecting any form of argument.

The Greensider got up and walked out, to face a black bouncer who didn't look too happy at all. In fact, he looked as if he'd never been happy. His friend checked the cubicle, while the black guy ordered Stacey to stay put. Soon enough, his white colleague came back.

'Didn't do much did ya?'

Stacey shrugged, doing up his jeans and tucking his shirt-tails back in. 'I only jus' started innit. Don't even feel like shittin' now mate. Can I go?'

'Give 'im a search Phillip,' the black bouncer said in a monotone, his dark stare never leaving Stacey's face. The youth had time to wonder if the bouncers might have any battyman tendencies, before holding his arms out in a resigned fashion and sighing.

'Go on den,' he said, knowing he was well in the clear by now.

They searched him quickly and methodically, finding the pouch at his ankle with no trouble. They opened it, then stared questioningly at him when the contents were revealed.

'My girl's birt'day,' Little Stacey explained, thinking fast.

The black bouncer didn't look convinced, but as there was no drugs to be found, the white one nodded and jerked a thick thumb at the toilet door.

'Go on den, hop it.'

'Cheers mate. Happy New Year.'

They didn't answer him, but Stacey didn't care. He emerged from the toilet like a rabbit from its burrow, to see that the crowds around the stairway had diminished almost entirely. Darting down the stairs, he ran straight into an army of people, all trying, as he was, to get into the Garage room. The ravers were throwing their bodies around with an abandon that belied any physical concern for themselves. The MC was bubbling at full throttle by now.

'One more minute to go my people, one more minute to go!' he chanted. 'One more minute to go now London, one more minute to go!'

Concerned, Stacey threw himself into the crowd of people at full force, and steamed his way through, ignoring the girls' curses and men's threats (though sometimes, it was the other way around). At half a minute, he was back by the bar. He looked around for Orin and the barmaid, but neither was in sight, so he kept on. The heat of the room made sweat pour from him in rivers. His heart was booming in his chest like the woofers of the big sound speakers, placed strategically around the hall. Then the music stopped.

And the waiting crowd went wild.

'Ten ... nine ... eight ...'

He was panicking. He struggled harder, seeing the looks of amusement on certain faces, but unable to heed them. It was imperative he started the New Year with his people.

'Seven ... six ... five ...'

There they were! They were standing like everybody else, looking in the direction of the stage, blowing their foghorns and clutching each other deliriously. Orin was with the barmaid he'd been lusting after, which wasn't unusual for the good-looking young man — Little Stacey was pleased for his friend, and glad things had worked out. Rochelle stood forlornly with Sissy, Carolyn and the other girls, holding Carolyn's hand and drinking.

Stacey ducked underneath a crew of mini-skirted girls and popped up by Ray, who almost jumped in shock — he'd been smoking a sly crack spliff while he was supposedly on the wagon. Stacey scooted past him and made a bee-line for his girl. At the last instant, Rochelle saw him coming; she screamed, making Carolyn grin in delight, and opened her arms out wide to meet him.

'Four ... three ... two ... one! Happy Millenniuuuuum!!!'

They held each other. She buried her head against him like she always did, her touch feeling familiar and welcoming after the madness he'd been through not long before. Everyone around them was screaming and hugging each other, whether they knew the person they were embracing or not. Bright white strobelights flooded the hall. Champagne bottles popped like kids' cap guns, the sound getting more and more frequent, until it reached an amazing crescendo which made Stacey want to duck for cover.

Instead, he kissed Rochelle warmly, and looked into her eyes, glad she was his, and he hers. They kissed again, and she smiled her cheeky grin.

'I love yuh!' she shouted, though he couldn't even hear over the noise. Of course it didn't really matter to Stacey — somewhere deep in his mind, he'd been hoping she'd say those three magic words, and the feeling it gave him when he saw them on her lips was impossible to describe. All the stress and the worrying over the realities of his life were over for just this moment — he was carefree, he was healthy, and he was happy. That was all that mattered here and now.

He clutched Rochelle's body a little harder, and shouted those three magic words in return.

Douglas Rushkoff

'IS EVERYBODY HERE?'

Is everyone here?
Who? Henry is upstairs? That's fine.
And the children? Good. Bring them around.
Hello dears. Beautiful.
Let's have some music.
Ahh good. That's nice. Mmm.

What's wrong Martha?
You look — you look so worried. Yes, you do.
Don't think about anything but right now.
Nothing at all, you understand?
All is bliss. We're here together.
Good. You get it. Nice.

Mmm. Yes. Mmm.
Someone bring down the lights a bit.
Do we have any candles? Two of you.
Yes, go and find them.
Then come right back.
We'll be waiting. Right here. No rush.

Henry, you're back.
You've got it all set up? Good man.
Someone give Henry a hug. Madeline.

That's nice. It's all love.
Good now. Sit down.
Is everyone here? Great. Now.

How is it we found one another?
How is it we knew?
What strange attractor brought us to this time?
Brought us to this moment, this place, this space?
An evening like any other. Just like any other.

Stephanie. Sit with me.
Make room.
Let her through.
Stephanie. Daughter of Marcelle.
My first. So beautiful.
You're not afraid. No.

She's not afraid because she knows.
Darkness falls as a natural consequence.
The passage of time is circular.
From day into night, then night into day.
Circles within circles. Moments within moments.
As above so below.
So it is below.

And you think you have a choice in the matter.
The world, your world, it's in no time at all.
You think you go from beat to beat, as if
Your choices, step by step they take you from
Place to place. But they don't, do they? Not really.
No. It's not like that, is it Steph?

Of course not, no, sweet thing. You know the truth.
The pond we swim in. Infinite in its
possibilities. Infinite in its destinies.
Not just one of you, but many, more than millions.
Another for each thought. Another Henry,

who has just come down the stairs. This one
with a horn from his forehead. That one
having just finished making love, and
Another still, who chose to sit there, no there.
Or maybe he went out the door and never
came back.

Each Henry spawning another universe
of possibility. No, not spawning,
but finding, touching, discovering. They all
exist right now. Each past, each present, each future.
You wander aimlessly between the moments.
Everything has already happened. Nothing
left to chance. There's nothing you can do
that would surprise the universe now.

You don't move along a line of time.
There's no such thing. Hear just this:
Every possible way your life could work out
is already in existence. You can only
choose which one to visit. The one you dream
is the one you get. You don't make them
happen. You just float about in the sea
of possible worlds, of possible yous. Every
feasible future and even those that are not
live side by side in a metaverse already here.

Janet,
bring a candle
to the front of the room
and tell us how you came to find me.

Yes,
that's right.
We let you in the dream.
That night, I took your hand. You knew
it was me, I looked in your eyes. There was no

other way it could have worked out for you, not after
that.

I love you all so much.
And I know how you love me.
As best you can.
As you are now.

How lucky it is we found this space together.
With all the many ways you could have gone.
This moment. This time. Precisely now.
What you call nineteen hundred and ninety-nine.
What we call the moment of infinite possibility.
Where fate and coincidence kiss to form
an opening.

Because you can crash the gates.
A single act of will. An act
of faith.
Creates a portal.

Is everyone here?
As above, so below.
Bring me the wine.

To pass through the veil keeping you
trapped in a dimension of singularity.
Flitting blindly from consequence to
consequence. Caught in the illusion
of cause and effect. Action reaction.

No matter how many lifetimes you live
No matter how many highs and lows
good deeds and evil acts, loves and murders,
births and deaths. There's only the possible.

'Is Everybody Here?'

I want you to taste the im-possible.
Not the end of the story, not after the story.
But beyond the story. Beyond the many stories.

Why have you forsaken me? He asked.

Yes, God's own son, who saw the many stories.
The man-God who knew that a life was merely
a piece of a puzzle that fit into one whole,
feared to imagine what lay beyond infinite choice.

He would move beyond the boundaries themselves.
Beyond the possible lives he could live.
God gave his only begotten son, to show us the way.
The way to break the cycle of joy, the cycle
of pain. To move outside the realm of everything.
To cheat the death foisted on him by those who
couldn't understand.

Even He was forced to pass through the moment
of doubt. To abandon the certain. To leap
through the portal through which he emerged
two thousand years ago this very night.

God always saves the best and last for those who endure.
Take this cup away from me.

There is no death in absolute freedom.
There is no death in moving beyond life.
There is no death in refusing to be reborn.
There is no death in finding the only real way
to make a choice.

Drink, Henry. Now, yes. That's good.
Then pass it on.

Imagine, my friends, you are reading a book.
And in that book are lines filled with words.
A story that follows the words of a man.

271

A teacher with strange notions, but who
seems to know something more than you can conceive.

You follow the words, line after line. But
sense that the only way out is through,
or to start it again and maybe next time
it will make more sense. The picture
will come together. That picture that
seems to elude you every time you come back.

Because each time it's anew. You just start
again. Endlessly repeating the same things
as different people in different places.

That's it, Marcelle. So beautiful. Just drink.
Help the children now. They don't know
yet how they've been saved. Spared the fear.
Spared the pain in their short, glorious lives.
They made it here just in time, lucky souls.
Touched by light. Here for one purpose alone.

Someone hold Madeline. No, not the door.
Hold her down, Henry. She's only afraid.
Help her, friends. Help her defeat the mindless
protests of the flesh.

Imagine that you can break from the trance
of the mundane illusion you're so sure is real.
To break from the story — has everyone drunk?
It's as simple as lifting your eyes from the page.

Tania Glyde

'PAVLOVS BITCH AND YOGA COW REACH 2000'

I've done many things in my life, but I've never been in jail. And I've never fucked my mother either. It's 7 p.m. on 31 December 1999, so if I want to get those in before the new millennium I'd better get going.

It's like the last days of the Roman Empire, the Friday and the Saturday, innit, says Yoga Cow, unwrapping something small. Sometimes Yoga Cow thinks she's God, bless 'er.

No it's not, I say, don't be such a fucking media victim. It's just another year over. Another jerk of death's crowbar!

I pick up the vodka and drink.

This New Year's Eve will *not* be like the time we spent two hours in the back of a small hatchback going to Crouch End on the hunt for pills, then another four hours trying to find a rave in Kent that was cancelled anyway, and then the pills didn't work and made us puke; it will not be like the time you spent stroking the back of my neck while I threw up outside that trattoria with a giant fibreglass mullet hanging in the window while that fat guy tried to force us to drink Pink Ladies; nor will it be spent hanging around with people we hate or despise in general; nor under the rule of overpaid, bad DJs; nor waking up on a pile of rubbish bags with my face stuck in a discarded, barely-touched pasty; and nor will it be spent watching the *Harry Hill* or *Father Ted* or *This Life* specials which are all right but—

275

Shut the fuck up and have a line, says Yoga Cow, you'd better get your act together. We've got a lot to do.

I know! I snarl, tramping around and around the big table where she sits, jerking my body slowly in time to the music.

A big roasting beast of a man's voice growls and ululates and imprecates while the hyper-rich sweet scent of a rising rhythm pulls me up and up.

> *The only gang sign*
> *That I ever knew*
> *Was people turnin their backs*
> *'We don' wan' you!'*
> *So I said Fine*
> *On my own I'm gonna shine*
> *To mine own self*
> *I will be true.*

Skagga, I call this. Shiatsu Breaks. Yoga Cow's starting to stick her leg up and out at odd angles. Always a bad sign if I know anything. Yoga Cow leans round and kisses me full on the mouth.

Not now.

Oh, go on then.

Yoga Cow can get both legs round the back of her neck. I always make sure I never act impressed by this. After all, what good is it to me where her feet are? I'm not into feet. Yoga Cow runs her hand over my left breast and takes my nipple between two fingers and squeezes. We know now just how many drugs we can take before sex stops being good and starts being like sorting out a pile of old clothes. And it is a fine line. She bends and pulls my top to the side and sucks at me. I slip my hand between her legs. She is firm. I stroke upwards, up her thighs to her pussy. I stroke her clitoris with the side of my finger. It slips back and forth in her fresh juices. She rubs the back of my neck with her toe. Her lips are soft—

The bell goes. Oh no. It's Luke Roadkill, The Person Who Was There At The Beginning.

Hi Luke. Have a line and there's the vodka. What a lovely blue fur anorak. Luke barely acknowledges us before launching into a tirade.

Oh my God you wouldn't believe it! I went to this club last night and the DJs were *awful* I mean the people there were all so bloody young, they don't know anything about what's *going on*. Fuckin' *dingy* tunes, it was all really manky, all kind of housey techno-ey trancey drum 'n' bassy — I mean they just weren't *there*, were they? Oooh, halls of residence are gonna be *swinging* to that derivative crap. It's not like the old days I can tell you. I can't believe all these people are trying to enjoy themselves to that shit when they weren't even there at the beginning.

Beginning of *what*? I hiss. Tip when chatting about musical trends of the last twenty years to someone like Luke Roadkill: Think of what style you're on about, take the year you think it 'all started', and then go back a couple more, just to be safe, e.g. 'but Afrika Bambaataa was doing that in '78, surely?' etc.

Luke responds.

Well, they weren't *there*. When it all started.

How could someone who's seventeen years old in 1999 have 'been there' in 1986, at the age of *four*? I mean, even if they were actually in Ibiza that year, they'd have been making sandcastles, wouldn't they?

Club fascists are a race all their own. Luke pisses me off.

We've got to go! Yoga Cow stands up quickly. We've got to get the stuff. Mack'll be so hurt if we don't get it. Come on, think about what she's been through.

Oh all right.

Yoga Cow goes to a drawer and pulls out a grubby white velveteen-covered plastic mini-suitcase. It looks really cheap an' all, not like Yoga Cow.

Don't ask questions, she says, this is for Mack.

Okay then.

Silence.

Right. We're gonna do it now. Come on, something to tell our grandchildren.

We take a bit of acid and some speed because we're on a mission. And head for the door.

Hold on, hold on, what about Lily?

Oh she'll be fine. She always is.

Kids grow up fast these days.

Yeah, thank God.

First stop in our hunt. A trendy pub not far away. We heard rumours that what we need will be available there. We sit down. Yoga Cow grabs a menu.

I can't believe we're gonna get sorted so quickly.

People always notice us so our order won't be difficult except that we haven't sat at a table but on barrels waiting to be loaded into the cellar.

Can't sit there loveys.

Oh go on. Go on, Slab Cake — you know what I mean, she whispers.

You'll be lucky luv. He laughs.

I look over at a woman at a nearby table who has ordered a whole crab. It is quite big, at least relative to the plate. I look and look at the crab which I decide is moving, or about to. I get the beginnings of a phobic reaction, cold shakes, fuzzy panic vibration, a feeling of being about to burst into tears.

Yoga Cow is shouting, disproportionately loudly for this time of the evening, even given that it is New Year's Eve 1999.

Whadyer mean no Ruby Slab! The man looks weary.

No steaks! Come on you know we'd lose our licence.

Oh come on mate!

Sorry love.

Yoga Cow grabs me and we skitter off down the street. She is firm with me.

Come on Bitch. Get yer act together. Don't pull that crab shit on me either. 'Oooh it's the legs, it's their legs!' You're not tripping and you're not going to be.

Awright, awright, calm down you old slag!

Fuckin' 'ell. Okay, we'll go to Paul's party for a while, he's sure to have something in the freezer. We go out into the street and narrowly miss getting caught by a random Stop 'n' Search team. Stop 'n' Search round here is like shooting fish in a barrel. They may as well arrest people who *don't* have any anything on them for wasting police time.

We get a cab to Paul's.

Paul's got a nice flat where people with long coloured nails sip things and listen to light jazzy fusiony stuff. Paul loves his straight friends. I mean straight as a lifestyle generalisation, not a sexual one. The mediocracy are quite happy with their petty adulteries and tweaks at joints of pot. I chat up a man.

God this music's gacky, I say. Hey! Remember that cartoon where a grasshopper called Chester gets together with this little lost puppy who says 'Gimme a ham roll' and they all live together in Times Square behind some dustbins. Imagine the puppy going 'Gimme a ham roll or I'll blow a hole in your face that'll make the Grand Canyon look like a gnat's jacksy!'

I giggle.

Hey, do you wanna fuck me? I say to the man. I notice simultaneously that Yoga Cow is disappearing down to the basement with purpose.

The man is tall and black with a v. expensive suit, and looked a bit bored until I said that. Now he looks even more bored.

Bitch! Get down here now! Yoga Cow needs me. The man looks bemused as I skip off.

Look! A freezer! There's sure to be some in here!

Yoga Cow pulls up the lid of the freezer to reveal boxed pizzas and all kinds of stuff in ice-cream cartons. I boredly suppose to myself that there'll be a body chopped up in there. Human slicing action very dull now we've reached this date. Killer chic done 'n' gone I hope. Yoga Cow starts maniacally rummaging among the contents. I pace up and down. It's cold in here, of course. I hold a frozen, bagged-up salmon. Paul loves to cook. Bet *he's* not gonna be cowed by no laws or death scares, eh Paul.

Imagine being a supermodel! I say suddenly. Imagine being one of those women for a minute. After all, if the parts of your body that are publicly valued are so freakish, imagine all the other really *out there* parts of you that the public doesn't see. Heh! heh! Really *massive* feet, for example, which you can tell photographers are obviously warned to conceal — and we're taking *men's* sizes here, *large* men's sizes. And hands like whopping great hams or talons like that bit in *The Thing* where the bloke runs away and then we suddenly see him pull out this giant claw thing; and no tits at all (which, of course, is freakish for every other woman to have *apart* from models). And that's only the *outside*! What about *inside*! Oesophaguses and intestines all stretched out — maybe it takes them longer to swallow and digest their food so that's why their metabolisms are so fucked that they really *can* eat twenty pie an' chips and not get fat! Odd how you never see any cases of kwashiorkor among supermodels eh?! And then of course there's *massive* tunnely weird fannies—

Shut the fuck up and help me prop the lid open! hisses Yoga Cow. Put some of that stuff on the floor or something.

The salmon gets stuck to my hand.

There's no fucking meat here!

Strangely, Yoga Cow is sweating. I am swaying to the music now.

Right we're going to Luna's.

Now?

Bitch, you losing the plot. We're taking Mack some meat and that's that.

Christ can't she make do with fish? We can just borrow it off Paul, can't we?

We get out of there and go to Luna's, on a houseboat in Battersea.

It'll be full of NA people, cybores and veggie told-you-so

sanctomaniacs, I warn you. They definitely won't have any meat on them.

We'll try. She's a bit of a wide one, old Luna. You never know what she's got tucked away.

After a terrifying voyage over ramps and down ladders in the pitch dark, we reach Luna's boat. The party is full of NA people, cybores and veggie told-you-so sanctomaniacs. However, Luna is the egalitarian type and they can't all be that bad. Most of the guests are crowded around Luna's fab new giant Huge-Screen MacroMac. The screen really is two metres across like the ad says!

They are watching a riot. A terrible, mass riot. A screaming woman runs towards the camera, in flames.

Shit where's all that going on? I ask.

They look at me as if I am stupid and mad.

Come on, where?

Here, of course, says a stringy looking blonde woman who glares at me with scorn before rapidly turning her face back to the screen, where a huge man with a massive helmet is dragging a couple of nuns along a road. He throws them to the ground. One tries to run, but he grabs her, pulls out a machete and chops her face in half. He pulls up her habit and kicks her cunt as her body jerks. She is wearing only tights, no knickers. I drag my eyes from the screen to the backs of the audience's heads.

Yes yes but where *really*?

Here. Someone snarls viciously at me.

Stupid of me! The revolution will not be televised. It will be on-line! I say. What a cliché ...

Luna, tiny with dark curly hair, takes me by the arm and into the kitchen.

Some mates of mine set it up, it's pretty amazing, isn't it. Here's our card. You can get it on http://www.millennium.riots.co.uk.

Actually I don't have that much respect for Luna. Once she pulled up her top and showed me her pierced belly button and tattoos. I love my body ornamentation, she said, because it helps me commune with tribal peoples.

Oh really, I replied, surely if you want to *really* commune with tribal peoples, why don't you spend eight hours a day grinding maize, or try walking six miles and back each morning with a metal tank of water on your back? But she did not get it. She also has a boyfriend called Twat Sunblest or something like that. Oh shit and he's here!

God I've been through so much. At my meeting last night I just couldn't stop talking—

I offer him a drink to shut him up but he refuses.

Sorry! I've been going to AA as well! Just to meet people, you get me?

I offer him a cigarette but he refuses it, pulling out this little plastified card with a condensed version of the twelve steps on it.

So sorry, I say.

I ask what he is addicted to, having heard a bit about it from Luna. I am expecting tales of crack psychosis and babies hurled from upper floors.

Cannabis, he says, I was having a spliff *every morning*.

If there's one thing I can't stand it's an addiction addict. I concentrate on wiping my face, then remember I have to distract Luna while Yoga Cow picks the lock on Luna's fridge using only her little finger (she really can do it you know, she told me) and searches for meat.

Luna suddenly looks over my shoulder and rage enters her face. What the fuck's Yoga Cow doing in my freezer compartment?

Yoga Cow has one hand in there, and looks guilty. Luna grabs her and yanks her arm away, savagely.

Oh, for fuck's sake Luna, okay we're gonna come clean. Please, please can we take this beef. *Please*. It's for Mack. Come on, you know she's been in that fucking weirdo hospital for six months. She's gagging for it.

Have you any idea what I went through to get this meat?

We are silent. Knowing exactly what she must have gone through.

I turn back to her.

You selfish slag! Have you any idea what *Mack's* been through? Luna spits.

And have you, Bitch, not read any of the newspapers or seen any of the information bulletins we've been getting through the door? WE ARE ALL GOING TO DIE. And I am going to enjoy this joint of beef that someone was nearly killed acquiring for me. I'm probably going to have to sell my car to pay him off. How dare you spoil my New Year's Eve party! Get out of here!

Awww, Luna, please, *pleeeeze*. Anyway, New Year's Eves are always crap. Look at all those fucking boats going up and down the river. There'll be pissed drownings, firework incidents, drug overdoses—

Get out.

We go. I lift a bottle of tequila on the way. Me and Yoga Cow stand for a few moments on the jetty, barely able to hear ourselves think for the vast soundclash going on around us on the Thames and its banks.

Life Before Meat = LBM (well, there never was one, unless you count the Carboniferous Period and before). Life After Meat (there isn't one, for most of us, now) = LAM. Lamb!

Ages ago, I was working in Lancashire and I wanted to buy a black pudding and I asked my friend, 'Do you know any good butchers?'

There are no good butchers, Bitch, she replied, ominously.

Vegan, I forgot! And I sneered to myself. But look now. And I look down at my and Yoga Cow's bodies, and the timebomb that exhales gently inside us. God has many mansions etc., and the butcher's shop was the sleaziest one of the lot.

So goodbye to the nineties, says Yoga Cow, and goodbye to us, she says, sensing my mood. Suddenly her face becomes urgent.

Okay, I didn't mention this before, but Harrods still has a secret meat store, guarded twenty-four hours. Hardly anyone knows about it. Apparently, if you buy anything, they make you sign an indemnity certificate and claim their stuff's all pure anyway. Even if you're royalty.

Don't royalty types have their own stash? All those burning cows and pigs and sheep!

I think back to the drama of the news six months ago.

I don't know, Bitch. Come on. Let's go.

We get a bus to Harrods. There are no cabs. It takes ages. The streets are full of people. I hate this shop a lot.

How are we going to get in? Yoga Cow pulls something like a small metal pineapple from her bag.

That's a World War Two hand grenade. What are you doing with that? I ask.

Never you mind. I'm not just a mother you know, she says loftily. The meat safe is actually in the food hall. We take two lefts and a right. We throw this and we run.

She hands me a kitchen knife. There are people everywhere. It's only nine thirty and the overpriced Knightsbridge bistros are full of rich trash and coining it in. I want to bomb *them*. We creep down some basement steps and each take a hit of crack from an ugly, creamed-up plastic bottle and cracked Biro.

Now! We run towards the shop window.

We duck behind a car. Yoga Cow pulls the pin and chucks the grenade. It explodes, to my surprise. We run through the hole, our feet crunching on glass. I trip on a dummy's dismembered arm. Security people run at us. Yoga Cow pulls out a fucking handgun! I'm getting pissed off because now I will have to top all this with some higher high of female machodom at a later date. I follow Yoga Cow to the meat counter.

Madam! You can't come into this establishment dressed like that! shouts another, trying to get me in an arm lock. I slash at his hand and pull down a stack of Luxury Shortcake Biscuits.

Yoga Cow fires off a few rounds at the meat safe and screeches with triumph as she emerges from behind the counter with a hand-ful of dripping thin-cut fillet steaks. They soon start to slip through her fingers. She fires a couple of shots at the security men.

Get me a carrier bag! *Now!* Another one scuttles behind a counter and comes back.

Not a paper one you stupid fucking cunt!

One of the security men has fallen to the ground and appears to be begging for something.

For God's sake at least sign a form, he moans. I realise that I am bigger than the security man who tried to get me in the arm lock. Yoga Cow fires a few more shots and we run out again. All this takes under a minute.

Where are the bizzies?

Pissed! What do you think!

Yoga Cow hands me the dripping bag and pulls out a small codebreaker thing and we get into a small, low sports car. This is getting stupid.

Where did you get a small codebreaker thing for a car lock?

She smiles, and one edge of her smile says she is doing this for me, in homage for me, she has organised a sexy incident *for me*.

Maybe.

Anyway, I am excited. She also has a skeleton key which starts the car.

But we said men's type of crime's crap, didn't we?

I am pretending now. I love having beliefs and values, but we humans tend to forget we are also part of the animal kingdom. I had briefly forgotten.

I know we did, I know we did, she sounds impatient. I laugh.

Right Mack, here we come. I drive. Yoga Cow puts the music on loud. And then—

Wait, she says, let's just stop here and lock the doors and have a drink.

We find a parking space by the busy road. Yoga Cow turns to me and puts her hand on my face. She takes the bottle of tequila and takes a mouthful from it. She passes it to me. The brown alcohol burns in my mouth.

I look her in the eye. The car is small but both the seats go back.

What are you doing? she asks.

I lean over on to her and push her back in her seat. I am still tied by the seatbelt which somehow in all the mayhem I actually put on. The restriction is enjoyable but I undo it and undo my top and let my breasts show. The engine is still running. Yoga Cow laughs loudly and reaches out with her hand. I swing some more tequila as she squeezes my nipple. Her pussy is wet. I slip my finger in and then run it up and over and through her pubic hair, and up over her stomach. Our activity starts to attract attention.

Wahey!!! Fingers and fists tap on the windows. Faces leer and slaver. I climb on top of Yoga Cow. My legs strain to find a comfortable position on the narrow seat. I rub myself against her, licking her face and neck. She sucks my left nipple — my favourite nipple — hard. The car begins to shake as the people round it start to push. The car rocks so violently I need only stay still. I take more tequila.

Shit! It's quarter to eleven! shouts Yoga Cow, we've got to get going.

The car is surrounded as if by bees. I scramble back into the driving seat and rev the engine. I drive slowly, men climbing on the car, ripping, tearing impotently at anything they can get hold of. When the road seems a little clearer I speed up, then slam on the brakes, causing the men to fall off. Then I accelerate down the street, scattering them like empty bottles on a kitchen floor.

We drive, pushing and pushing through crowds and crunching cans until we get to Vauxhall Bridge. It seems to take years to get across, across and down through Brixton and down some more. The building is big, with a little drive in front.

We get out, Yoga Cow first of all hiding the steaks in the tops of her stockings.

Hello we've come to see Mack. We've got an appointment. Music emits from somewhere at the back of the building. We get searched, but the steaks are thin and pass unnoticed.

We are led through doors and other doors with buzzers. Mack is at a level where visits don't always have to be supervised.

Someone said Mack had the meat-madness quicker than normal and needed to be locked up for observation. Actually I think she accused some other people of a crime or of being racist or something, and people thought she was too much of a shaman. And she took her DJing skills a bit too far and did something weird with a crowd. Mack used to run a smackadelia shop in Clerkenwell. Everything in art etc. to do with heroin, and souvenirs of famous people who used it, books, records, art. It was quite good. Mack is six feet tall and her hair has stopped growing. Come to think of it, mine's not moved much recently either.

I grope the duty psychiatrist as we walk down the corridor. Then I notice that Yoga Cow is dripping watery blood down her legs.

You dirty old slag! Getting your period and not even noticing! So sorry doctor! I hustle her to the toilet where we wipe up and wash the steaks.

Mack greets us with war signs and laughter. We giggle over the steaks. She shrieks with delight. She has been forced to eat chickpea bake and tempeh roundlets for six months and it shows.

Gotny? I say to Yoga Cow.

Gotny wot?

Y'know. That.

She sighs. We have a routine where smack's concerned. We never ever say the word out loud. This is in homage to a dead friend who was always the same. Then she OD'd and died when pissed which was slightly our fault. I mean not massively but you know what I mean. So this is our eternal flame for her. Well, eternal chase. Sort of. Not that we feel good about it or anything.

That.

That?

Yeah that.

Er, try the, er, in here.

Here? I get her purse out.

Yeah.

Yoga Cow gets the make-up case out of the bag.

Drugs! I think, *even more* drugs. Yoga Cow opens the case for Mack. I peer over.

So! What's in here then! I rattle a lipstick case expecting to hear the sound of pills, and open a powder compact expecting to see a small bundle of jiffy bags with white powder in. But no, it really is face powder.

I wanted make-up, says Mack. She has been allowed a small stove in her room — a privilege — and we cook the steaks. First of all sealing round the door with tape. Before we start cooking Mack eats one raw, cramming it in, staining her white teeth. It is 11.30 p.m. The hospital rave bangs on.

I can't wait for the bongs! giggles Yoga Cow.

How many do you need, for fuck's sake? asks Mack, getting out an improvised water pipe. Yoga Cow has more rocks with her. She is so organised.

Four minutes to go. It is as if Father Christmas had revealed that he really does exist — we are all getting really excited. I mess about with some foil.

We're all gonna die, says Mack, I know it. And soon. We don't need to go to the street called Straight, the one in Damascus, to get this revelation.

Straight, what is straight? I ask, as I watch Mack, still holding in a lungful, stretch out her long brown arm and touch Yoga Cow's hair.

Mack yowls with laughter and bites Yoga Cow's neck in a sudden rush. My heart retches with jealousy.

Sodom, Gomorrah, Gomorrhoea. The death of us all! It's coming, she chants.

A horrible image of a human sucking pig dances in front of my eyes, and memory of the dying lamb from the virtual riot. There is a bit of steak left, I cut it in half and run one of the pieces, warm by now, along Mack's bare shoulder, leaving a wet trail.

Hysterical countdowns are going on in the streets and everywhere. I jump to the window to look out. Every radio is on, every television. Like all New Year's Eves, the cheering you overhear is always staggered, everybody's got a slightly different time on their watches. I turn laughing. They are still snogging.

Have some meat guys, it's New Year 2000! They share the bits. I then begin to tell a joke, hoping they will choke laughing. But they do not. The great bellow that erupts from London Town is so long and loud that I have plenty of time to slit Yoga Cow's throat and stab Mack through the heart.

I slip away and pace into the screaming night. I've done them both a favour.

Steve Beard

'RETOXICITY'

The Hwang family forgot to pay off the Corporation's drug cops and I barely escaped with my life. It's being written up as a jurisdictional dispute on the London datanets. Just one of those things, accidents will happen, etc. You know the score.

They're withholding casualty lists at St Thomas' Hospital. Most of the victims had no ID. Lost in the digital jungle. So they don't really count in any final census, *capische*?

It was a bad night if all you wanted to do was load up on rocks and dance. But then that's been the case for a long time in England. It seems that there are bigger stories to rack up on UBC Global. Like which of the warring factions from some damaged European blood-line is going to be running things out of the Palace of Westminster. Or how the Chamber of London lost a pile on the futures market.

Real smalltime stuff. No room, you see, for the big picture, for the nightly sacrifices which keep the whole machinery of power sparking. Which is the reason why I cut loose down in South London with my CAMnet. Now I had a choice, here. I could have dropped into any of the pleasure dumps which ghost the industrial leys of the South Bank — Crucifix Lane, Clink Street, Tinworth Street, Goding Street, Bondway, Nine Elms Lane. But my contacts in Kyoto tell me that Battersea Park Road is where the furnaces of ecstasy are really *stoked*.

Drop-off at Bat Hat at eleven in the p.m. Like Westminster,

an old island in the Thames. Unlike that old crowning ground —
and far distant from the corporate temples and occult quadrangles
of the City of London — Battersea and the South Bank have always
been where the effluent of empire has been discharged.

Take a core sample from its deep and teeming sediment. Run
back through paper switching centres and refuse tips to electrical
generators, gasometers and railway yards to lime kilns, chemical
works and windmills. Go back further to the farms and the markets
and the timbered marshlands. Track all the way back . . . and the
legacy of quarantined populations and slum landlords persists like
a dark stain.

Now one thing I do know is you have to take your pleasures
where you can find them. And always on the South Bank, deposited
in the shells of each receding layer of industry, have been the
factories of joy.

Blue lasers cutting up the night sky, traffic and commotion,
the drums of London like an underground tattoo. The party was
on tonight just like it had been every night since the end of the
millennium. Some people just didn't know when to stop. They
were drawn in their thousands from all over London — the
barricaded wastes of Brixton and Stockwell, the low-rise estates
of Whitechapel, Plaistow and Bow, the pavements of Fulham
and the tenements of the Holloway Road. The old power station
crouching on the Thames was like a beacon reeling them in with
its promise of solace, adventure and sex.

But some of us have a job to do. I've been to the melt fields of
Sao Paolo and the war zones of Trebona. I've seen it all before.

Drifting through the shanty town crammed up against the
eaves of the sheltering ruin, home to a blinkered population of
the nomadic, the exiled and the lost. Shaved heads, laser eyes,
whiplash antennae poking out of the industrial moraine. The graft
of the homeless is the same the world over. Sheets of polythene,
sporting colours, recycled tech. The only difference here is that
the debris is plush. You remember your Jaguars, your Mercs
and your BMWs? Burnt-out skeletons for improvised dwellings,

dressed with the gaudy remnants — chipped tiles, metal railings, stripped marble — of an abandoned Twentieth Century past.

You see what I see? Realtime video eye flashing red, CCD witness tech catching it all.

Take a look at what's left of the cathedral once built by the London Power Company in Battersea. Crumbling brick façade, exposed joints of steel lashed with neoprene and plastic, internal armature of generators, turntables and lights. Only the four ribbed chimneys of reinforced concrete — towering over the shambles like a paired brace of dead rockets — still marking the skyline with a Promethean glower.

Bat Hat is what the South London homies call it. For them, it's a quarry of renewable resources and a temple of carnal delights. This was why I was here. For its absentee landlords, it's something different. The Hwang family overlook this distant riverside patch from their revolving satellite watch with the same lazily speculative eye they reserve for the rest of the slum properties shuffled to the back of their global investment portfolio. Looking at the last set of Hwang accounts filed in HK, I can see that they've done to Battersea in London what they've done to similar under-performing land assets in Bombay, St Petersburg and Kuala Lumpur. Contracted out management of the place to a local strand of the family, paid off the native chieftains, patched in their drug connections and tried to make a quick buck in the interval before the market picks up.

The Soho end of the Hwang mob had things sorted down here. Or at least that's what they thought. Dance events seven nights of the week, rock franchises, the Met turning a blind eye to the contravention of health and safety regs in return for a cut of the action, the Brixton Yardies pacified. They'd really carved out a space for themselves. Pity they weren't paying attention to the war going on between the Crown of England and the Corporation of London north of the Thames. A lot of people would pay for that omission with their lives.

But it didn't feel that way when I was there. It felt like it was an event. Cabs and rickshaws running up and down the Battersea Park Road. Roisterers and carousers streaming into the pleasure ground dressed in industrial face masks, skin-tight Versace and luminous Caterpillar boots. Smoked-glass limos trailing through the throng into the underground car parks. The party kicking off right there in the squatlands outside the dancehall. You see what I see? Drug pedlars togged up in Replay and Chevignon shouting their wares ('Trips! Rocks! You sorted?'). Indian chai ladies sitting on rush mats selling tea, cigarettes and naan. TiNi datasuit vendors and pirate CD-ROM merchants blocking the path. Paramedics setting up emergency field tents. The Met boys nowhere to be seen.

It was a special evening. That much I did know. A date reserved for a fire festival in the local pagan calendar. November 5th. The Hwang family had rented out space on the outside of the building to the usual motley crew of water companies, drug distributors and record labels. The logos of Thames Valley Water, GlaxoWellcome, TDK and Sony burning their way into the distressed brickwork like projected core memories. Nothing new there.

What was distinctive was the string of artcore messages popping up in between the shuttle of ads like subliminal reminders of a utopian past. Local VJs pumping out wish images of the Westminster mob in jeopardy. Burnings, hangings and shootings wrapped around kitsch patriotic footage of the old queen at play. Well, she was dead anyway. So what did it matter? Plenty, as it turned out.

Rolling up to the massive ornamental gates at the entrance to the dancehall. Shakedown at the door. T'ai chi goons puffed up in Antarctic camo and pink Oakley shades — with an underarm flash of gun-metal grey — exuding an aura of cool. Weapons check, digicash card swipe, an extra tax for the CAMnet. It's all over and I'm in.

So you want to know what's happening in London?

'Wicked and wicked and wicked and rough!'

Hidden speakers punch out a slew of garbled syllables. Ranting

DJ boxed up on one of the dance floors beyond my immediate gaze. I'm losing my footing. Edges of darkness, shafts of light. Slammed against a press of bodies on the threshold of the building. CCD video eye blinded. Vapourised bass rocks the foundations and I'm caught in a hurtling backwash of sound.

'Yes, yes, yes, yes, London Town.'

A volley of drums slams through my body like a digital pulsar and I stumble.

This was going to be tough.

Time to reorientate. I pull down the blueprints of Messrs C.S. Allott & Son, engineers of Manchester from the days when the Ukrainians knew how to build suspension bridges, railways and dams. Checking east, checking west, checking east again. I've got two sets of Boiler Houses, two sets of Turbine Halls and two sets of Switch Rooms either side of the door. I'm looking for the Control Room above the Turbine Hall on the west side so flip back to realtime and head left. I don't know where I'm going. The attempt to navigate from old maps is senseless, the internal architecture has changed so much.

Time to surrender to the flow of the crowd. See how I'm dragged through a labyrinthine warren of improvised dance floors rigged up from cannibalised industrial plant and recycled techno-organic fibres. Flashing on stainless-steel banisters, Worcestershire brick, dead electricity cables, sheets of Kevlar and PVC, alumimium spars and neoprene sails.

Losing it. Sample a quicktime CAMnet image from one of the floors. DJ erected high on a podium, chocked up in metal platelet jacket with a gold sleeper in his nostril and a ring of bone in his lobe. Two thousand dancers at his feet dressed in feathers, jewels and luminous threads working the drift of his hands over the decks in an open feedback loop. Dizzying sweep of overhead gantries, rotting stairwells and drop-dead shafts of light. The void filled with seething bass turbulence, euphoric speedkill drum loops and sampled shreds of London slang. 'Buss off your head and set you 'pon fire!' Panic images of fear and flight — Lockheed F-117s, trance bucks, aerospace salamanders, windowless UAVs — racing over the screens above the DJ's head.

Calibrating. Resisting the siren call of the rock vendors and the champagne hawkers — later! — I twist and turn my way through a maze of black corridors before catching the logo over the lintel of the old Control Room. TEMPLE OV ISIS picked out in holo red with the eye of Horus flashing alongside. I slide through the sound-proofed airlock rigged up beneath the sign and step into an intense cabin of flailing limbs, throttling bass and whiplash drums.

The acrid smell of burning rock hits my nostrils. There are huddled packs of dancers refuelling at the margins of the dance floor from delicately wrought Turkish pipes. Jets of flame spurt high into the air from hidden butane gas canisters. The stars are visible in the broken roof above.

CAMnet casting around the room. Totemic images and graffiti tags are visible on the touch-screens embedded in the skirtings of Belgian black marble which still line the walls. Hobo signs, website numbers, strings of alphanumeric code. Dog-headed astronauts, Blakean angels, cartouched Mayan glyphs. An inverted image of Bat Hat folding its legs beneath it like an insect about to unsheath its wings. Planets, star signs, computers. An aerosol portrait of Isis at the prow of an aerodynamic barge with a handmaiden attending her on either side. Raw data for my colleagues at Kyoto. Enough to keep them busy for a year.

'Here's to all the liberty-takers, the nutters and the ravers. Taking it to the other side.'

This is what I've travelled three continents and multiple time zones to witness. The orgiastic cult of Isis at its peak, a chiliastic dance craze whose seismic fallout has been rocking the planet's datanets for the last year. Three decades of aggravation, pressure and intimidation falling down from the north of the Thames has led the natives of London to revolt in the only way they know how. You've heard about it. They've invented a homegrown cargo cult from the trash washed up on the shores of empire, a hybrid santeria fusing elements from ancient American and African myth, Haitian voodoo rites, interplanetary fantasies and occult techno-science. They want to do more than stake a claim for themselves in the evacuated wastelands of London. They're going further. They want to *disappear*.

One of them made it, too. But you'll never believe it will you? My CAMnet was confiscated by the Corporation of London goons before I had a chance to file the event. But there's always the evidence of my own eyes. Sitting here pressing the keys in a rented room in Vauxhall, I can hardly believe it myself. But it happened. There's nothing more I can say.

The thing about the Isis posse was ... they really thought they could make it to another world with only rock, the gods of London and a DAT archive of snarling drum loops to send them on their way. They had it all figured out. Sirius C was the destination, the missing planet in the constellation of the Great Dog (source: the tribal mythos of the Dogon in Mali); Isis the presiding deity of teleportation, old Portmaster demon from the banks of the Thames (source: local mythology); and 2012 the deadline, the year when the cosmic switches would be hit and a new planetary kiva would come on-line (source: the trans-millennial calendar of the Mayans).

The Temple ov Isis had kicked off at the start of the year. It was still going eleven months later. The celebrants were running out of time. I was witness to the ecstatic ravings of a para-millennial cult which was approaching endtime with no release in sight. The dancers — kitted out in transparent TiNi datasuits, VR shades and tribal markings — had been putting out a call to Isis for the last year in an attempt to escape the bonds of gravity and take flight through the electronic ether. Their mission was to transform the archaic ruins of Bat Hat into an interplanetary craft which would arc high over the degraded landscape of London and find the wormhole which connected with Sirius C. Who says they weren't going to do it? Everyone, of course. Luckily your faithful correspondent has more of an open mind. Someone had to.

Two hundred London natives snaking their hips from side

to side as their hands flip up and down and their feet weave intricate geometric patterns in the floor. Their separate bodies — exhibiting signs of sexual arousal through the metal tracework of their prosthetic skins — knotted and spliced into a single corporate entity which was dancing up a storm in the virtual world.

Eerie synth moans drifting round the temple, the bass dropping low as if waiting to attack. A moment's pause ... and then the drums kick in with a deafening fusillade of reprocessed beats. The dancers skid and dive as if caught in the cross-fire of a digital warzone. Some have already collapsed.

I flipped the CAMnet eyepiece to one side, stooped to retrieve a pair of discarded VR shades and put them on. A landscape of plush grasses filled with madly cavorting figures — quicktime avatars comprised of Deleuzian body parts, baroque Meccano rods and Lathamesque crustaceans — scrolled past at 170 bpm. I blinked rapidly and tracked back to take in the full widescreen view of what was now a distant planet wrapped in an cocoon of alien stars. The planet was covered in a net of purple micro-filaments which was in the process of being rapidly colonised by the swarm of avatars. You ask me what they were doing? Obviously reconditioning it for flight. One of the stars in what appeared to be the southern hemisphere was throbbing and flickering with an insistent urgency, its phase-shifted modulations in synch with the shattering tattoo of the drums. Here was the homing signal, the pinpoint navigational code which the craft needed to make its unimaginable journey.

It was too much. I flung the shades to the ground. Flocks of drum loops arced and rolled across the old Control Room as I made my way to the rickety podium of scrap metal at its centre on which the DJ was placed. She towered above the throng of celebrants like a voodoo priestess addressing the ancestor gods of the astral plane or an air-traffic controller plucking longhaul carriers from faraway holding patterns. Her long needle-tipped fingers tugged purposefully at the atoms around her as if shuttling thread from an invisible loom. She would keep on beating the drums like this all night. I stood quietly before her.

So this was Voodoo Ray. Her fame preceded her on the datanets. It was whispered that she could conjure the spirits from their hiding places in rocks and machines and trees, that she was a keeper of the keys which unlocked the hearts of men. I watched her. Her dark face was enclosed in an enveloping wimple of Sennheiser cans and skin-tight TiNi hood and her lips were parted in an ecstatic grin. Sweat poured from her brow and collected on the rim of the VR shades which shielded her eyes. She looked like the image of a pagan saint or a blind prophetess. CCD video eye catching it all.

The drums crashed at my feet. I needed to smoke some rock. That way I could plug into the London dreamtime and participate in the collective attempt to boot up rediscovered shamanic flight vectors and exit the rotting shell of Bat Hat. But, like I say, some of us have a job to do. It was down to me to keep a clear head.

You ask me to specify the tech jammed into the Temple ov Isis? I'll do it. Like its sustaining mythos, its operating system had been scratched together from a bundle of found objects. Check One. Bat Hat had fallen off London's electrical grid, so all power was sourced from protected banks of flaking generators which chugged quietly outside in the improvised marketplace. Check Two. The suits and shades had been imported from the sex arcades of Soho. (Old Hwang family connections.) Check Three. All virtual avatars had been custom-built in the coding basements of Brixton. Check Four. The celebrants had managed to grab hold of some junked Chamber of London software and were tripping on the back of its immersive store of images. It didn't matter to them that the writhing grasses, the purple planet and the winking stars coded the records of old financial transactions. But it mattered to the Corporation of London.

You ask me to go on? Then I shall. Check Five. Distributed ranks of old SPARC clones formed a local area network which plugged each of the dancers into the same virtual space at the same time. The shape-memory alloys embedded in the threads of their datasuits powered a collective force-feedback mechanism which was helmed by the figure of Voodoo Ray. She was the usher. Her own avatar was the lodestar in cyberspace which fine-tuned the collective rhythms of the planetary mass spread before her. Now do you understand?

It gets more intense. Check Six. The whole virtual envelope had been retro engineered so that it coincided with a computer-generated audio-tactile field. Infra-red sensors grafted into the datasuits sent coded burts of data to the SPARC clones based on the movements of the dancers. They entered the feedback loop and were ushered back into physical space by the kabuki hand jive of Voodoo Ray. Check Seven. A Matsushita DAT machine encased in a Kamecke black box rested at the base of the podium, its hermetic surface carved with Tzolkin calendrical glyphs and an Egyptian votive inscription. It was here that Voodoo Ray had hoarded her stock of digitally reprocessed breakbeats, her inheritance of old vinyl memories.

Check Eight. The speakers blasting out the punishing sonic fragments which Voodoo Ray retrieved from the DAT with a flick of her wrists. Her nails were sheathed with infra-red needles which glittered like claws as they scratched signs in the air. In front of her was the sample space. Behind her was the play space. She was suspended in the trigger plane.

I moved closer to her perch.

'Oh my gosh. London Town. Yes, yes, yes, yes, yes, yes, YES!'

She stood like a tiny colossus with her legs apart, the damp patch of her sex visible beneath the sheen of her suit as her hips rode the shuddering battery of sound. Spittle flew from her lips as she chanted her mantras. She plucked beats from the air with a manic glee, her arms wheeling and darting as if weaving a shroud or connecting a call. It seemed impossible that anyone could be so quick.

It was then that I understood. Voodoo Ray's podium marked the quadrivium in this cathedral of sound, the digital switchboard from which the gods of London were signed in. Devotional smartcards bearing images of local media saints – Jimi, Gerald, Jezebel — were pinned to the scrap-metal tower on which she was placed. Her feet were supported by a grimy slab of limestone which capped the whole edifice like the bridge of a ship. This was her stage, her scaffold, her gantry. It was the platform from which she would turn herself off.

Inside the mesh of iron and steel the Kamecke box reclines like a voluntary captive or a protected savant. You see what I see? Wicker machine.

I ended up dancing. What else could I do? Once the drums were racked up to 220 bpm, it was the only way to keep sane. Look at it. That's why the CAMnet footage is so spasmodic at this point. It's obvious that things were getting out of control.

Needlepoint rhythms unseaming my head as I struggle to keep up with their murderous pace. Voodoo Ray's claws a blur of deft cutwork. The drums looping and writhing in undulations of panic. I know I can process it all if I concentrate ... but the stress is too much. My body picks up the slack with its twitches and spasms and for a moment I slide into the groove. Stretched envelope of sound. The drums tripping higher and higher, weaving harp bolts of colour into a diaphonous labyrinth. I can almost reach out and touch it ... the internal architecture of a fantastic dream vessel. But none of this survives on the tape.

Look what is there. The crowd is demented, as if caught in a vortex of conflicting demands. Its members stagger and reel and hold out their hands. Some of them roll on the ground. There are nosebleeds, babblings and spontaneous orgasms. Do you think that maybe there was something coming in?

The Corporation goons had made their big entrance. Thrown a temporary exclusion zone around the perimeter of Bat Hat and sealed off all exits in advance of the bust. Roadblocks in the Battersea Park Road. Media blackout. Chinooks slung with Exocets clattering in the sky. The takedown sheet specified software piracy and drug trafficking. But that was just a paper construction. Battersea Power Station had been declared an autonomous bar of the City of London. The Corporation could do what it liked.

You heard the story of how they loosed off a missile? I don't know. It could have been the drums.

'Yes, yes, yes, yes. Let it come down.'

Voodoo Ray ... she warps the beats up into an even higher dimension. You have to slow down the CAMnet tape to even get close. It was then that I came to the end of my senses. The dance floor span away from me and I fell to the floor.

Mass panic and awful confusion. The Corporation's enforcers threshing the crowd with a relentless attack. Heckler & Kochs flailing, radio chatter, blood on the walls. What exactly is it they want? Quarantined inside white biohazard suits, the dreadful seals of the Corporation of London masking their faces, ribbed cables humping their backs like red dragons' spurs. They were breathing their own oxygen. As if the prospect of some awful contagion was what they most feared.

They were moving in on the stone mount where Voodoo Ray danced. She rained down her DAT gods upon them in invisible tongues of fire. The drums shrieking and squealing in an orgy of judgement. It was too much for the human metabolism to bear. But they could hear nothing. All orifices were plugged. The one thing they knew was protection.

Voodoo Ray's last move. She swings round — a full 180 degrees — and exposes her back to the advancing legions. It's then that I notice the tattoos beneath her TiNi suit. Seven of them descending from the crown of her head to the base of her spine like a wrathful serpent or a coiled flame. This was her last line of defence.

She squats on the stone with her legs wide apart and places her final calls to the gods. Her tattoos are like baroque circuit diagrams or compressed voodoo dials imprinted on a wafer of carbon. With the infrared needle attached to her left index finger she quickly signs each one. Her hand gently trips down her spine as if she were unzipping the skin of her datasuit in order to wriggle free. Sampling and playing the drums simultaneously there in the heat of the SPARC trigger plane. The clamour of the breakbeats was terrible. Her body shivered with the pleasure of it.

It's too weird for the Corporation goons. They have most definitely lost it. Someone releases a catch and there's the panicky stutter of gunfire.

Then they all open up in a roundel of lust.

'Stop, stop, STOP!' It's my own voice. Last thing I said before my CAMnet was trashed and my head opened up. You see what I see? Identification number on the goon doing me over is a blank. Bzzzp! End of transmission.

I was dazed and leaking. What happened next was what you would have to call an unexplained phenomenon. Because there is definitely no way I hallucinated the event.

Voodoo Ray is bowed with her head between her knees. She is unbloodied. They didn't catch her. The drums are still roaring. It's a miracle. She's scratching the stone with her needle, tracing a sigil she maybe sees in her head. Her face is a mask of awful recognition. Is she being called? The Corporation goons are closing in for the kill. Their blood is up. What do they care?

I was thinking that someone would be shot.

The dance floor seemed to lose its moorings for an instant. Quantum fissure. The desperate chatter of automatic fire. Voodoo Ray went up in smoke.

Let me rephrase that. A blue shaft of light inundated the stone and wrapped her tired body in a spectral cocoon. She raised her hand in greeting and waved farewell. Rapture. She was transported as her atoms dispersed.

I saw her tattoos glow red and burn themselves into the back of her TiNi suit. It dropped to the stone like a charred mantle from Heaven as the light died away.

Pick-up.

The drums were seething with a fierce imprecation. They shouldn't have been.

'Forgive.'

After that, it was just a matter of tidying up the mess. There was no future for Bat Hat, of course. The Corporation evacuated the building and detonated the remains. I guess there was some evidence they just didn't want to collect.

The strange thing about it all. Mass arrests, no charges. Blinking survivors left massaging their wrists on the Battersea Park Road as the power station retracted its sublime fluted chimneys and sank to its foot in a cushion of dust. The Corporation dezoned the territory soon after and relinquished it to the Crown. Shipped out its troops as quickly as it had choppered them in. It was a ten-line item in the domestic tabs. Bat Hat a death trap. Isis a Waco cult. Et cetera, et cetera. Blacks, guns and drugs.

Slightly more on the NEK WipeNet. Another ethnic skirmish in a Euro civil war. The Hwangs to sue for loss of capital assets. All of which leaves the big questions hanging. How many people were killed by the Corporation of London? Where are they buried and what are their names?

Information on this matter is very hard to come by.

One thing I do know. Voodoo Ray may be reckoned among the dead. But her name shall live for ever in the binary devotions of the digital shamans.

Neal Stephenson

'CRUNCH'

The condemned man showers, shaves, puts on most of a suit, and realises that he is ahead of schedule. He turns on the television, gets a San Miguel out of the fridge to steady his nerves, and then goes to the closet to get the stuff of his last meal. The apartment only has one closet and when its door is open it appears to have been bricked shut, Cask of Amontillado-style, with very large flat bricks that are mostly bright red. It is a cool red with strong bluish overtones, not a warm orangy red, and this impression is reinforced by the intensely blue uniform of the venerable and yet oddly cheerful and yet somehow kind of hauntingly sad naval officer whose image is printed upon each one of the bricks. They were shipped over here, directly to Randy's apartment door, several weeks ago by his boss, who was on this touching and somewhat annoying campaign to lift Randy's spirits. He sent a whole pallet load of them, perhaps (for all Randy knows) a whole shipping container full of them, with the remainder still sitting on a Manila dockside ringed with armed guards and dictionary-sized rat traps straining against their triggers with immediate-pre-orgasmic coiledness, each baited with a single golden nugget. Randy selects one of the bricks from this wall, creating a gap in the formation, but there is another, identical one right behind it, another picture of that same naval officer. They seem to be marching from his closet in a peppy phalanx of grinning Myrmidons. 'Part of this complete balanced breakfast,' Randy says. This is part of the ritual. Then he slams the door on them and walks with a measured, forcibly calm step to the living room where he does most of his dining, usually whilse facing his thirty-six-inch television set like a Victorian bachelor entertaining lady friends at opposite ends of a long table. He sets up his San Miguel, an empty bowl, an exceptionally large soup spoon, so large that most European cultures would identify it as a serving spoon and most Asian ones as a horticultural implement. He obtains a stack of paper napkins, not the brown recycled ones that can practically be immersed in a tub of water without getting moist, but the flagrantly environmentally unsound type, brilliant white and cotton-fluffy and desperately hygroscopic. He goes to the kitchen, opens the fridge, reaches deep into the back, and finds an unopened box-bag-pod-unit of UHT milk. UHT milk need not, technically, be refrigerated, but it is pivotal, in what is to follow, that the milk be only a few microdegrees above the point of freezing. The fridge in Randy's apartment has louvres in the back where the cold air is blown in, straight from the Freon coils. Randy always stores his milk-pods directly in front of those louvres. Not too close, or else the pods will block the flow of air, and not too far away either. The cold air becomes a visible gas as it rushes in and condenses moisture from the air and so it is a simple matter to sit there with the fridge door open and observe its flow characteristics, like an engineer testing an experimental minivan in a River Rouge wind tunnel. What Randy would like to see, ideally, is the whole milk-pod enveloped in an even jacket-like flow to produce better heat exchange through the multi-layered plastic-and-foil skin of the milk-pod. He would like the milk to be so cold that when he reaches in and grabs it, he feels the flexible, squishy pod stiffen between his fingers as ice crystals spring into existence, summoned out of nowhere by the disturbance of being squished.

Today the milk is almost, but not quite, that cold. Randy goes into his living room with it. He has to wrap it in a towel because it is so cold it hurts his fingers. He launches a videotape and then sits down. All is in readiness.

'Crunch'

This is one of a series of videotapes that are shot in an empty basketball gym with a polished maple floor and a howling, remorseless ventilation system. They depict a young man and a young woman, both attractive, svelte, and dressed something like marquee players in the *Ice Capades*, performing simple ballroom dance steps to the accompaniment of strangled music from a ghetto blaster set up on the free-throw line. It is miserably clear that the video has been shot by a third conspirator who is burdened with a consumer-grade camcorder and reeling from some kind of inner-ear disease that he or she would like to share with others. The dancers stomp through the most simple steps with autistic determination. The camera operator begins in each case with a two-shot, then, like a desperado tormenting a milksop, aims his weapon at their feet and makes them dance, dance, dance. At one point the pager hooked to the man's elastic waistband goes off and a scene has to be cut short. No wonder: he is one of the most sought-after ballroom dance instructors in Manila. His partner would be too, if more men in this city were interested in learning to dance. As it is, she must scrape by earning maybe a tenth of what the male instructor pulls down, giving lessons to a small number of addled or henpecked stumblebums like Randy Waterhouse.

Randy takes the red box and holds it securely between his knees with the handy stay-closed tab pointing away from him. Using both hands in unison he carefully works his fingertips underneath the flap, trying to achieve equal pressure with each one, paying special attention to places where too much glue was laid down by the gluing-machine. For a few long, tense moments, nothing at all happens, and an ignorant or impatient server might suppose that Randy is not doing anything. But then the entire flap pops open in an instant as the entire glue-front gives way. Randy hates it when the box-top gets bent or, worst of all possible worlds, torn. The lower flap is merely tacked down with a couple of small glue-spots and Randy pulls it back to reveal a translucent, inflated sac. The halogen down-light recessed in the ceiling directly overhead shines through the cloudy material of the sac to reveal

311

gold — everywhere the glint of gold. Randy rotates the box ninety degrees and holds it between his knees so its long axis is pointed at the television set, then grips the top of the sac and carefully parts its heat-sealed seam, which purrs as it gives way. Removal of the somewhat milky plastic barrier causes the individual nuggets of Cap'n Crunch to stand out, under the halogen light, with a kind of preternatural crispness and definition that makes the roof of Randy's mouth glow and throb in trepidation.

On the television, the dancing instructors have finished demonstrating the basic steps finally. It is almost painful to watch them doing the compulsories, because when they do, they must wilfully forget everything they know about advanced ballroom dancing, and dance like persons who have suffered strokes, or major brain injuries, that have wiped out not only the parts of their brain responsible for fine motor skills but also blown every panel in the aesthetic discretion module. They must, in other words, dance the way their beginning pupils, like Randy, dance. It is not a pretty sight, and Randy is all too conscious of the fact that he does not even have a dance-gigolo's ameliorating face, hairstyle and physique.

The gold nuggets of Cap'n Crunch pelt the bottom of the bowl with a sound like glass rods being snapped in half. Tiny fragments spiral away from their corners and ricochet around on the white porcelain surface. World-class cereal-eating is a dance of fine compromises. The giant heaping bowl of sodden cereal, awash in milk, is the mark of the novice. Ideally one wants the bone-dry cereal nuggets and the cryogenic milk to enter the mouth with minimal contact and for the entire reaction between them to take place in the mouth. Randy has a set of mental blueprints worked out for a special cereal-eating spoon that will have a tube running down the handle and a little pump for the milk, so that you can spoon dry cereal up out of a bowl, hit a button with your thumb, and squirt milk into the bowl of the spoon even as you are introducing it into your mouth. The next-best thing is to work in small increments, putting only a small amount of Cap'n Crunch in your bowl at a time and eating it all up before it becomes a pit of loathsome slime, which takes about thirty seconds in the case of Cap'n Crunch.

At this point in the videotape he always wonders if he's inadvertently set his beer down on the fast-forward button, or something, because the dancers go straight from their vicious Randy parody into something that obviously qualifies as advanced dancing. Randy knows that the steps they are doing are nominally the same as the basic steps demonstrated earlier, but he's damned if he can tell which is which, once they go into their creative mode. There is no recognisable transition, and that is what pisses Randy off, and has always pissed him off, about dancing lessons. Any moron can learn to trudge through the basic steps. That takes all of half an hour. But when that half-hour is over, dancing instructors always expect you to take flight and go through one of those miraculous time-lapse transitions that happen only in Broadway musicals and begin dancing brilliantly. They never show you how the transition works, which is the really mysterious part where creativity or inspiration or something happens. Randy supposes that people who are lousy at maths feel the same way: the instructor writes a few simple equations on the board, and ten minutes later he's deriving the speed of light in a vacuum, having jumped over the part where he does something brilliant and miraculous, because not even he himself knows how he did it.

He pours the milk with one hand while jamming the spoon in with the other, not wanting to waste a single moment of the magical, golden time when cold milk and Cap'n Crunch are together but have not yet begun to pollute each other's essential natures: two Platonic ideals separated by a boundary layer a molecule wide. Where the flume of milk splashes over the spoon-handle, the polished stainless steel fogs with condensation. Randy of course uses whole milk, because otherwise why bother with the whole exercise? Anything less is indistinguishable from water, and besides he thinks that the fat in whole milk acts as some kind of a buffer that retards the dissolution-into-slime process. The giant spoon goes into his mouth before the milk in the bowl has even had time to seek its own level. A few drips come off the bottom and are caught by his freshly washed goatee (still trying to find the right balance between beardedness and vulnerability, Randy has allowed one of these to grow). Randy sets the milk-pod down, grabs a fluffy napkin, lifts it to his chin, and uses a pinching motion to sort of lift the drops of milk from his whiskers rather than smashing and smearing them down into the beard. This happens without thinking about it; all his concentration is fixed on the interior of his mouth, which naturally he cannot see, but which he can imagine in three dimensions as if zooming through it in a virtual-reality display. Here is where a novice would lose his cool and simply chomp down. A few of the nuggets would explode between his molars but then his jaw would snap shut and drive all of the unshattered nuggets straight up into his palate where their armour of razor-sharp dextrose crystals would inflict massive collateral damage, turning the rest of the meal into a sort of pain-hazed death march and rendering him Novocain-mute for three days.

Randy has over time worked out a really fiendish Cap'n Crunch-eating strategy that revolves around using the nuggets' most deadly features to his advantage by playing them against each other. The nuggets themselves are pillow-shaped and vaguely striated in a way that he has always thought is supposed to echo piratical treasure chests or something. Now, in a flake type of cereal, Randy's strategy would never work, but then Cap'n Crunch could never be manufactured in flake form because then it would be all surface area, and it must have been obvious to the cereal engineers at General Mills that this would be suicidal madness, that Cap'n Crunch stuff in that configuration would last about as long, when immersed in milk, as snowflakes sifting down into a deep fryer. No, they had to find a shape that would minimise surface area, which ideally would be a sphere (this is why healthy cereals tend to be flakes and sugary ones tend to be round). As some sort of compromise between the sphere that is dictated by

Euclidean geometry and whatever sunken-treasure-related shapes that the cereal-aestheticians were probably clamouring for, they came up with this hard-to-pin-down striated pillow formation. The important thing about which, for Randy's purposes, is that the individual pieces of Cap'n Crunch are, to a very rough approximation, shaped kind of like molars. The strategy, then, is to use the Cap'n Crunch against itself by grinding the nuggets together in the centre of the oral cavity, making the cereal chew itself, like stones in a lapidary tumbler, minimising any contact with gums and palate — contacts bound to be bloody, violent and painful. Like advanced ballroom dancing, verbal explanations (or for that matter watching videotapes while sitting on your ass) only go so far and then your body has to learn how to do this.

By the time he has eaten a satisfactory amount of Cap'n Crunch (about a third of a twenty-five ounce box) and reached the bottom of his beer bottle, Randy has convinced himself that this whole dance thing is a practical joke. When he reaches the ballroom, the people who sent him the invitation will be waiting for him with mischievous smiles. They will tell him it was all a joke and then take him into the bar to talk him down.

He puts on the last few bits of his suit. Any delaying tactics are acceptable at this point, and so he checks his fax machine. There is one fax from his palimony lawyer in California, which he puts into his breast pocket to savour while he is stuck in traffic. He takes the elevator downstairs, and catches a taxi to the Manila Hotel. This (riding in a taxi through Manila) would be one of the more memorable experiences of his life if this were the first time he had ever done it, but is the millionth time and so nothing registers. For example, he sees two cars smashed together directly beneath a giant road sign that says NO SWERVING, but he doesn't remember it.

Robert Anton Wilson

DALI'S CLOCKS

No malfunction! Number five is alive!
— *Number Five*

I am not a number! I am a free man!
— *Number Six*

A census taker tried to quantify me once.
I ate his liver with some fava beans
and a big Amarone.
— *Hannibal Lecter*, MD

First Predicament of Perspective

Get the crow-bar, Gloria.
Rock'n'Roll Wrestling Women Versus the Aztec Ape

Although Dubliners claim that a Cork man is only a Kerry man in human form,[1] there is reason to believe that Cork men are the

[1]Dubliners also believe, or claim to believe, that the wheelbarrow was invented to teach Kerry men to walk on their hind legs. On the other hand, Kerry people claim that to house the insane of Ireland one would have to build a mental hospital in Belfast, another in Limerick and then put a roof over Dublin.

most Irish, and therefore the most subtle, persons on the planet. It was a Cork jury which once voted a defendant, 'not guilty, if he promises not to do it in this town again.'

The town hall of Cork City has four clocks facing the four quarters. They are all consistently inconsistent, to introduce an appropriately Irish bull. That is, no two of them ever tell the same minute and they usually don't even agree as to the hour. Locals call them the Four Liars.

A visitor from some heathen and exotic place — possibly England — once commented, 'How typically Irish — even the clocks don't agree!'

A Cork man, overhearing this, quickly explained, 'Well sure now, if all four of them agreed, three of them would be superflous.'

Cork people all believe that time was invented by the English as a treacherous way of making a man work more than is altogether good for him.

And the only Irish philosophers to have world class status, Erigena and Berkeley, both denied that time exists at all, at all.

All Irish bulls are pregnant.

Second Predicament of Perspective

> Tao fa tsu-jan.
> Lao-Tse. *Tao Te Ching*

It was the most reverend televangelist Jowly Fallow[1] who inspired Simon The Walking Glitch to devise the Anti-Millennialist Organisation (AMO). Neither of them knew anything about the vast insectoid intelligences and the mad Arab who would

---

[1] The Revd Fallow daily informed his fourteen-million TV audience of such arcane secrets as the control of the Rock industry by the Illuminati, the fact that all UFOs were demons in disguise, and all Feminists were witches, lesbians and practitioners of cannibalism in their secret Satanic rituals.

intervene in both their designs and, incidentally, send millions of humans flying into the wild blue yonder.

Simon founded Anti-Millennialism on 3 Absolu 124 EP[1] when Fallow's followers and all sorts of Christians and New Agers were starting to prepare for a millennium which they claimed would happen in only two years, three months and nineteen days. Simon The Walking Glitch insisted that their damned millennium would not occur for *three* years, three months and nineteen days, which proves they couldn't count, and besides the real millennium, the first, wouldn't occur for over eight hundred years.

Simon believed that, since 'pataphysics is *the science*, the 'pataphysical calendar is *the* calendar. Just as all other sciences deal with the general and 'pataphysics with the exceptional, the 'pataphysical calendar is the only one deliberately designed so that every month would have a Friday the 13th, just to keep people careful.

Simon The Walking Glitch was not the son of Mr and Mrs Walking Glitch, you must understand. His parents were Tim and Molly Moon, who would have spelled their last name Muadhen if they had remained in County Cork, but in the United States people tended to pronounce that noble old Celtic name as if it were mud-hen, so Tim's parents approximated a phonetic spelling. Simon, an obsessive-compulsive in all things, knew enough Gaelic etymology to realise that Mo'on would be more accurate, but Americans are not very good at pronouncing aspirates, so he let the Moon shine as it would.

---

[1] *Era Pataphysique.* Simon had been converted to 'pataphysics when he discovered that Alfred Jarry, the founder, was born on the date called 8 September (1873) in the pagan system. Since 8 September is also the birthday of the Blessed Virgin Mary in the Vatican mythos and Molly Bloom in the Joycean mythos, Simon recognised synchronicity and was immediately attracted. But it was Professor Timothy F.X. Finnegan's extension of Jarry's 'pataphsycis into 'patapsychology that really hooked Simon, as we shall see. (8 September in the old system is I Absolu in the 'pataphysical system, of course.)

It didn't really matter because all his friends called him The Walking Glitch anyway.

'Here comes Simon The Walking Glitch,' they would say. Or:

'Who's that lurking there like the kiss of death? Isn't it Simon The Walking Glitch?' Or;

'Protect your hard disks, boys — Simon The Walking Glitch is in the building.'

Simon had earned this reputation by his labours in 'pataspace, which he virtually invented after exploring all the possibilities of cyberspace and cryptospace.

Cyberspace was available to anyone with a computer, but cryptospace, where the real fun happened, was only accessible to those with the proper PGP-variants for that week: the true subterraneans and troglodytes of the night side of cyberpunk.[1] 'Pataspace, like ordinary cyberspace, was open to all — but comprehensible only to those with Fully Illuminated Minds, i.e. Simon and the eleven other members of the Invisible Hand Society.[2]

Actually, although Simon had a strong resemblence to Bigfoot, except that he didn't have big feet, he was a gentle soul. If he

---

[1] According to *The Encyclopedia of Social Inventions*, Institute of Social Inventions, London 1990, the first non-interest-bearing electronic currency began in a section of cryptospace between Vancouver, Canada, and San Diego, US around 1982. Such currency does not require usury paid to bankers and remains invisible also to tax investigators. As T.C. May writes, 'Strong cryptography, exemplified by RSA (a public key algorithm) and PGP (pretty good privacy) provides encryption that essentially cannot be broken with all the computing power in the universe ... '—tc may @ netcom.com

[2] The Invisible Hand Society was based on Adam Smith's doctrine that an Invisible Hand guides all free markets and on Prof. Timothy F.X. Finnegan's addendum that even in unfree markets (those with Government Interference, monopoly, conspiracy, corruption etc.) the Invisible Hand still governs. 'What you can depart from is not the Tao; what you can violate is not Natural Law; what you can subvert is not the Invisible Hand.' — Finnegan, *Nightmare and Awakening*. Royal 'Patapsychological Institute.

ever broke his early-sixties imprint and got a haircut he might look like any middle-aged middle-rank executive in Silicon Gulch. His 'pataphysical glitches never harmed anyone (he was scrupulous about that): they just left behind an aura of inpenetrable mystery and a faint suggestion that inhuman, maybe extraterrestrial, minds had penetrated the Net.

Those advanced hackers who knew about Simon and his labours spent many hours among themselves debating which Websites were Simon's work, which came from imitators of his style, which from genuine certifiable nuts, and which might be actual extraterrestrial come-ons.

If you've ever had a seeming-virus that did no real damage but kept coming up at odd moments to incite you to send lasagna to the starving aliens in Area 51 you might — just *might* — have intersected one of Simon's 'pataphysical invasions of ordinary mindspace. Or then again, maybe it was just another joker – or maybe it was real starving aliens down there under the hot south-western sand. You never know what the CIA is up to.

Third Predicament of Perspective

Computers in the future may weigh no more than 1.5 tons.

Popular Mechanics, 1949

In its tragically brief career (it only lasted twelve billion years, and by then its best minds had migrated to Zeta Reticuli), planet Earth produced approximately 845,000 species of animals, an about average figure for a planet that tiny and transient.

Among the less numerous species, this included only around 2,100 (twenty-one hundred) different kinds of amphibians, including frogs, toads, salamanders, newts, caecilians and other croaking or creeping critters of that ilk.

Earth did better with mammals, producing over 4,500 (forty-five hundred) species, such as the much-loved dog, the loathed but indestructible rat, the bumbling human, the imperialistic lion, the vivacious voles, the bland bovines, the sagacious equines, the grizzly ursines, the suave suidea (including pigs, hogs, wild boars, several families of distinguished swine and various LA peace officers), along with foxes, dingoes, hippopotomi, and a variety of aquatic cousins such as the dolphin, the orca, the sperm whale, the allegorical white whale and the stupefyingly great blue whale.

In one of its more creative moods Earth also gave birth to more than 7,000 (seven thousand) species of reptiles, among them the brachiosaurus, the stegosaurus, the tyranosaurus, the crocodile, the alligator, the boa constrictor, the asp, the rattlesnake, the king cobra, the black snake, the mamba snake, the asp, the viper and the Revd Jowly Fallow.

Earthlife also had its psychedelic and neo-surrealist, or 'exuberant' varieties. It galloped along producing well over 9,000 (nine thousand) species of birds, varying from the unbelievable peacock and the splendid robin to the nondescript sparrow, the finch, the jay, the scrubjay, the hawk, the falcon, the seagull, the mudhen (never to be confused with the muadhen, native to Cork and, although an odd bird, more human than avian), and the egregious pelican whose beak holds more than his belly can as all students of classic poetry know ...

On the side it added 21,000 (twenty-one thousand) species of fish, from the shark and salmon to the guppy, the squid and lobster.

Mostly, however, in a kind of creative delerium, it gibbered a plethora of insects — its favourite invention, evidently — over 800,000 (eight *hundred* thousand) different kinds of them, most of which were various kinds of beetles. That is of the 845,000 (eight hundred and forty-five thousand) species of animals, more than 800,000 (eight hundred thousand) were bugs.

Earth also produced the kingdom of plants, including bird of paradise flowers and cacti, along with giant redwoods, the holy-healing-hilarious hemp, roses, violets, mums, fuchsia, buttercups and broccoli. Then it added the kingdom of fungi.

Mostly, however, it went on adding more and more beetles, and more and more different species or kinds of beetles.

Earth just never seemed to think it had enough beetles. You might say the whole planet suffered from acute incurable beetlemania.[1]

One very clever mammal named Dr J.B.S. Haldane — a primate and a Marxist biologist who, oddly, did yoga ever day — was once asked, 'If you would accept the idea of a Mind behind life's evolution, what outstanding trait would you attribute to that mind?'

Dr Haldane answered without hesitation, 'An inordinate fondness for beetles.'

The ants, who didn't give a damn what mammals like Haldane thought about anything and had even less regard for beetles, had taken over Earth midway through its history.

At least, they had taken over in the only timeline they knew about.

Vtttrl had spent most of her modest life as a worker ant in the Institute for Historical Correction in Bqfszn, but a strange, unworkerlike yearning to know more had haunted her all her life. Since omnipresent radiation and the mutations it caused were constant factors in her world, Vtttrl knew that she probably had a few freaky genes. She had been born defective.

Of course, some mutations were improvements. But it was immodest and anti-social to think that way. She accepted herself as a pervert.

The Institute for Historical Correction, where she worked, was popularly called the It-Never-Happened-Department. The

---

[1]Some scholars regard the last twelve paragraphs as an invasion from 'pataspace by Simon Moon and or his cohorts in the Invisible Hand Society. This theory is probably a romantic fiction, like the Bacon-Shakespeare schlemozzle.

workers there spent all their time fine-tuning the Big Bang. They did not need wormholes and time-travel to do this. They simply exploited Qgwwkwe's application of Adkk's Theorem, which showed that, since all nuclear systems are non-locally correlated, any nuclear adjustment here-and-now has effects there-and-then — non-locality meaning in this case, that here-and-then is anywhere-and-anywhen. By use of Fukgiikwt's tensors, anywhere-and-anywhen became, at the experimenter's choice, a specific there-and-then, i.e., the Big Bang.

'Everything started with the Big Bang,' went the antennæ-vision bromide whenever the work of the Institute was discussed on a pop science show, 'so if there's anything wrong anywhere, the place to fix it is to start right there, at the beginning.'

Almost all her life, Vtttrl had accepted this as a kind of Article of Faith, although she called it Scientific Fact.

Vtttrl and the other giant ped-ants were inclined, like some earlier species, to confuse their Articles of Faith with their Scientific Facts. Some of them were clever enough to notice this, so they founded a Committee to Separate the Articles of Faith from the Scientific Facts. Under ideal conditions, this much-needed work of analysis could have clarified every ped-ant's thinking and working.

Unfortunately, the members of the Committee firmly believed that their own Articles of Faith were actually the only real Scientific Facts, and they only added a great deal of acrimony to the existing general confusion.

Vtttrl had been part of that Committee once, before she saw through their errors. She had spent her life seeing through the errors of one group of ped-ants after another. The only error she had not seen through, yet, was the error shared by all black ants.

This error held that the world would be perfect once all the *red* ants were exterminated. All the work on the Big Bang — the endless fine-tuned adjustments in the fabric of space-time — had the single purpose of impossiblising potentia. This meant limiting the number of possible universes, and limiting again, and again, and again ... until *eventually one* perfect universe would remain, without a single red ant in it anywhere.

Vtttrl's Heresy and her Forbidden Experiments all began when she calculated, one day, how many universes had to be impossibilised before that one perfect universe appeared. The number seemed to be higher than Xzbrie's first kind of infinity, and her second kind of infinity ... and, as Vtttrl calculated further, it gradually emerged as higher than any kind of infinity known to (or invented by?) all the clever account-ants who had ever lived.

No finite number of adjustments in the Big Bang, however many were made, would ever produce a whole universe without red ants. Vtttri inscribed her proof in proper notation, just to check her calculations. The result was just what she had reasoned. Only an infinite number of adjustments, requiring infinite time, could abolish those damned *Reds*.

Vtttrl had learned something about the confusion of Articles of Faith and Scientific Facts when she was still attending meetings of those who thought they could make that distinction easily. She did not tell any of her hivesibs or co-workers about her discovery. She destroyed her inscribed proof. But she went on thinking her private thoughts, privately.

Eventually, she realised that the Big Bang was too far back to begin the process of Historical Correction. She started researching the period just before the dawn of history, i.e., before the Rupture.

Both of Earth's intelligent species had appeared after the Rupture — i.e., the wise and kindly black ants, who were devoted to peace, high art, and pure reason, and only wanted the territory that belonged to them by Natural Law; and their bitter enemies, the wicked red ants led by a mad queen (with a 'dictatorial lust for power') who wallowed in war, vulgar art, vile superstitions, and wanted territory that did not belong to them by Natural Law. And the Rupture came of the White Dawn, which came of the silly conflicts of the absurd two-sexed mammal species that once dominated this planet.

Vtttrl studied archaeological history more avidly than any ped-ant before her. Eventually, she was sure she could place the blame for the White Dawn on one group among one obscenely two-sexed species.

That group had been called the Christians. Not knowing that everything is produced by thought and does not exist apart from thought, they did a lot of thinking about the End of the World. Worse yet, they talked about it, which made other people think about it. They had almost produced a real End of the World out of their Apocalyptic fantasies, and the Rupture was the result.

Now she simply had to find a way to travel backwards in time and eat those Christian bastards one by one.

She started studying the literature of wormholes. They were theoretically possible, but all learned opinion held that it would cost a quintillion (a billion billion billion billion) megaztuykkpz to build one and the project would take at least four hundred and seventy millenniums.

She despaired — but only for a little while. Having weird genes, she always cheered up fairly soon, no matter what happened.

Vtttrl advanced to her wildest Heresy yet. Having found that many alleged Scientific Facts were only Articles of Faith, she decided to investigate whether some Articles of Faith might actually be Scientific Facts. She began studying the 'superstitions' of the stupid, brutal soldier ants — huge louts despised by all workers. Everybody knew the soldiers were only good for killing millions and millions of the damned red ants every year. Vtttrl began studying the soldier ant Faith, which posits the Great Szn which maintains all things in balance by renewing the universe every nanosecond.

She wasted years with divinations that were only correct about 50 per cent of the time, longevity oukka that only made her irritable and insomniac, and other balderdash. But more and more the Yspist meditations and visualisations opened her mind to vistas of worlds that seemed as real as the Institute for Historical Correction — worlds of mammalian horror and beauty and boredom. And she came to understand the great mystic teaching at the heart of the Szn cult. Vtttrl soon realised this formula — the opening cweaw of the ancient *Szn Sd Bghmh* — would lead her to her own secret wormhole: 'THE SZN THAT CAN BE THOUGHT IS NOT THE TRUE SZN.'

She walked through everywhere/everywhen and began searching for the proper here-now.

In this distance, dimly, she heard a voice complain about dirty socks and denture breath ...

Fifth Predicament of Perspective

This carrot, as you call it, has constructed an aircraft
capable of flying millions of miles through space,
propelled by a force unknown to us.

The Thing

'And all these baby-killing abortionists and the men who lie with other men, as St Paul said, and the UFO hell creatures — and Hillary Clinton, too,' Jowly Fallow ranted into the television camera, 'They'll all get their come-uppance on the great day of the Rupture — I mean, the day of the Rapture ...'

Simon Moon, toking deeply on his hash pipe, grinned, and clicked the remote over to the Playboy channel.

The interpenetration of the universes had begun ... The Anti-Millennialism meme was infiltrating the Christian reality-tunnel.

Sixth Predicament of Perspective

The deity ain't no nickle-dime bum show.

James Joyce

When Abdel Rahman Massoud, director of the Institute for

Serious Investigation of Claims of the Preposterous, decided to send himself two hundred years backwards in time, from the Sixteenth Century to the Fourteenth, he knew he might be making a huge mistake.

None the less, he sincerely felt his choice was necessary. He was on a mission from God. Besides, he consoled himself by contemplating the great quote from the Unspeakable Infidel, which he kept on his office wall:

> DON'T WORRY ABOUT THE END OF THE WORLD:
> ALLAH IS SMART ENOUGH TO KEEP A BACK-UP DISC

Abdel, had inserted the name of Allah. The infamous infidel, in addition to her other heresies, had said 'Goddess'.

Abdel in fact, was not a normal Muslim for his time, or any time. He had studied the forbidden works of Hassan i Sabbah, Abdul Alhazred, Noble Drew Ali and Hakim Bey, and perhaps he had studied them all a bit too assiduously. Even in his sleep he sometimes saw the most shocking sentences of their works dancing before him: 'Nothing is true, all is permitted', 'Past, present, future: all are one in Yog Sothoth', 'Let's smoke this shit,' 'The chains of the law have been broken!'

And he also had this infamous (only mildly expurgatged) wall plaque, taken from the infidel philosopher — and a mere woman, too! — the notorious witch-queen, Lola of Capitola. She had lived two hundred years ago, contemporary with the Great Mistake. Lola had lived during what Abdel called the Fourteenth Century [1] (which the uncircumcised white-skinned Euro-American dogs — floating way out there in the infidel *dar al-harb*, or space stations — still called the Twentieth Century, even though none of them were Christians any more).

Abdel had an obsession about Lola. She seemed to know something that even Sabbah, Alhazred, Noble Drew Ali and Bey

---

[1] Lola had been born in fact in 1358 AH and did not leave this world until 1393 AH. She left by starship, bound for Sirius.

didn't guess. 'Allah has a back-up disc': the more you contemplated it, the less sure you were that you had understood it fully. But you remained sure it was worth understanding.

Besides, when all was said and done, Abdel had lost faith in the mullahs who ruled the *dar al-Islam* (formerly, planet Earth). Islamic mullahs, Abdel thought, were like the priests of all other (and hence, lesser) religions. They didn't really know shit from shinola about metaphysics. Why, most of them even thought his Institute for Serious Study of Claims of the Preposterous was some wacko kind of Sufi joke! They even called Abdel 'the goofy Sufi'. They hadn't even begun to notice all the little clues, in dull ordinary places and in the expanses of space itself, showing that the world was far more preposterous than pious minds ever realise, factors which added synergetically made up what Abdel called the Cosmic Giggle Factor.

Abdel had built himself a wormhole — a simple way of connecting two black holes, which was an elementary project he had found in the Erector Set of the third son of his second wife. These gizmos were common nowadays, but the mullahs said you should only use them to look back into the past. You should not use a wormhole to change the past.

Worse: the mullahs had their opinion on this matter written into the law. What Abdel planned was a high crime, punishable by the worst penalty allowed in current law — the madness-or-suicide option. Those sentenced to this Extreme Penalty were given a box containing one cyanide capsule and then locked up for life in a small room with a television set that broadcast videos of ancient Jowly Fallow tapes twenty-four hours a day. Almost all of the wretches punished this way swallowed the poison capsule within the first year.

The mullahs wanted people to use wormholes as if they were mere television sets for history majors. Abdel gritted his teeth at the thought. In the whole city of Los Angeles — from the opulent Santa Barbara neighbourhood in the north to the run-down Phoenix section in the east — there were more great Islamic scholars than had ever lived in one place in the whole history of *dar al-Islam*. And none of them dared to disobey the mullahs, dive into a damned wormhole, and actually *change* the past. The past could not, should not and would not be changed, the mullahs said, because Allah Himself had ordained and written it.

Religious conservatives are the same everywhere, Abdel thought bitterly. None of them realises Allah is smart enough to keep *more than one* back-up disc ... and He knows when to send things to the Rewrite Department.

He probably even knows when to send some things to the It Never Happened Department.

Abdel was ready; his mind was resolved. He would hesitate no more. He would open the wormhole, go back in time to the One Wrong Turn in history, kill Jowly Fallow, that Great Shaitan who had ruined everything, and come back to a world which, in logic, must be very different, and much better, than the world he had left.

He flick-clicked the positronic electroframmis, checked the quark compactor on the neurofranz one more time, opened the sub-space Finagle junction and boldly stepped into the wormhole.

The first thing he saw was a huge black ant the size of a full-grown male rhinoceros.

The ant saw Abdel, too, and addressed him in precise, almost finicky Arabic: 'O contemptibly insignificant molecule of camel turd, what are you doing in *my* wormhole?'

Seventh Predicament of Perspective

> Orson Welles didn't wear angora sweathers!
> *Ed Wood*

'Well, I'm a Thelemite,' Mavis Celine explained. 'At midnight, the new year for me will be 97 y. H.'

'That's year of Horus, I assume?' Simon asked politely.

'Hoor-par-Kraat, or Harpocrates,' Mavis said. 'I'm a reformed Thelemite.'

The Anti-Millennial bash was in full swing as the clock passed eleven and everybody looked forward to the non-millennium in less than an hour. Simon had even redecorated his pad, adding a reproduction of Dali's *Persistence of Memory* to the seawall, melting clocks speaking mutely against grids of all kinds.

'For us,' Juan Tootreegro was telling Marvin Gardens at the other end of the room, 'the year changes on 31 October. The year 79 ended last 30 October and the new year, 80 psU, begins at midnight in ten months, when 30 October turns to 31 October again.' He saw Marvin's confusion and added quickly, 'We date things psU. That means *post scriptum Ulysses*, because Joyce wrote the last sentence of the Good Book on 30 October 1921 and thus ended the Christian era.'

The whale-like bulk of Blake Williams loomed over both of them. 'So you have 920 years to go before the first millennium?' he asked, making notes. (He had invented neurosemantic topology and was researching an article.) 'The only group that has longer to wait is the 'pataphysics folk whose calendar started in 1873 e.v.'

Standing by the patio door, a little man named Ginsberg was telling Carol Christmas, 'I only came to this party because tonight isn't my millennium either. I didn't realise there'd be so many weird types hanging around ...'

'And how many years until *your* next millennium?' Carol asked warmly, trying to put him at ease. Her blonde head leaned forward intimately.

'Uh, well, the next millennium um 6000 that would be for the Orthodox like me is ah oh yes 239 years away,' Ginsberg calculated rapidly somewhat befuddled by the approach of a great deal of persistence of mammary. 'Orthodox Jews,' he added, not sure she understood that part.

Simon The Walking Glitch was wandering about distributing blotter acid to anyone who was interested.

'Dates? Faith, I don't care about dates. Sure the universe has no single Big Clock now, does it? What interests me is what I found on Mars when I employed computer analysis to the Face.'

Simon recognised the voice — Professor Timothy F.X. Finnegan, the man who had converted him to 'patapsychology and then to 'pataphysics.[1]

'The Face on Mars?' Mavis Celine asked dubiously. 'I thought with close analysis the "face" turned out to be just rocks and shadows.'

'Hah!' snorted Finnegan, and passed the cocaine. 'With holistic computer enhancement,' he pronounced slowly, 'I have positively identified the face as Moses Horwitz! The only man to be honoured on two different planets. Jumping blue Jay-sus, won't that knock the scientific and theological establishments on their arses!'

'Moses *who*?' asked at least five voices at once; but at the same moment Mamie van Doren said quite distinctly, 'Dirty socks and denture breath.'

When the hell did she get in, Simon wondered uneasily, and what the flying fuck was she talking about?[2]

But then he was even more confused by the streets of 1904 Sandycove. The mix of horse-drawn carriages and infrequent

[1]Professor Finnegan, in addition to founding the science of 'patapsychology (the study of puzzling but uncertain mental events that could not be replicated or even remembered exactly by six o'clock the next morning), also created CSICON, the Committee for Surrealist Investigation of Claims of the Normal. It was CSICON's claim that no person, place or event was ever totally normal in all respects, or even average, and that those who believe in 'normal events' are believing in spooks (abstractions). 'There is no such thing as a normal European, a normal dog, an average sunset or even an ordinary Beethoven symphony,' Finnegan wrote in his *Life After Life*.

[2]Although Moses Horwitz has not yet been identified (and the editors would be most happy to receive any information on this matter) Ms van Doren's remark has been traced to a comment she made after her affair with Henry Kissinger: 'All I remember is dirty socks and denture breath.'

'automobiles' seemed normal for that time-space predicament, but few of the citizens looked at all Irish. Most of them were Arab boy-prostitutes and they propositioned him twenty-three times before he reached the corner to hop on the tram to Dublin Central.

'—with his brother Jerome, you see, and a friend name Lawrence Finestein—'

'The Subliminal Syndicate as pale as his shirt ... dirty socks for our Irish poets—' There were flutes and pan-pipes playing nearby ... wormwood, too much in the sun ...

The tram was drawn by a giant black centipede. The driver, Madonna in one of her more pointy-type bras and a ballet skirt above army boots, kept a flamethrower at her side and had to use it a few times, sending warning blasts of fire over the centipede's head when it made obviously hungry lunges at passing Jesuits and Mugwumps.

'I hate pleonasms,' Simon Moon moaned mournfully, 'but where the fornication am I?' He knew he had taken acid a while ago but this was unlike any Trip in his experience.

'Let me explain,' said the large red ant — it was about the size of a Greyhound Bus — 'We dragged you through a wormhole. You and your Discordian friends are messing up the pivot point of all history and aiding the Evil Black Ants. I will tell you the awful truth in plain English, your own language.' (That was a mistake: Simon still regarded Gaelic as his 'own' language and English as the tongue of the *Sassenach* invaders.)

'Yes?' Simon prompted. The ant was frowning thoughtfully (as far as Simon could judge, not being an expert on insect physiognomy).

'It has been known as swim-two-birds from ancient times,' the ant went on in rudimentary West County Irish Gaelic, 'and I a mere lad at the time I learned it — God and Mary and Patrick and Bridget be praised—' (He can read minds, Simon decided.) '—that the ant is neither the first nor the last of Earth's masters. We know of you, and your odd, faintly silly, two-sexed culture.

We have studied you with our vast, cool and unsympathetic intellects. We know you as the nose knows the rose and the rose knows the nose.' (Trouble with Gaelic syntax often produces such effects in non-native speakers, Simon remembered.)

'Because of your Erisian interference with the fan of fan-shaped fate,' the ant said, groping towards his point, 'a Totally Wrong universe emerged. It included a most unfortunate species — large, and totally vicious, *black* ants, led by a mad queen with a dictatorial lust for power. They are illogical and superstitious and backward and, *a chara*, in simple Irish, man, they are a royal pain the arse. I have built a wormhole to eliminate their time-line from the possible predicaments of energy. And you are messing with me by sending 'pataphysical momes in pursuit of the Christian memes.'

'The mome rath hasn't been born that can outgrab me,' Simon protested.

A huge black paw crashed through the floor and seized Ingrid Bergman from between Bogart and Henreid. The pongoid head appeared briefly, glared at Simon and cried 'Now look what you made me do!' It disappeared down the hole to the centre of fumes.

'But what have I got to do with that?' Simon objected.

None of the Mugwumps answered. They were all walking about the Berlin streets naked, their skin the colour of penis-flesh, sipping cuntjuices from laboratory jars, occasionally masturbating, their cat faces impassive.

'Jerome was always the most popular, but Moses didn't object. You know the ancient Terran motto, "If it works, don't fix it." Then Jerome died and the whole synergy seemed on the verge of implosion—'

Professor Ubu reads the last of his reports over TV: 'Seventeen per cent of juvenile delinquents and 23 per cent of Senatorial delinquents believe Ingrid Bergman, not Fay Wray, was the bride of Kong. Clinical paranoids shown inkblots in the standard test often say spontaneously that they see Major Strasse rubbing chocolate syrup all over Bergman's endless curves and labyrinths. In most dreams (80 per cent) it is George Washington, not Robert Armstrong, who sails to Skull Island to confront Black Gorilla rage. We conclude that Kong's mythically necessary six-foot penis obsesses males over seventy years and accounts for the panic-stricken bombing of Iraq and other insufficiently caucasian nations ...' He lapses into incoherent mumbles: 'Rats in the lemonade ... denture breath ... The Merovingian kings round up the usual suspects ... strawberry mice ... no more constipation worries ...'

Blake Williams is more concerned with the telegram that was just delivered by an osteopath in a gorilla suit. He reads it aloud, as Jowly Fallow leaps from the window in terror:

DEAR FORTINBRAS TERRIBLE NEWS STOP OLD KING NEW
KING QUEEN AND PRINCE ALL DEAD STOP ALSO DEAD
PRIME MINISTER AND HIS SON AND DAUGHTER STOP ALSO
DEAD TWO COLLEGE STUDENTS WHOSE NAMES NOBODY
CAN REMEMBER STOP ALSO COURT JESTER PREMATURELY
EXHUMED STOP BRING SHOVELS HORATIO.

'You know,' Mavis said thoughtfully. 'I think somebody cut the acid with Saniflush. To me it looks like Jowly isn't falling but rising ...'

'It's not just him,' said Blake Williams in awe. 'Look, I see thousands and thousands rising and flying ...'

Eighth Predicament of Perspective

> I pick the goddam terror of the gods out of my
> nose!
>
> J.R. 'Bob' Dobbs

By the dawn of 7 Absolu 124 EP Simon had enough data to figure out, more of less, what had happened. He convened a meeting of the Invisible Hand Society to discuss what they might learn.

'Are we ready to discuss identified flying objects?' he asked cheerfully.

'There is no doubt that the levitations occurred,' said Dr Horace Naismith. 'Millions and millions of witnesses — not to mention millions of missing humans.'

'Not missing humans, *per se*. Not random humans,' Simon said. 'There was selection involved.'

'You noticed that, too?' asked W. Clement Cotex. 'Yeah, it's like one of old man Fort's segregating whirlwinds. Only it was even more choosy. It only picked up Christians.'

'Well,' Naismith said, 'that fits with a pet theory that a lot of us hold. If enough believe in something hard enough and long enough, their thought waves eventually make a quantum jump in the quantum foam from which matter and energy emerge ...'

'That's just what I think,' Mavis said. 'The guns-and-Jesus fringe kept thinking about "being lifted up in the rapture" and talking about it and writing about it and, well, when the right date came on their grid, they did get themselves picked up ... but by what?'

'Giant red ants,' Simon said. 'I thought it was just the acid at the non-millennial party, but now I believe it. They got picked up in a rupture, not a rapture. I met one of the ants involved. Several reality-tunnels collided. I talked to one of those red ants. They seem to think Christians are especially tasty.'

'That's awful,' Naismith said. 'Being torn up and chewed apart by giant insects ... it's like Lovecraft ...'

'Well, they did believe in hell,' Simon said. 'And most of them could not live up to that silly taboo system they held, so they expected to go to hell.'

There was a long pause, and then they all looked at their newest member, who had not spoken yet.

'What do you think, Abdel?' Naismith asked.

'I'm new around here,' Abdel Rahman Massoud said softly.

'But I have a hunch that a world without Christians will be a quieter and saner place. Already fifteen wars have ended in three days ... Maybe we don't understand all the forces and intelligences that worked together — or even worked in opposition — to "accidentally" produce the final resultant that we remember as non-millennium day.'

They exchanged thoughtful glances.

'The Invisible Hand,' said Professor Finnegan raising his glass of Jameson's, and they all drank piously.

Douglas Coupland

'FIRE AT THE ATIVAN FACTORY'

Wyatt has worked overtime in the latex room, carefully sculpting the skin texture of an alien needed for shooting after the weekend. His hands, of which he is inordinately proud — long-fingered and hairless after years of chemical exposure — are poxed with resins and paints, his fingernails irretrievably pitted and scratched. These are the scars of his unusual work as creative director in the prosthesis division of a local special effects production company named Flesh. This week, a quickie low-budget movie-of-the-week for a US cable network is being squeezed through the production mill like so much meat byproduct through a sausage maker. 'Grinding out the quickies,' as Wyatt had said just to the staff that afternoon which raised smiles among his Flesh coworkers, all of whom have become virtuoso moulders, flensers and painters of latex and fibreglass bodies over the past five years. Crime shoots are a specialty with Flesh — the creation of dozens of tortellinis and raviolis of fake blood embedded within torso moulds, all of which is electrically wired to explode in synch once the cameras roll. Lately Flesh has moved heavily into the production of aliens. Aliens, in their own way, are easier craft than humans because aliens, like the future, don't really exist; any blank or difficult spots can be easily filled in with flights of fancy.

Wyatt glances at the window: the sun has already gone down. Through the walls Wyatt can hear the thrums and parps of vehicles rushing home, gleefully preparing to celebrate the passing of 1999 into 2000. Earlier in the afternoon when Wyatt had made an emergency epoxy run to London Drugs up on Lonsdale, he could sense the lifting of a large weight of concern off the shoulder's of North Vancouver's citizenry. It felt to Wyatt as though an enormous asteroid had been floating over the city for at least the past month, threatening to clomp down like a sack of potatoes at any minute. This sensation had made this year's Christmas an oddly dour event. 'The last Christmas of the century,' Wyatt's family members kept on saying — for whatever that was worth.

Wyatt's wife, Kathleen (no kids), had sat through an agonisingly long ritual gift-opening ceremony at his parents' house — nieces and nephews and in-laws squawking and cooing, sending subtle signals to Wyatt and Kathleen: *Why no kids?*

But now the impending asteroid has tumbled away. The city is popping upward like newly sprouting seeds twisting up to the sun and Wyatt feels slightly martyred for staying to work late while everybody else packed it in early to go home and prepare for midnight.

Wyatt thinks of the movie plot around which his current alien — now flopped across his left knee as he pokes it and texturises it — revolves. Honey-blond aliens, disguised as real-estate agents lure prospective human beings to houses secretly equipped for biological experimentation. The only Earth food the alien real-estate agents are able to eat is birth-control pills. At night they rampage the city's drug stores foraging and killing for their needs.

Needless to say, the hero and heroine link the pill thefts to the housing sales and arrive in the nick of time to prevent two adorable tots (in real life cell-toting vain-at-thirteen monsters) from being vivisected. The final scene involves a Pontiac Sunfire convertible full of starving alien agents which is surrounded by guns and flashing police cruisers. The trapped aliens pop out of their false human bodies and reveal themselves in full, gluey millipedal horror, and are then promptly shot by local police (whose bodies are embedded with bloody raviolis) but not before the neighbourhood lies in ruins.

The End.

The cable network is getting a true bargain. Aside from special effects, the whole film can be shot in under twelve working days with only a minimum of exterior shots and the Canadian dollar hasn't been worth less against the American in years. Fully a third of the budget is going into the final scene, and this is a testament, Wyatt feels, to the studio's high evaluation of his skills.

Wyatt has been quiet the past few days — and so has been, basically, everybody in the shop — cutting latex, mixing aniline dyes and testing glass eyeball sizes as they mulled over history's impending magnificent odometer turn. But Wyatt has more on his mind to be concerned with than mere numbers. Since September he and Kathleen have been seeing fertility specialists both down in Seattle and up in Vancouver and the results, now in, have been, after endless pap tests, forced ejaculations, pH checks, blood samples and endlessly rehashed personal histories ... *inconclusive*.

'What do you mean you don't *know*?' Wyatt had spat out at Dr Arkasian. 'You *must* know.' Through the windows Vancouver looked grey and overcast, as though the entire city had been manufactured rather than built.

'Sorry Wyatt, there's no real answer.'

'Is it my sperm? My fault?'

'Not — particularly.'

'Kathleen then — no eggs? Bad eggs? Damaged eggs?'

Dr Arkasian tried to cool Wyatt down. There was no clear answer. In Wyatt's mind he saw his sperm rushing towards Kathleen's eggs only to slow down as they approach and then one-by-one fall asleep or die. Wyatt sees Kathleen's eggs as though they were chicken eggs, all yolk and no white — eggs that exude a spermisomnolent spray. Can eggs sleep? Can sperms sleep and dream? They're only half a creature, really — yet how can they be alive — how can they dream?

Kathleen has no brothers and sisters and wanted nothing more with her marriage to Wyatt than to have fifteen children. Wyatt's enormous family was to Kathleen, as it can so often be with single children, a great aphrodisiac. The two of them certainly give it every try they can but—

But *what?*

'There has to be a single cause,' Wyatt said, thinking aloud to Dr Arkasian back at the office just before Christmas. 'Something I ate, maybe. Something Kathleen once breathed. A medicine we took as children—'

'That *could* well be the case,' Dr Arkasian replied in a platitudinous way, visibly anxious to hustle the childless couple from his office in the absence of any clear explanation for their infertility.

And so now Wyatt has been mulling over his and Kathleen's position within the world. For the past week he's been rerunning memories in his head — memories of the things his body has ingested and absorbed since being born in 1964: vaccinations as a child; antibiotics, sulfa drugs and antifungals as a teenager; the car exhausts breathed the two years he worked as a mechanic; food additives, recreational cannabis, cocaine, amphetamines and recently (and just once, ecstasy) and ... And what else? That strange smell that pervaded the outdoor café in Rome back in 1986. Spraying the house's yard with pesticides. Pesticides! Jesus — not even *God* knows what they put into those. And then there's Kathleen with her birth control pills which, although Kathleen disclaims it, must surely have been sapping away at least a fraction of her reproductive capacity.

He puts down his alien and holds his body tightly around his chests and whoops in a gulp of air. *Shit: the chemicals he uses for his models.* He's using cleaner chemicals now but for years his days were rife with toluene, xylene, resins and—

Wyatt feels sick.

He wasn't always a body maker. He ended up there by way of building miniatures for television and films. It had been a hoot and he hadn't quite wanted to leave miniatures, but Kathleen and he had just married and they needed the extra money because they wanted to have a . . . *kid.*

Part of the reason for Wyatt's initial success model-building was that he could build alien space crafts that looked genuinely *alien.* Most other alien craft designers would glance through a book on insects, choose one that they liked and then just build a modified version of them in metal. Not Wyatt. Instead he went to the library and scanned the books on pharmaceutical and plastics molecules — forms that had no need to respond to the mundanities of gravity, light or biology.

'Honestly, Wyatt,' said Marv, his boss, years ago, 'where do you get these ideas from? They're so — *new. Fresh.*'

To Wyatt the real architecture of the Twentieth Century was at the microscopic level: cloned proteins, superconductors, branch-chained detergents, prescription medicines . . . Why, the molecular shape of the anti-depressant Venlafaxine (aka Wellbutrin) alone had paid for the house's down payment — by way of its becoming the overall blueprint of an alien space cruiser in a B film that did lousy in theatrical release but which cleaned up on video and overseas. Now *there* was a molecule that looked like something that only the meanest and scariest aliens would design. Good for them. Good for Venlafaxine.

Wyatt would have actually liked to have *tried* Venlafaxine. Over the past two years his childlessness has given him an increasing whack of anxiety and depression — yet he balked at taking Venlafaxine for reasons of jinx. In the end he wound up with an unshakable addiction of Ativan, innocuous tiny white pills chemically related to all the other sedatives such as Xanax, Darvon, Valium. Miss one pill and Wyatt's brain felt as though it had been epoxied solid. Titred reductions proved doomed. His twice-daily dose was finite and loathed. He hated his addiction but saw no way around it. Wyatt was happy that nobody except Kathleen knew about it.

Kathleen, on the other hand, had tried a host of space-cruiser anti-depressants, finally settling for an old stand-by, Elavil, a drug once given to shell-shocked Second World War British pilots to get them back into their planes and back into the fight. She flowed through her days more peacefully now (if not a little spacey) and she endured the holiday season which was more than she had hoped for.

And now Kathleen was in Saskatchewan tending to her father, laid low with alcoholism and touting a liver as soft and puffy as a water balloon. Wyatt, back in Vancouver, had an invitation to attend Donny and Christine's New Year's Eve party but doubted he would attend. Donny and Christine's New Year's party was *not* the place where he had always envisioned himself at century's end. Since childhood he had pictured himself — where, on that special midnight? Eating champagne Jell-O cubes with Diana Ross at the top of the Empire State Building? Copulating in zero-G on a Space Shuttle? Swimming with bilingual dolphins in the Sea of Japan? No, Wyatt had never seen himself at 11.59:59, 31 December 1999 at *Donny and Christine's place*, 60 per cent drunk on a microbrew-of-the-week, remembering to take his meds shortly after the stroke of twelve, and ringing in the New Year with U2's 'New Year's Day', a song Christine chose each year with a numbing repetition she had successfully converted into a cherished personality quirk.

And then the idea hits him: it's not Kathleen and it's not himself that's to blame — it's the whole bloody *century*. A hundred years of extremeness. A hundred years of molecules never before seen in the universe. A century of action and progress and activity and destiny. A century that had slowly infiltrated Wyatt's system — the fat cells in his brain, the neurons of his spine; the flesh of his palm and eyeballs — his liver and kidneys and heart — a century now pulsing within him — a century with which he is unable to detach himself. Or can he?

Wyatt reaches for a paper cup from the Dixie-cup dispenser, the cups used for mixing fibreglass resins, not for the drinking of water.

Wyatt fills the cup from the cafeteria tap and looks at its

contents — clear and harmless. Or maybe not. Copper. Chlorine. Bacteria. Viruses. He leaves the cup on the counter and walks out of the back door, turning out the lights and alarming the building.

The traffic is quite heavy for that part of town for that time of day — five thirty, and everybody is excitedly preparing for the night. The rain is also heavy but the rain comes as no surprise at that time of year. There's a bit of a traffic slowdown on the highway near Lonsdale but minutes later, Wyatt arrives home to the small house up in Edgemont Village. In the house there are two messages on his machine. Kathleen calling to say she'll be phoning just before midnight and one from Donny asking if he can bring ice to the party. Wyatt erases both messages and stands in the front doorway area of the house: some bills, a throw rug with a kink in one corner, some boots and an unread newspaper.

I want every damn bit of that hellish century out of my system. I want it clean. Whatever the Twenty-first Century brings me, that's fine, but I want the Twentieth Century out of my system now.

This idea takes him with a jolt. It is a *real* idea, not a confabulated whiff of impulse. It is instantly clear to Wyatt that he must cleanse his system.

Very well then.

From the bedroom he retrieves a pair of handcuffs, remnants of an earlier sexual era when he and Kathleen could have sex without sweet darkness. From there he goes to the front hall where he puts on three coats over the top of each other and then he walks through the sliding glass upper balcony door, into the dark and on to the wood balcony. There, he sits down on a $9.95 white plastic stool — a chintzy stackable drecky chair of a type that appeared one summer a few years ago, and erased all other patio chairs in the world. 'A category killer,' the salesman had called it.

He sits on this chair and handcuffs himself to the metal railing beside him. Before allowing himself time to reflect, he throws the key through the bushes and down into an adjoining creek running at a full alpine swoosh.

And it is then, while there is the noise of the creek and the rain, that there is also the silence. Great silence. Rain slopping down on to the yellow hat attached to the outermost jacket layer.

It's jarring at first, the clash between the cold wet outdoors and the warm dry indoors. But then his eyes adjust to the foggy wet dark, his skin to the dank, and his ears to the weather and the landscape.

This is how I want the Twentieth Century to end, he thinks. Personally — alone – in contemplation — during an act of purification.

He looks at his watch. The time is 10:45 — where did the hours go? And then he becomes aware that he has been looking at his watch. He removes it and throws it down into the creek along with the handcuff keys.

He shivers and then shivers some more. His fingers feel rubbery and chilled. His core temperature is falling. He can hear cars roaring around the suburb. He hears a few bangs — premature fireworks by the overeager.

Shortly Wyatt's teeth begin to chatter and he wonders if he's made a dreadful mistake. He stands up and tries to yank at the railing and in so doing slips and sends his chair flying towards the balcony's other end, banging his knee in the process, forcing him to sit on the wet planks. And it is at this point that his phone rings and he curses himself and the world. It rings ten times and dies. And half a minute later party-goers across the city bang and carouse and ignite, welcoming three fresh new zeroes into their world.

Goodbye, 1999.

And after an hour the kerfuffle ends. It is still the world. Not much has changed, or has it? Wyatt is unable to sleep — and won't be able to sleep for days; within his body the idea of sleep and Ativan are one and the same.

His core temperature lowers and he shouts for his neighbours to come and retrieve him from this stupid idea but the creek and the rain are too loud, drowning out his voice so that even to himself his words seem smothered before they can get away from his ever-chilling body. His efforts at uprooting the steel railing from the porch have merely sapped his energy. He is truly stuck.

Around 3 a.m. his brain begins to revolt against him. His eyes flutter and soon he will go into seizure. A bony hand clenches his scalp's top. His breathing shortens and becomes non-automatic. He is aware of every breath but increasingly removed from this awareness at the same time.

I am cold, he thinks. *I am cold and this is how I'll be ending — cold.* His three coats are soaked through. He thinks he hears the phone ring again, but can't tell if he's imagining it. All he wants is for the cold to end and as he wishes for this, he remembers the first time he tried Ativan and he remembers how much he loved it. And he remembers joking with his GP about possible addiction. 'What if I get hooked on this stuff?'

'You won't get hooked.'

'What if I do get hooked and what if the Ativan factory burns down — what would I do then?' They both had a forced laugh over that one.

And now, somewhere across the Pacific, somewhere west of Honolulu, the century ends absolutely. The International Dateline is crossed and as it does so, Wyatt pictures the burning factory and he imagines he is standing next to it, warming his hands, warming his body and warming his core as he leaves the Twentieth Century and the Twentieth Century leaves him.

PAT CADIGAN

As a child, Pat Cadigan had been spotted at numerous showings of The Wizard of Oz, hollering, 'Don't, Dorothy — are you *crazy*?! Stay in Oz! *Stay in Oz!*' As an adult, she served a total of twenty-three years without parole in the state of Kansas, before being pardoned by the Good Witch of the Zeitgeist.

Now she lives in North London with her son, the Bobmeister, and her husband, the Original Chris Fowler. She is the author of three published novels, two of which, *Synners* and *Fools*, have won the Arthur C. Clarke Award. Her next novel, *Tea From An Empty Cup* will be out in Autumn 1998.

NICHOLAS BLINCOE

Nicholas Blincoe is the author of the already classic crime 'n' clubbing novels *Acid Casuals* and *Jello Salad*. Between books, he finds time to be a street-walking cheetah with a hide full of napalm. His latest novel, *Manchester Slingback*, tells the story of two Bowie boys, running around Manchester in the early eighties, high on beauty, amphetamine and betrayal. As Biggie Smalls once said, 'Somebody's gotta die.'

GRANT MORRISON

Grant Morrison is the writer of a number of successful graphic novels and comic book series, including *Batman: Arkham Asylum*, *The New Adventures Of Hitler*, *St Swithin's Day*, *Doom Patrol*, *Kill Your Boyfriend* and *Flex Mentallo, Man Of Muscle Mystery*. He is currently writing the monthly titles *The Invisibles* and *JLA* for

DC Comics. He is also the author of the award-winning plays 'Red King Rising' and 'Depravity' and numerous other things besides.

JONATHAN BROOK

Jonathan Brook was born in 1967. Before he started writing fiction, he was a musician for eight years. He has published three novels and a novella and is working on his new novel, entitled *Joe*. He lives in London and his story in this collection is dedicated to J.J.

POPPY Z. BRITE

Poppy Z. Brite has published three novels, *Lost Souls*, *Drawing Blood* and *Exquisite Corpse*, and a short story collection *Swamp Foetus*. She is the editor of the anthologies *Love In Vein 1* and 2. Her most recent project is the biography *Courtney Love: The Real Story*, published by Simon & Schuster (US) and Orion (UK) in 1997. She lives in New Orleans with her husband Christopher, a chef and food writer.

CHARLIE HALL

Heading headlong forwards to the next Century. World traveller, adventurer. Collecting nothing, no hobbies, no past. Play the records, feel the rhythm.

DOUG HAWES

Doug Hawes became an archaeologist just as the jobs ran out.

He is now retraining as a health worker. He lives in Manchester with his son Brendan and cat Maslow. This is his first story.

PAUL DI FILIPPO

Born the year Elvis first hit the recording studio, Paul Di Filippo lives with his mate, Deborah Newton, in the hometown of H.P. Lovecraft, Providence, Rhode Island. His books include *The Steampunk Trilogy*, *Ribofunk*, *Fractal Paisleys* and *Ciphers*, the latter being his first novel. Occasionally he feels, like Billy Corgan, that despite all his rage, he is still just a rat in a cage. More often, he is inclined to hum the Talking Heads' 'Naive Melody'.

STEVE AYLETT

Steve Aylett is the author of three novels, *The Crime Studio* (Serif), *Bigot Hall* (Serif) and *Slaughtermatic* (Four Walls Eight Windows), a new one about crime as creative play. Aylett was born in the late sixties, grew up in Bromley, and was recently punched in the stomach by a nun.

BILL DRUMMOND

Money burner. William Ernest Drummond, 29 April 1953, Butterworth, Transkei, South Africa. Father, Church Of Scotland minister (Presbyterian); mother, minister's wife and political activist. 1955, Newton Stewart, Galloway, Scotland, Penningham Wee School, Penningham Big School. 1964, Corby, Northants, Beanfield Secondary Modern, Kingswood Comprehensive, 4 'O' levels, no 'A' levels. 1970, Northampton School of Art. 1972, Liverpool College Of Art.

1973, steelworker, gardener, milkman, trawlerman, ward orderly, carpenter. 1976, Science Fiction Theatre of Liverpool. 1977, Big In Japan. 1978, Zoo Records, Echo And The Bunnymen, The Teardrop Explodes. 1987, Justified Ancients Of Mu Mu, Timelords, KLF, K Foundation, K2 Plant Hire. 1997, doing things with Jimmy Cauty and writing. Five children.

Books: *The Manual* (How To Have A Number One The Easy Way), *Bible Of Dreams*, *Bad Wisdom*.

MARTIN MILLAR

I come from Glasgow. I've lived in London for a long time. I spend my time playing the flute, reading ancient history and sitting at my computer.

I've had five novels published, fairly successfully: *Milk Sulphate and Alby Starvation*, *Lux the Poet*, *Ruby and the Stone Age Diet*, *The Good Fairies of New York* and *Dreams of Sex and Stage Diving* — but it's taken me a long time to get my new book out. It should be out by the time you read this. If not, it won't be long. It's called *Love and Peace with Melody Paradise* and it's published by Prolesec. It's a romantic comedy set at a free festival among hippies and travellers. No wonder no one wanted to publish it. You'll find more details about my books on my Website. (You can read all the rejection letters for *Love and Peace* there as well.) My Website has the most stupid address in the world: http://dspace.dial.pipex.com/town/street/kbh38/mmindex.shtml

HELEN MEAD

Born in Utopian Harlow, Essex. Helen Mead fell into music journalism at the age of fourteen when a chance letter to Radio One turned into a live interview with her teen idol Adam Ant. After skipping gym classes to edit a local music page for which she won a national award at fifteen, she joined NME at sixteen and became their first female section editor at nineteen. We became one nation under a groove thanks to her early coverage of acid house, KLF, Stone Roses, Primal Scream and the Manchester scene.

Helen went on to be assistant editor of *i-D* and inaugurated the ground-breaking 'Trance Europe Express' compilations and parties. Now the director of innovative Blood Records and management, Helen shakes her tail feathers worldwide, but lives in London.

COURTTIA NEWLAND

Courttia Newland was born in Hammersmith in 1973 and raised in Shepherd's Bush, West London. After four years of unemployment, he borrowed a word processor in 1994, and began writing his first novel, *The Scholar*, published by Abacus in April 1997.

He has written numerous short stories based in and around West London and is currently involved in community film-making using a youth-oriented crew and actors at a project in Ladbroke Grove. Forthcoming projects include a second novel, *Altered Minds and West Side Stories*, short stories and films.

DOUGLAS RUSHKOFF

Douglas Rushkoff wrote *The Ecstasy Club*, *Children of Chaos*, *Cyberia*, and *Media Virus*. He lives in New York, writes a column for the *Guardian*, talks about media, and hangs out in quiet places. He is not part of the chemical generation, and hasn't met anyone who is. You can find him at http://www.levity.com/rushkoff.

TANIA GLYDE

Tania Glyde lives in London. Her first novel, *Clever Girl*, was published in Britain in 1995, and Germany in 1997. According to one newspaper reviewer, the book '... manages to mention in the first few pages a dog's sexual excitement, dildos, various bodily fluids, child abuse, loveless sex, lavatory paper and all the usual four-letter words, not to mention a girl's irresistible lust for a thick Habitat pottery lamp, a blasphemous 'joke' about the Christ Child and various other things too crude to reprint. And that was only up to page 47, at which point I threw Ms Glyde's nasty little book across the room.'

Her second novel is called *Junk DNA*. 'It's hard to satirise the world we live in but she has succeeded,' said one reader. She is now working on her third book, an endorphin-soaked celebration of British sexuality.

She also does spoken-word performances and poetry. 'My favourite piece I've done so far is set in Purgatory, and ends with Christ dispensing methadone to all the junkies via his penis.' Her latest project is a cycle of useful art for the benefit of white liberal intellectuals. 'The first one's called *Poverty Porn*. More will follow.'

STEVE BEARD

Steve Beard was born in the Thames Valley and lives and works in London. He is the author of the cypherpunk novel *Digital Leatherette* and the conceptual novel *Perfumed Head*. He has been sifting the wreckage of the post-modern crash scene for the past ten years now, trying to figure out how it all went wrong. The results of his forensic labours are now published in *Logic Bomb*.

NEAL STEPHENSON

Neal Stephenson is from a clan of rootless, itinerant hard-science and engineering professors. His novels include *The Big U, Zodiac:*

The Eco-thriller, The Diamond Age and the huge cult hit *Snow Crash*, which was written between 1988 and 1991 (as the author listened to a great deal of loud, relentless, depressing music).

Neal Stephenson now resides in a comfortable home in the Western hemisphere where he spends his time — when not side-tracked by his computer, rollerblading or parenting — attempting to write more books.

ROBERT ANTON WILSON

Robert Anton Wilson has written thirty-one books, including the *Illuminatus* trilogy, the *Cosmic Trigger* trilogy and, most recently, *The Walls Came Tumbling Down*. He lectures and gives workshops frequently in both Europe and North America, dealing with neurosematic and neurolinguistic strategies for deconstructing obsolete belief systems. His next book will be *Everything Is Under Control*, an encyclopaedia of conspiracy theories, coming in June from Harper Collins. His website is http://www.rawilson.com

DOUGLAS COUPLAND

Douglas Campbell Coupland was born a Canadian citizen on 30 December, 1961 on a Canadian NATO base in Baden-Sollingen, Germany. Shortly afterwards he moved to Vancouver, where he still lives. Coupland's books to date include *Generation X, Shampoo Planet, Microserfs, Polaroids From The Dead* and *Girlfriend in a Coma*. They have been translated into twenty-two languages.

SARAH CHAMPION

Manchester 'wild child,' now grown up and living in Camberwell in a big shared house. Likes curry, lager and clubbing. A former

Contributors

NME hack and compiler of the drum'n'bass CDs 'Breakbeat Science', Sarah Champion is also the editor of the bestselling *Disco Biscuits*, and co-editor of a forthcoming Irish fiction anthology. She can be found at www.discobiscuits.org.

Acknowledgements

Acknowledgements

'Dali's Clocks' copyright Robert Anton Wilson, 1997
'Fire At The Ativan Factory' copyright Douglas Coupland, 1997

The words of 'Peace In The Valley' and 'Mao Tse Tung Said' by Love, Love, Love, Rev D. Wayne Love, Sir Real and L.B. Dope, appear courtesy of Chrysalis Music. Both are taken from the Alabama 3's album *Exile On Coldharbour Lane*

Collect the set

Disco 2000: Various Artists (*bokå*) bokå 2

The soundtrack, nineteen tunes for the last hours of 1999. Futuristic music for the end of the millennium. Especially recorded as a companion to this book by the top names of drum 'n' bass, big beats, trip-hop, techno and house. Available as a limited edition pop-out package.

Disco Biscuits (*Sceptre*) *ISBN 0 340–682655*

Disco 2000 is the follow-up to *Disco Biscuits*, the bestselling and definitive chemical anthology. Nineteen stories about drugs, sex, dancefloors, dealers, police and DJs. Featuring Irvine Welsh, Jeff Noon, Nicholas Blincoe, Q, Alan Warner, Martin Millar, Charlie Hall, Alex Garland, Douglas Rushkoff and more. Already a cult classic.

Disco Biscuits: Various Artists (*Coalition*) *0630–181924*

The soundtrack, celebrating the tenth anniversary of Acid House with nineteen classic anthems including: 808 State 'Pacific State'; Future Sound Of London 'Papua New Guinea'; Underworld 'Rez';

LTJ Bukem 'Horizons'; Goldie 'Inner City Life'; Green Velvet 'Preacher Man'; Orbital 'Halcyon'; Leftfield 'Not Forgotten'; Sueno Latino 'Sueno Latino'; Hardfloor 'Acperience'; The Beloved 'Sunrising'. Also features a history of Acid House and pictures.

Irish anthology (Sceptre) ISBN 0 340–712694

The third book in the *Disco Biscuits* series, forthcoming in Autumn 1998. An anthology of cutting-edge Irish fiction, co-edited by Sarah Champion and Donal Scannell, Radio Ireland DJ and promoter of Dublin's drum 'n' bass night, Quadraphonic.

'We pride ourselves on a literary tradition that guarantees coach loads of tourists, but name the last Irish author you actually related to?' writes Donal. 'They do exist you know – Irish people who can write about more than twisted famine legacies and sexual repression.

'This book proves that there's more going on here than retirees fondly remembering slums, and that we're not a nation whose aspirations extend to running chip vans, or forming a dodgy covers band. We've our OWN stories . . .'

The Website

For more information on *Disco Biscuits* and *Disco 2000* check: www.discobiscuits.org
The website is designed by Lateral.Net.

Write to us at Disco Biscuits, PO Box 15021, London SE5 92R.

RESPECT DUE

Special thanks to top geezer Simon Prosser for looking after me and coming clubbing.

Thanks to Anna-Maria, Katie, Diana, Al, Camilla, Petra, and all at Hodder for their enthusiasm; to Paul Basford from *Bokå*; Tim Perry for technical, moral and alcoholic support; Steve Aylett and Douglas Rushkoff for providing contacts; Christine Kellogg for software navigation and gossip; Bigson and John @ lateral for the website; Robert Blincoe for suggesting the title; Geremy O'Mahony and Fraser Jopp for advice; and Steve Redhead for accidentally getting everything started.

A 'shout going out' to the Cormont Road posse, Denise Moore, Denise Madden, Gonnie (Doctor of House), Mandie James, DJ Bee and the Alabama 3. Big up SE5 and SW9.